STUDENT LAB MANUAL

Are Flågan

PHOTOGRAPHY

Seventh Edition

BARBARA LONDON

JOHN UPTON

KEN KOBRE

BETSY BRILL

PRENTICE HALL, UPPER SADDLE RIVER, NEW JERSEY 07458

Prentice Hall

Upper Saddle River, New Jersey 07458

10 9 8 7 6 5 4 3 2

ISBN 0-13-041340-2

Printed in the United States of America

CONTENTS STUDENT LAB MANUAL

▼

INTRODUCTION

Welcome to the Student Lab Manual for Barbara London and John Upton's Photography – 7th edition. The manual has been developed to serve as a study guide and journal for beginning as well as more advanced photography students. The chapters correspond to the chapters in the textbook, and the manual has been written and designed to encourage a close collaboration between the two resources. Refer to the textbook for a solid grounding in photographic techniques and practices, and actively use this manual as you start to explore these principles in your own practical work. Photography is ultimately an integrated system that demands close attention to precision and detail to secure the results you desire. The numerous tables and charts prepared for you in this Student Lab Manual provide a framework where you can easily enter your decisions and results into a structure that immediately supports them in a way that makes sense. You will effectively be working in partnership with an instructive outline that somewhat squarely but accurately fits the equipment and processes that constitute photography. The User's Guide below offers a more comprehensive introduction to the contents of this manual. Once you have efficiently framed photography through the boxes on the following pages, take another look through the viewfinder frame and explore your own vision. Good luck with your photography!

USER'S GUIDE

Each chapter in this manual is divided into the following subheadings:

GLOSSARY

The terms included in the glossary are all chapter-specific. Density, for instance, is a term used in relation to both film and paper. In chapter 6, Developing the Negative, the term will focus on how density is understood for film and negatives, while in chapter 7, Printing the Positive, the term is explained with regards to paper in printing.

SUMMARY

All summaries are structured to reference Photography – 7th edition. The left-hand column of each summary contains the page numbers where this material can be found in the textbook. The bold topic sentences are repeated from the book throughout to serve as a reference. If the abbreviated summary does not give you an adequate explanation, simply use the bold text as an index to find a more comprehensive treatment of this point in the textbook. For example, if the following summary in chapter 3 – **The most important way lenses differ is in their focal length**: Focal length is technically the distance from the rear nodal point in the lens to the focal plane when the lens is focused on infinity. – is short on the explanation you were seeking, look up the bold text in the textbook (on page 42) for a more comprehensive treatment of focal length.

TEST

The tests are devised to help you digest the material covered in each chapter. They will undoubtedly also prepare you well for any quizzes offered by your instructor. There is one module of Fill-in-the-blank and one module of Multiple-choice per chapter - a total of 20 questions. The answers are found in chapter 18 with a score-sheet to record your own frustration or enjoyment, depending on the results.

PRACTICAL TIPS

Practical tips are offered to introduce a transition from theory to practice. Most of them are invaluable pointers gained by practical experience with photography. Please refer to these tips before you try the processes described in the textbook and this manual.

JOURNAL

These informative sections are prepared to guide you through the technical aspects of photography. The entries will familiarize you with your equipment, introduce you to the most important principles of photography, and they provide useful records and charts for all your practical work. Extensive use of the Journal will assure you predictable results during exposure, development, and printing almost immediately. Please use a colored pen to make your entries stand out from the printed text.

COMPANION RESOURCES

Companion Website – www.prenhall.com/london

A Companion Website has been developed for Photography – 7th edition at http://www.prenhall.com/london. The site features interactive simulations that allow you to practice technical aspects of photography prior to the expense of developing film and printing negatives. There are also chat rooms reserved for photography topics available. Please visit the Companion Website to broaden your learning experience and have some fun with contents only the Internet can offer.

Companion publication – Photography on the Internet

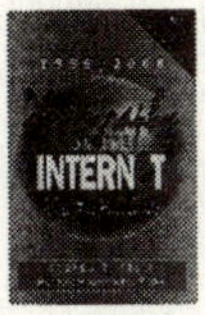

Prentice Hall annually publishes a comprehensive guide to Photography on the Internet, which is available for free when packaged with Barbara London and John Upton's Photography – 7th edition. Please ask your instructor to order this guide with the textbook. The guide covers Internet navigation with a special emphasis on the search for and display of images on the World Wide Web. It also features a very extensive listing of sites related to photography.

ACKNOWLEDGEMENTS

I would sincerely like to thank Kimberly Chastain, my editor at Prentice Hall, for her ardent support of this project. The concept has gradually developed into the Student Lab Manual you are currently holding, and it is our common belief that it will prove a valuable resource for students of photography. Without this kind of shared enthusiasm, it is at least twice as hard to get something accomplished. A genuine expression of gratitude is also extended to my past students at the University of New Mexico, who taught me what I know about teaching. Thank you for making the classroom both educational and enjoyable.

1 GETTING STARTED

1.1 GLOSSARY

Aperture An adjustable opening within the lens used to control the intensity of the light falling on the film during exposure. The aperture, given by an f-number, refers to the size of this opening.

Aperture-priority An automatic exposure mode. The camera operator sets the aperture and the camera sets the shutter speed.

Automatic camera A camera where one or more functions are performed automatically by the camera without user input.

DX-code A checkered code found on the film cassette. Some cameras are equipped to read the code and automatically set the right film speed and number of exposures.

Exposure An exposure describes the amount of light falling on the light sensitive film after the shutter is released. The exposure is controlled by a combination of aperture and shutter speed.

Exposure readout The metered exposure values seen in the camera's viewfinder or in a data panel.

Film Film is used to permanently record the image formed by the lens. It consists of a light sensitive emulsion on an acetate or plastic base.

Film cassette A light proof container for light sensitive 35mm film. The film speed is often inscribed in a DX-code on the side of the cassette.

Film speed A measure for the light sensitivity of film.

Focal length The distance from a point in the lens to the focal (film) plane when the lens is focused on infinity. Longer focal length lenses bring you closer to the subject by increasing magnification.

Focus In focus refers to the point where rays of light converge on the film to form a sharp image. To focus involves adjusting the lens to film distance by turning the lens barrel until the desired subject in the scene appears sharp (in focus).

ISO (International Standards Organization) The most common measure for film speed. Used in combination with a numerical rating to describe a film's sensitivity to light.

Lens A lens consists of one or more optical glass elements arranged to sharply focus a scene in front of the camera on the film.

Light-meter An instrument, built into the camera or used hand held, that measures the amount of light either falling on a subject or reflecting off a subject. The measurement is used to calculate an exposure setting of shutter speed and aperture.

Manual camera A camera where the functions are controlled by the user.

Manual exposure A camera mode where the user sets both aperture and shutter speed before making an exposure.

Negative The tones in a negative image recorded on film are reversed in relation to the original subject. Light becomes dark and vice versa.

Shutter The shutter mechanism opens and closes to control the length of time the film is exposed to light.

Shutter speed The actual time that the shutter remains open to expose the film.

Shutter-priority An automatic exposure mode. The camera operator sets the shutter speed and the camera sets the aperture.

SLR camera Single-Lens-Reflex cameras reflect the image formed by the taking lens onto a ground glass for viewing. A mirrored pentaprism in this path turns the image around so it is viewed the correct way. Most 35mm cameras are SLR cameras.

Transparency/ Slide A positive image recorded on transparency film where the tones are the same as they were in the subject. Slide usually refers to a 35mm transparency mounted for projection.

Viewfinder A small window on the camera used to frame the subject. The viewfinder image seeks to be an exact representation of the image seen by the lens.

1.2 SUMMARY

3

Getting started

The steps in this chapter are a basic checklist: The chapter introduces you to the basic principles of photography and photographic equipment. **Cameras have become increasingly automatic, often including automatic exposure and focus:** Automatic cameras have many useful features, but manual cameras allow you, the photographer, to make all the decisions. **Once you have gotten the basics down, how do you get better:** Take more pictures. Practice your technical skills to develop your aesthetic sensibilities.

4

Camera and film

A camera's main functions: View the scene, focus the subject, and expose the film. View through the viewfinder, focus the lens, and expose the film using a combination of shutter speed and aperture. **If you want prints:** Select a negative film. **If you want slides or transparencies:** Select a reversal film. **Film speed:** Describes a film's sensitivity to light. Most commonly rated on the ISO scale. Films with higher numbers are more sensitive to light, which means that they require less light to make an exposure compared to slower films with lower numbers.

5

Loading film into the camera

Make sure there is no film in the camera: Check the film frame counter. Turn the rewind knob to make sure that it rotates freely. **A camera that loads film manually:** If the camera has a film rewind knob, lifting the knob usually opens the camera back. **A camera that loads film automatically:** Turn on the camera and slide the release lever to open the camera back. **Check for dust in the camera:** Remove dust from inside the camera and especially from the pressure plate located in the camera back. **Insert the film cassette:** The film casette only fits one way, normally in the left side of the camera body. **Manual loading:** See the description on page 5. **Automatic loading:** See the description on page 5. **Close the camera back:** Make sure that the back is securely closed. If it opens after you have started advancing the film, all frames outside the film cassette will be ruined. **Manual film advance:** Turn the film advance lever. Frame numbers will appear in the film frame counter. Advance to frame 1 before you start taking photographs. Check that the film is advancing properly by observing the film rewind knob. If it turns counterclockwise, the film is pulled correctly out of the cassette and onto the take-up spool. **Automatic film advance:** Close the camera back, and the camera will automatically advance the film to frame 1. For some cameras, you may need to press the shutter to advance the film to frame 1.

6 - 7 **Focusing and setting the exposure**

Film speed is a measure of a film's sensitivity to light: Film speed is rated with a number on the ISO scale. It must be set on the camera to get the correct exposure readout. **Manually setting the film speed:** On manual cameras, the film speed dial is usually combined with the shutter speed dial. Set the number to correspond with the ISO number on the film packaging and the film casette. **Atomatically setting the film speed:** The camera uses a DX-code on the film cassette to automatically set the film speed. **Focus on the most important part of your scene:** Focus on your main subject to ensure that it will be sharp in the photograph. **Manual focusing:** Use the ground glass, the microprism, or the split-image device found in the viewfinder to aid you in focusing. **Automatic focusing:** Press the shutter release halfway down to focus the lens on a subject central in your viewfinder. **To get a correctly exposed picture:** You use a combination of aperture and shutter speed to ensure that the film receives the right amount of light according to its rated sensitivity. **Exposure readout:** Cameras with a built-in exposure meter usually give you a recommended exposure setting as a combination of shutter speed and aperture in the viewfinder. **An LCD data panel:** Automatic cameras often display the exposure readout in a data panel. **The viewfinder:** The same information is frequently also displayed in the viewfinder. **The needle-centering display:** Another type of exposure readout. Adjust combinations of aperture and/or shutter speed until the needle is centered to get a recommended exposure setting. **With manual exposure, you set both the shutter speed and aperture yourself:** You set both shutter speed and aperture on the camera using the appropriate controls. **You can use a camera's built-in meter for manual exposure:** You use the exposure meter in the camera to measure the amount of light reflected off your subject. You base your exposure on this reading. **With automatic exposure:** The camera sets the shutter speed or aperture for you. **With programmed automatic exposure:** The camera sets both the shutter speed and aperture for you. **With aperture-priority automatic exposure:** You set the aperture and the camera sets the shutter speed based on the exposure reading. **With shutter-priority automatic exposure:** You set the shutter speed and the camera sets the aperture based on the exposure reading.

8 **Taking your picture**

For horizontal photographs: Keep your arms against your body to steady the camera. Use a shutter speed of 1/60 or faster to ensure that your photographs will be sharp. **For vertical photographs:** Keep the shutter release button pointing down and brace both your arms against your upper body. (The illustration in the textbook shows an unstable stance.) **A tripod steadies the camera for you:** Use a tripod for long exposures or careful compositions. **Make an exposure:** Check focus and composition again, then gently press the shutter release button down. **Make some more exposures:** Try several compositions and exposure settings to ensure the best results. **Keep a record of your exposures:** Use the records provided with this manual to keep track of your initial exposures. They will help you to get predictable and repeatable results faster. **NOTE: What to do when your camera won't let you take a picture:** Check for film, test the battery, clean the battery contacts, change the exposure or focusing mode, lift the film advance lever, or try a new roll of film. **After your last exposure on the roll:** Check that the frame counter has reached the right number of exposures. Rewind the film before opening the camera. **Manual rewind:** Press the rewind button (frequently found at the bottom of the camera) and turn the rewind-crank until the tension is released. **Automatic rewind:** At the end of a roll, the camera will rewind the film automatically. You may need to press a button to start the rewind.

9 **What will you photograph?**

One place to start is by looking around through the viewfinder: Use the viewfinder frame to compose different elements in various ways. **Often people photograph from too far away:** Isolate your main subject by getting close to it. **How do the edges of the photograph intersect the subject:** Use the edges of the frame to decide how much of your subject is shown and how it appears within the frame. **How does your subject relate to its surroundings:** Consider the influence of the background and/or the foreground on your main subject. **Is the light more or less even overall:** Look carefully at the light in a scene to decide if it creates the kind of mood or appearance you want. **See what happens:** There are no rules. Surprise yourself and others with daring angles and compositions.

10 - 11 **Photographing people**

A good portrait shows more than merely what someone looks like: Photography can be more than a record of likeness. Explore expressive possibilities in a subject's reactions or envrionmental props. **Put your subject at ease:** Relax and be confident about technical decisions to put your subject at ease. **Don't skimp on film when shooting portraits:** Catch that small change of expression that could make a difference by making numerous exposures. **Try to use a fast enough shutter speed:** Be ready to make an exposure when your subject strikes an interesting pose. Longer exposures will demand that the subject holds still on your instruction, which inevitably results in a much less spontaneous look. **Photographing close to home can be an easy place to start – or a difficult one:** Working with people close to you can often result in personal and rewarding photographs. **Some pictures of people appear to be unplanned:** Candid or unposed shots are often considered more revealing about a subject than planned and posed shots. **Set your camera's controls beforehand:** Set exposure and focus before photographing a scene to concentrate on the subject and to work in a fast and unobtrusive way. **A fast shutter speed is even more important for unposed photographs of people than for planned portraits:** Use a fast film to enable the use of a fast shutter speed when you work with moving subjects.

12 - 13 **Photographing places**

How do you photograph a place: Consider your own responses to the place and try to communicate these through your framing and exposure decisions. Work with viewpoint and distance to express your impressions.

1.3 TEST

FILL IN THE BLANKS

1 The camera uses a combination of shutter speed and ____________________ to expose the film.

2 A sharp image is achieved by ____________________ the lens.

3 The abbreviation ISO followed by a number refers to a film's ____________________ to light.

4 A ____________________ on the film cassette allows some cameras to set the film speed automatically.

5 Reversal or transparency film produces a ____________________ image.

6 In aperture-priority mode, you set the aperture and the camera sets the ____________________.

7 Consider the influence of both the foreground and the ____________________ on the main subject of your photograph.

8 The ____________________ determines the length of time light strikes the film during an exposure.

9 The ____________________ determines the intensity of the light striking the film during an exposure.

10 Check the film-frame ____________________ to make sure that you have reached the end of a roll.

MULTIPLE CHOICE – CIRCLE ONE OR MORE

1	The camera light-meter usually gives an exposure readout in:	a.	a combination of film speed and focusing distance.
		b.	a combination of shutter speed and aperture.
		c.	an ISO number.
2	After loading the film in a manual camera, you should:	a.	open the camera back to ensure that it was loaded properly.
		b.	set the film speed on the film-speed dial.
		c.	advance the film to the first frame in the film-frame counter.
3	You can improve on your photography by:	a.	taking more pictures.
		b.	looking at the work of other photographers.
		c.	keeping records of your technical decisions.
4	A tripod is useful for:	a.	slow shutter speeds.
		b.	careful compositions.
		c.	fast moving subjects shot on fast film.
5	For candid shots, it is beneficial to:	a.	ask the subject to say "cheese".
		b.	work without looking through the viewfinder.
		c.	set the camera controls beforehand.
6	To capture a telling expression in portraiture, you must:	a.	always dictate a series of poses.
		b.	make several exposures to get more than one expression to choose from.
		c.	use a tripod to get an unplanned feel.
7	In shutter-priority mode, the camera sets the aperture and you set the:	a.	shutter speed.
		b.	ISO distance.
		c.	shutter distance.

8	If you primarily want prints from your photographs, choose a:	a.	reversal film.
		b.	negative film.
		c.	slide film.
9	Use the viewfinder to:	a.	creatively frame your subject.
		b.	determine if your subject is in focus.
		c.	adjust the amount of light striking the film during exposure.
10	The main function of the camera is to:	a.	view and frame the scene.
		b.	focus the image.
		c.	expose the scene on film.

1.4 PRACTICAL TIPS

Loading film

Watch the rewind crank to make sure that your film is winding on properly.

If you have a camera with manual film loading, you use the film advance lever to advance the film from frame to frame and a rewind crank to rewind it after the last exposure. On most camera models, there is a chance that the film slips out of the slot or the sprockets attaching it to the take-up spool when you close the camera back. If this happens, your frame counter will keep counting even if you are not actually advancing the film. You could end up shooting an entire roll of imaginary photographs before finding the roll unexposed in your camera.

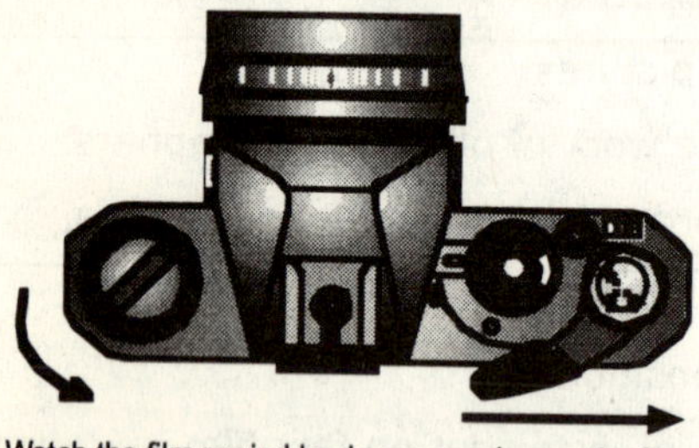
Watch the film rewind knob as you advance the film

To ensure that the film is winding on properly, watch the rewind knob as you use the advance lever. If it turns counterclockwise, you are pulling film out of the film cassette and onto the take-up spool like you should. Finally, once you have reached frame 1, turn the rewind-crank clockwise to check for tension. After any slack in the film cassette has been taken up, you should feel the tension of the film attached to the take-up spool. With most automatic cameras, you have to rely upon the camera to notify you of any problems with film loading.

Film speed

Insert a piece of the film packaging in the pocket on the camera back.

In order to get the right combination of shutter speed and aperture from your exposure reading, you must set the correct film speed for the film you are using. On automatic cameras, this is done automatically with the aid of the checkered DX-code on the film cassette. If you have a manual camera, you set the film speed yourself on the film speed dial. Always do this when you first load the film, so you don't forget. As a reminder of the type of film currently loaded, many cameras have a small pocket on the camera back where you can insert a piece of the film packaging. Tear the lid or the bottom off the paper box and keep it in this holder as a record of film type, film speed, and number of exposures. You can refer to this memo and verify your settings at any time.

1.5 JOURNAL

1.5.1 INTRODUCTORY CHECKLISTS

Consult these checklists the first few times you use your camera. They will help you establish correct procedures for some basic operations. Most of the material relating to the camera, film, focusing, and exposure will be covered in the next chapters.

✓ **Loading film manually**

❑ Make sure that there is no film in the camera. Check for tension on the rewind crank and consult the frame counter.
❑ Open the camera back by lifting the rewind knob.
❑ Remove all dust particles from the inside of the camera using a blower and a brush. Do not touch or interfere with the shutter curtains. You may easily damage them.
❑ Insert the film cassette in the camera and secure it by lowering the film rewind knob.
❑ Pull out a few inches of the tapered film and attach it to the take-up spool.
❑ Close the camera back.
❑ Advance the film to frame 1.
❑ Test to see if the film was properly loaded. See 1.4 Practical tips above.

✓ **Loading film automatically**

❑ Make sure that there is no film in the camera. Check the frame counter in the data panel.
❑ Open the camera back with the release lever.
❑ Remove all dust particles from the inside of the camera using a blower and a brush. Do not touch or interfere with the shutter curtains. You may easily damage them.
❑ Pull out a few inches of tapered film and align the end of the film with the appropriate mark inside your camera.
❑ Close the camera back.
❑ The film should automatically advance to frame 1. You may need to press a button. Check to see if frame 1 appears in your data panel as an indication of successful film loading.

✓ **Setting the film speed manually**

❑ Consult the film packaging and/or the film cassette to ascertain the correct film speed. It is rated in ISO, ASA, or DIN. ISO and ASA use the same numerical scale. The sequence from slow to fast films: ISO/ASA 25, 50, 100, 200, 400, 800, 1600, 3200. You may come across films rated at intermediary steps, such as ISO 64 or ISO 125.
❑ Locate the film speed dial on your camera and set the correct speed.

✓ **Setting the film speed automatically**

❑ You should consult the film packaging and/or the film cassette to ascertain the correct film speed. It is rated in ISO, ASA, or DIN. ISO and ASA use the same numerical scale. The sequence from slow to fast films: ISO/ASA 25, 50, 100, 200, 400, 800, 1600, 3200. You may come across films rated at intermediary steps, such as ISO 64 or ISO 125.
❑ The camera will consult the checkered DX-code on the film cassette and set the film speed for you. Just make sure that the film cassette actually has a DX-code. If it does not, the camera will use the default setting which may be wrong. Very few, if any, films are without a DX-code. If you use film cassettes intended for bulk loading, you can purchase stickers with the appropriate DX-coding for the film you are using.

✓ **Focusing manually**

❑ Look through the viewfinder at your subject.
❑ Choose an important point of focus in your subject. Remember that the lens can only focus on one plane at a time.
❑ Rotate the lens barrel until the chosen part of your subject appears to be in sharp focus. Use the ground glass, the microprism, and/or the split-image device in your viewfinder to aid you with focusing. See 3.4 Practical tips for use of the split-image device.

✓ **Focusing automatically**

❑ Look through the viewfinder at your subject.
❑ Choose an important point of focus in your subject. Remember that the lens can only focus on one plane at a time.
❑ Place the point of focus central in your frame. There might be a set of brackets in the viewfinder, which indicate the area chosen for focusing by the camera.
❑ Press the shutter release button halfway and observe elements of the central area come into sharp focus.

✓ **Setting the exposure manually and exposing the film**

❑ Ensure that the film speed is correctly set.
❑ Press the shutter release button halfway to activate the light meter.
❑ Note the recommended combination of shutter speed and aperture in the exposure readout.
❑ Set the aperture to the recommended setting.
❑ Set the shutter speed to the recommended setting.
❑ Check focus and composition.
❑ Press the shutter release button to make the exposure.

A large part of an introductory course in photography is devoted to learning about exposure. The reading recommended by the camera's light meter makes certain presumptions, which give you less than ideal negatives in most cases. By interpreting the metered exposure information in relation to your subject, you make manual adjustments in exposure to produce better negatives. Chapter 5 provides you with comprehensive coverage of these principles.

✓ **Setting the exposure automatically and exposing the film**

❑ Select the desired automatic exposure mode on your camera: Programmed mode, aperture-priority mode, or shutter-priority mode.
Choose the corresponding option below:
❑ In programmed mode, the camera sets both shutter speed and aperture based on the light-meter reading.
❑ In aperture-priority mode, you set the desired aperture for the subject and the camera selects a shutter speed based on the light-meter reading.
❑ In shutter-priority mode, you set the desired shutter speed for the subject and the camera selects an aperture based on the light-meter reading.
❑ Check focus and composition.
❑ Press the shutter release button to make the exposure.

A large part of an introductory course in photography is devoted to learning about exposure. The reading recommended by the camera's light meter makes certain presumptions, which give you less than ideal negatives in most cases. By interpreting the metered exposure information in relation to your subject, you make manual adjustments in exposure to produce better negatives. Chapter 5 provides you with comprehensive coverage of these principles.

✓ **Manual rewind**

❑ When the film advance lever will not turn and the frame counter has reached the right number of exposures, press the rewind button normally located at the bottom of your camera.

❑ Lift the handle of the rewind crank and turn it clockwise until the tension is released. See 5.4 Practical tips for the benefits of keeping a small portion of the film leader outside the film cassette.

❑ Open the camera back and remove the film cassette. Keep it away from humidity and heat. Develop within 72 hours.

✓ **Automatic rewind**

❑ When frame counter indicates that you have reached the end of a roll, the camera will either rewind the film immediately, or you may have to press a rewind button to start the process.

❑ Open the camera back and remove the film cassette. Keep it away from humidity and heat. Develop within 72 hours.

Notes

2 CAMERA

2.1 GLOSSARY

Aperture	An adjustable opening within the lens used to control the intensity of the light falling on the film during exposure. The aperture, given by an f-number, refers to the size of this opening.
Aperture-priority	An automatic exposure mode. The camera operator sets the aperture and the camera sets the shutter speed.
Automatic camera	A camera where one or more functions are performed automatically by the camera without user input.
Depth of field	The area from near to far in a photograph that appears sharp.
Electronic camera	A camera that uses a CCD (Charge Coupled Device) instead of film to record the image.
Exposure	An exposure describes the amount of light falling on the light sensitive film after the shutter is released. The exposure is controlled by a combination of aperture and shutter speed.
Film	Film is used to permanently record the image formed by the lens. It consists of a light sensitive emulsion on an acetate or plastic base.
Film cassette	A light proof container for light sensitive 35mm film. The film speed is often inscribed in a DX-code on the side of the cassette.
Film speed	A measure for the light sensitivity of film.
Focal length	The distance from a point in the lens to the focal (film) plane when the lens is focused on infinity. Longer focal length lenses bring you closer to the subject by increasing magnification.
Focus	In focus refers to the point where rays of light converge on the film to form a sharp image. To focus involves adjusting the lens to film distance by turning the lens barrel until the desired subject in the scene appears sharp (in focus).
Lens	A lens consists of one or more optical glass elements arranged to sharply focus a scene in front of the camera on the film.
Light-meter	An instrument, built into the camera or used hand held, that measures the amount of light either falling on a subject or reflecting off a subject. The measurement is used to calculate an exposure setting of shutter speed and aperture.
Manual camera	A camera where the functions are controlled by the user.
Negative	The tones in a negative image recorded on film are reversed in relation to the original subject. Light becomes dark and vice versa.
Rangefinder	Cameras of this type have a focusing device built into the viewfinder.
Shutter	The shutter mechanism opens and closes to control the length of time the film is exposed to light.
Shutter speed	The actual time that the shutter remains open to expose the film.
Shutter-priority	An automatic exposure mode. The camera operator sets the shutter speed and the camera sets the aperture.
SLR camera	Single-lens reflex cameras reflect the image formed by the taking lens onto a ground glass for viewing. A mirrored pentaprism in this path turns the image around so it is viewed the correct way.

TLR camera	Twin-lens reflex cameras have two lenses: a viewing lens projecting the image onto a ground glass for viewing and a taking lens mounted just below for exposing the film.
Transparency/ Slide	A positive image recorded on transparency film where the tones are the same as they were in the subject. Slide usually refers to a 35mm transparency mounted for projection.
View camera	Usually a large format camera where the image formed by the lens is registered directly (upside down) on a ground glass screen. Focus is set manually by observing the image as the front or rear standard of the camera is moved back or forth.
Viewfinder	A small window on the camera used to frame the subject. The viewfinder image seeks to be an exact representation of the image seen by the lens.
Viewfinder camera	Cameras of this type only have a simple viewfinder window for framing. Focusing is either automatic or set manually on the lens according to an estimate of the camera to subject distance.

2.2 SUMMARY

15

Camera

Why do you need to know how a camera works: In many cases, your subject does not fit average presumptions inscribed in camera design, and you may want to interpret the scene differently. Knowledge of how cameras work and the ability to control them manually is essential to take creative control of photography. **If you are learning photography, many instructors recommend using manual operation at first:** Using manual operation will allow you to fundamentally understand how the camera and photography works.

16 - 17

Basic camera controls

The basic controls on any camera are similar, helping you to perform the same actions every time you take a picture: The camera allows you to frame the picture, focus it sharply, and expose the film using a combination of shutter speed and aperture. **One of the most popular camera types is shown here – the 35mm single-lens reflex:** This is the camera most beginners start with and that many professionals favor due to its compact size and ease of operation. **As the camera's settings change, the picture changes also:** Your choice of shutter speed and aperture does not only determine the amount of light striking the film during exposure. It also affects the appearance of elements in the photograph. **Manually adjusted controls:** A shutter speed selector and aperture ring allow you to set the exposure. Settings are marked on the controls. A focusing ring on the lens allows you to focus the image. **On automatic cameras:** Buttons often replace knobs and rings on automatic cameras. Settings are displayed in a data panel. Automatic-focus cameras may have a ring on the lens for manual focusing or zooming. **The viewfinder:** Shows most (about 90%) of the scene included in the photograph. It aids focusing and may display exposure readout information. **The shutter-speed selector:** Controls the length of time the shutter remains open during exposure. Affects the impression of motion in the photograph. **The aperture selector:** Adjusts the size of the lens opening to control the intensity of the light during exposure. Affects the depth of field – the impression of sharpness from near to far in a photograph. **Interchangeable lenses:** Separate lenses of different focal lengths that can be used on the same camera body. Lens focal length affects the size of objects and the angle of view in the scene.

18 - 19 **The shutter and light**

Two controls adjust the amount of light that reaches the film: The shutter and the aperture must be set according to your visualization of the picture to get the desired result. **The shutter controls the amount of light by the length of time it remains open:** Shutter speeds are given in fractions of a second. Each speed is half the previous speed and double the next speed – 1/30 is half the time of 1/15 and double the time if 1/60. Manual cameras with mechanical shutters usually employ the following sequence of shutter speeds: 1, 1/2, 1/4, 1/8, 1/15, 1/30, 1/60, 1/125, 1/250, 1/500, 1/1000. Only the lower number of the fraction is usually displayed on your camera. Electronic shutters can operate at any speed, but you normally use the same sequence, perhaps with some intermediary speeds, in the manual mode on an automatic camera. Digital cameras turn their sensor chip on or off for the required time. **NOTE: The term "stop" refers to a change in exposure, whether the aperture or the shutter speed is changed:** The "stop" refers to the quantity of light that makes up the identical difference between two shutter speeds or two apertures. Changing the exposure by one "stop" means a change of one setting on either the shutter speed or aperture scale. **A focal plane shutter is built into the camera and is located directly in front of the film:** Two overlapping curtains move to expose the film. You can only synchronize the shutter with flash below a certain shutter speed. **A leaf shutter or between-the-lens shutter is generally located inside the lens itself:** A number of small overlapping metal leaves open and close to expose the film. Slower fastest shutter speed than focal plane shutters. Can be synchronized with flash at any speed.

20 - 23 **The shutter and motion**

The faster the shutter speed, the more likely a moving subject will be sharp: Fast speeds freeze action in a moving subject, while slower speeds create blur and an impression of movement. **Shown below are the effects of varying shutter speed and camera movement:** The direction of the subject and any camera movement along the same axis as the subject (panning) will affect the amount of blur. **Other factors besides shutter and subject speed also affect the amount of blurring in a photograph:** Distance between camera and subject affects the degree of blur in a photograph. Lens focal length also has an influence on how blurred a moving subject will appear. Longer lenses create more blur. **Panning keeps a moving subject sharp while blurring the background:** Moving the camera with a moving subject during exposure is called panning. Start the movement before pressing the shutter release button and follow through after completing the exposure. Please see pages 22 – 23 for some examples of how motion can be expressed in a still photograph.

24 - 25 **The aperture and light**

The aperture (the size of the lens opening) controls the brightness of the light that reaches the film: A diaphragm of metal leaves located inside the lens is opened and closed to control the amount of light passing through. **The size of an aperture is indicated by its f-number or f-stop:** The actual number of an f-stop is determined by dividing the lens focal length with the diameter of the actual aperture opening. A change of one aperture setting is often referred to as a change of one "stop". **The standardized, full-stop series of numbers on the f-stop scale runs as follows:** f/1, f/1.4, f/2, f/2.8, f/4, f/5.6, f/8, f/11, f/16, f/22, f/32, f/45, and f/64. Higher numbers mean a smaller opening. Each f-stop admits half as much light as the previous one and twice as much light as the next one – f/5.6 is half as much light as f/4 and twice as much light as f/8. Note how the relationship between f-stops equals the relationship between shutter speeds. This is the key to photography. **No lens is built to use the whole range of apertures:** This depends on the lens design and its application. **Lenses are often described as fast or slow:** These terms refer to the widest aperture opening. A fast lens has a larger maximum aperture than a slower lens.

26 - 27 **The aperture and depth of field**

The smaller the aperture size, the more of a scene will be sharp from near to far: The area of acceptable sharpness from near to far in a photograph is called depth of field. **The two large photographs shown on these pages were taken under identical conditions but with different aperture settings:** Consult pages 26 and 27 to see how a smaller aperture increases the depth of field. **Some types of cameras let you see the extent of depth of field:** The lens is normally set at its widest aperture to make the viewfinder image bright. Since the depth of field effect is very small at this aperture, it also makes focusing more accurate. By manually stopping down the lens, you can see, in the viewfinder or on the ground glass, how depth of field increases as the apertures gets smaller. Some cameras allow you to do this through a depth of field preview button. At very small apertures, the image is usually so dark that it is impossible to determine the degree of sharpness. **A rangefinder, point-and-shoot, or twin-lens reflex camera shows the scene only at the widest aperture of the viewing lens:** When there is no aperture present, depth of field can of course not be previewed. **Some lenses have a depth of field scale from which you can estimate the depth of field:** The depth of field scale is usually found between the aperture ring and the focusing ring. The distance range between two numbers, found on the focusing ring opposite a given aperture on the depth of field scale, constitutes the depth of field for that particular aperture. The infinity mark, ∞ , is the furthest point of focus. Focusing on infinity means that all parts of a scene farther away from this distance will be sharp.

28 - 29 **Using shutter and aperture together**

Both shutter speed and aperture affect the amount of light entering the camera: To get a correctly exposed negative, you need to let exactly the right amount of light in through the lens for the right length of time. You use a combination of aperture and shutter speed to achieve this. Since the difference between two apertures and two shutter speeds is the identical "stop", you can get the same amount of exposure by changing the settings in opposite directions. **Equivalent exposures:** If you let one "stop" *less* light in through the aperture, you can set the shutter speed for one "stop" *more* exposure and get the same amount of light striking the film. In practical terms, if you have an exposure reading of f/8 at 1/125, you can change this into many combinations. Changing the aperture to f/11 will let one "stop" *less* light in through the lens opening. If you change the shutter speed to 1/60 and one "stop" *more* light, you will have a new exposure combination of f/11 at 1/60. An exposure of f/8 and 1/125 is actually equal to an exposure of f/11 at 1/60. **Shutter speed and aperture also affect sharpness:** You change the exposure combinations of shutter speed and aperture to control the appearance of your photographs. Shutter speed choices affect the sharpness of moving subjects. Aperture choices affect the depth of field in a scene.

30 **Choosing a camera**

Choosing a camera will be easier once you decide what kind of pictures you want to take: For occasional amateur use, a point-and-shoot compact camera will do. To get more control over the photographs you produce, a 35mm SLR which allows for manual operation is a minimum requirement. **Shop around to compare prices, accessories, and services:** If possible, try the camera of your choice before purchasing. Look on the Internet for the best prices. You may be able to find a good used camera at a considerable saving. However, be careful about purchasing used equipment that shows considerable signs of wear. Ask your photography instructor to cover some easy tests you can do in the shop to determine if the camera is working properly. Make sure that there is a warranty or return policy. **The size of film used in the camera determines the size of the camera itself and the quality of the image the camera produces:** The degree of negative enlargement possible while retaining a high quality image increases with the negative size.

30 **Single-lens reflex cameras**

A single-lens reflex camera shows you the scene directly through the lens: A camera design involving a mirror and a pentaprism displays the image in the viewfinder. 35mm SLR camera systems are very versatile, with many useful components that allow you to practice almost every type of photography. Limit your choice of features to the ones you may conceivably need. Manual exposure mode is a necessity. SLR cameras are also available in medium-format with the added advantage of larger negatives and the drawback of bulkier equipment.

31 **Rangefinder/viewfinder cameras**

A viewfinder camera shows you the scene through a small window (a viewfinder): Simple viewfinder cameras use this window as a basic framing device, while rangefinder cameras have a built-in focusing mechanism. 35mm models are fast and quiet to operate, making them ideal for fast photojournalist type work under a wide variety of conditions. Due to parallax, these cameras are not suitable for detailed close-up work or careful framing. Medium-format models offer the same limitations, but their low weight makes them ideal for high quality negatives on location.

32 **View cameras**

A view camera has direct, through-the-lens viewing and a large image on a viewing screen: It features the oldest and simplest form of camera design. View cameras provide exceptional control over the image at the expense of large cumbersome equipment and slow operation. The film comes in single sheets, which makes it possible to develop each photograph individually. Fantastic image quality due to the large negative size.

33 **Twin-lens reflex cameras**

Twin-lens reflex (TLR) cameras: A fading medium-format camera model. Two-lens design struggles with parallax. Price is often agreeable compared to other medium-format cameras, but you pay for the lack of versatility.

33 **Point-and-shoot cameras**

Point-and-shoot cameras: Useful when portability is an issue and manual controls are not needed. Their price is very agreeable, but the lack of manual features makes these snapshot machines easy to outgrow for the serious photographer.

33 **Digital cameras**

Digital cameras: These comprise the future without film. A sensor is activated by light and the captured image is stored as data on a memory card. These image files are easily transferred to a computer for printing or electronic distribution. Many benefits with regards to use within an increasingly electronic culture, but image quality is a serious limitation compared to photographs caught on film, unless you can afford one of the prohibitively expensive models. Check Internet auction sites for yesterday's models at less than half the price today.

34 **Special-purpose cameras**

Special-purpose cameras: Immediate results, underwater photography, or extraordinary panoramic formats are some examples of special-purpose cameras. **Underwater cameras:** As their name suggest, these waterproof models lets you enjoy photography in another element. Protective housing is available for normal cameras. **Panoramic cameras:** These capture wide views on a variety of formats. Models with a fixed or rotating lens are available. **Instant cameras:** Polaroid cameras develop your photographs in a matter of seconds. Great for proofing or final prints.

Stereo cameras: Two lenses separated by a small distance take two photographs at the same moment. When viewed through a stereoscopic viewer, the two images merge into one for a three-dimensional effect.

35 **Keeping the camera steady**

Keep the camera steady during an exposure: Camera motion during an exposure will cause your photograph to blur and lose sharpness. **How much camera movement is too much:** Large enlargements of the negative will exaggerate any lack of sharpness. Fast shutter speeds are obviously less likely to show any camera motion that occurred during exposure. Longer lenses are inclined to register the slightest degree of camera movement. **If you are hand holding a camera, use a shutter speed faster than the focal length of the lens:** For a 50mm lens, use 1/60. For a 200mm lens, use 1/250 and so on. Support your body or the camera in any way you can, and squeeze the shutter gently to avoid camera shake. **Using a tripod and camera release is the best way to prevent camera movement:** A suitable tripod ensures the sharpest results. Keeping the camera in one position can also be useful for posed portraits, landscapes, or careful compositions of any kind. **Tabletop tripods are sometimes useful:** Their size is manageable and they can be used in a variety of creative ways. Monopods are another option.

2.3 TEST

FILL IN THE BLANKS

1 SLR is an abbreviation of single-lens ____________________.

2 A shutter speed is often chosen to control the appearance of ____________________ in a photograph.

3 A "stop" of exposure change refers to a change of either one full ____________________ setting or one full ____________________ setting.

4 Depth of field refers to the degree of ____________________ from near to far in a photograph.

5 Depth of field ____________________ as the aperture opening gets smaller.

6 Depth of field ____________________ with smaller f-numbers.

7 An aperture of f/11 is twice as much light as ____________________.

8 To avoid camera shake with a 50mm lens, it is best to use a shutter speed of ____________________ or faster.

9 The type of shutter used in the majority of 35mm cameras is called a ____________________ shutter.

10 A shutter speed of 1/60 is half as much light as a shutter speed of ____________________.

MULTIPLE CHOICE – CIRCLE ONE OR MORE

1	The ISO rating refers to a film's:	a.	maximum exposure.
		b.	speed.
		c.	minimum aperture.
2	An f-stop or f-number is:	a.	an aperture setting.
		b.	a camera to subject distance found on the lens.
		c.	the fastest shutter speed.
3	If an exposure is given by 1/250 and f/11, an equivalent exposure would be:	a.	1/250 and f/16.
		b.	1/500 and f/8.
		c.	1/125 and f/16.
4	Three shutter speed faster than 1/60 in full stop increments would be:	a.	1/125, 1/250, 1/500.
		b.	1/61, 1/62, 1/63.
		c.	1/30, 1/15, 1/8.
5	An aperture of f/8 is:	a.	half as much light as f/5.6.
		b.	twice as much light as f/16.
		c.	twice as much light as f/11.
6	A shutter speed of 1/125 is:	a.	twice as much light as 1/60.
		b.	half as much light as 1/60.
		c.	a quarter as much light as 1/30.
7	An aperture change from f/8 to f/16 will:	a.	increase the depth of field.
		b.	increase the degree of sharpness from near to far in the photograph.
		c.	alter the focusing distance.
8	The camera light-meter usually gives an exposure readout in a:	a.	combination of film speed and focusing distance.
		b.	combination of shutter speed and aperture.
		c.	combination of f-stop and shutter speed.
9	The following series represents part of an aperture scale in full-stop increments:	a.	f/2.8, f/4, f/8, f/11.
		b.	f/2.8, f/5.6, f/11, f/22, f/45.
		c.	f/5.6, f/8, f/11, f/16, f/22.
10	A one-stop exposure change from an exposure of f/8 and 1/125 is an exposure of:	a.	f/8 and 1/250
		b.	f/5.6 and 1/250.
		c.	f/11 and 1/250.

2.4 PRACTICAL TIPS

Focusing

Use vertical lines for split-image focusing.

Split-image focusing is usually the fastest and most accurate way of focusing your lens. If the ground-glass screen in your viewfinder has a central image made of a circle with a central line dividing it in two, you have a split-image-focusing device.

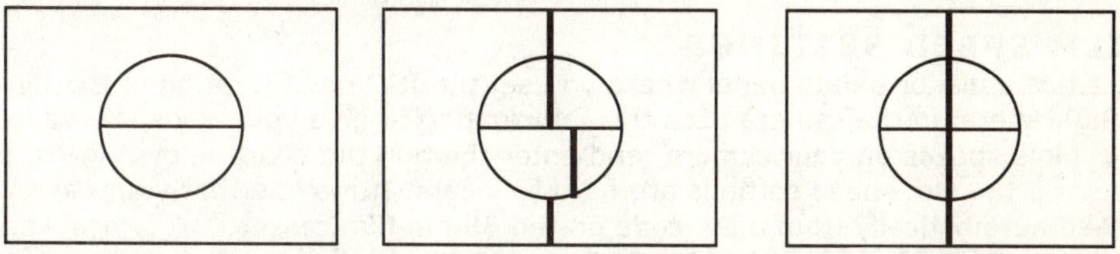

As the name implies, it splits the viewfinder image within the circle into two images, which become one at the distance in focus. A vertical line obviously makes an ideal subject to bring into focus with this device. When it is out of focus, the line is very clearly discontinuous (middle illustration above), and it neatly blends into one when it is in focus (right illustration above). If you are having trouble focusing your subject, find a suitable line at the same distance from the camera as your subject and turn your camera until the line intersects vertically across the circle. Focus on the line with accuracy, and keep the lens focused at this distance while you frame your original subject again. This time you can be absolutely sure that it is in perfect focus.

2.5 JOURNAL

2.5.1 SHUTTER SPEED SETTINGS

Your camera has a range of shutter speeds displayed on a shutter speed dial or in a data panel. Familiarize yourself with the sequence of shutter speeds on your camera by filling out the chart below. The flash synch speed is sometimes given as a shutter speed in another color or as a shutter speed with a lightning symbol next to it. B stands for Bulb and keeps the shutter open as long as you hold the shutter release button down. Ask your instructor, if you are in doubt about any of the shutter speed markings on your camera. A typical sequence of full stops would be 1, 2, 4, 8, 15, 30, 60, 125, 250, 500, and 1000. The next chapter will explore the lens and aperture settings in detail.

CAMERA MAKE AND MODEL ▸													
SHUTTER SPEED SETTINGS ▾													
Slowest													Fastest
Flash synchronization speed ▸													

CAMERA MAKE AND MODEL ▸														
SHUTTER SPEED SETTINGS ▾														
Slowest														Fastest
Flash synchronization speed ▸														

2.5.2 FILM SPEED SETTINGS

Your camera has a dial or a data panel where you set the ISO or ASA rating of the film you are using. The light meter in the camera uses this information to give you exposure readout. Find the range of films speeds on your camera, and enter them in the chart below. Again, consult your instructor if the film speed settings are hard to locate. It may be that your camera only sets the speed automatically from a DX-code on the 35mm film cassette. A typical sequence of full stops would be 25, 50, 100, 200, 400, 800, and 1600 with intermediary marks for speeds in between these.

CAMERA MAKE AND MODEL ▸										
FILM SPEED SETTINGS ▾										
Slowest										Fastest

CAMERA MAKE AND MODEL ▸										
FILM SPEED SETTINGS ▾										
Slowest										Fastest

2.5.3 AUTOMATIC SETTINGS

Your camera might have one or more automatic settings. These can be found either on the shutter speed dial, on the aperture ring (see the next chapter on the lens), or as a menu option in the data panel. Locate these settings on your camera and refer to the instruction manual to find out exactly what functions the automatic programs perform. The most common designations are P and A, which refer to a fully programmed mode and a shutter-priority or an aperture-priority mode. See the 2.2 Summary section above or the textbook for more information on these modes.

CAMERA MAKE AND MODEL ▸	
AUTOMATIC SETTINGS ▾	
Program abbreviation	Automatic mode

CAMERA MAKE AND MODEL ▸	
AUTOMATIC SETTINGS ▾	
Program abbreviation	**Automatic mode**

2.5.4 EXPOSURE READOUT

Your camera has a light meter, which measures the light and recommends an exposure for the subject you have chosen. It is important that you are familiar with the way your camera presents this information. Look at the illustrations below and select the method used by your camera. There are numerous variations on these three options, so consult with your instructor until you are perfectly clear on how the exposure readout in your camera works.

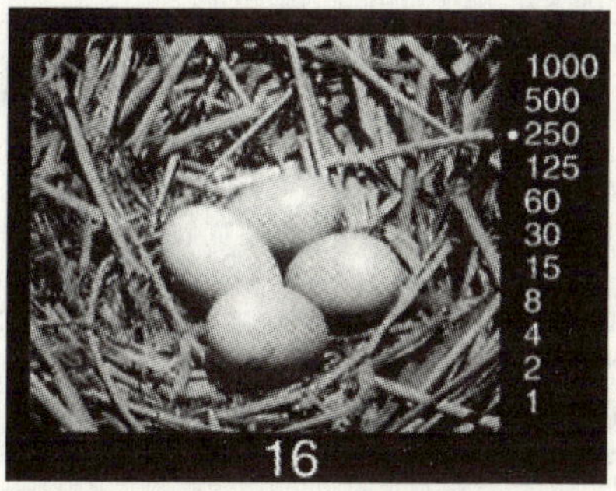

The small LED next to the shutter speeds indicates what speed the light meter recommends with the chosen aperture. In this illustration, an aperture of f/16 requires a shutter speed of 250 for this particular scene.

Is this your type of exposure readout?

Y❑ N❑

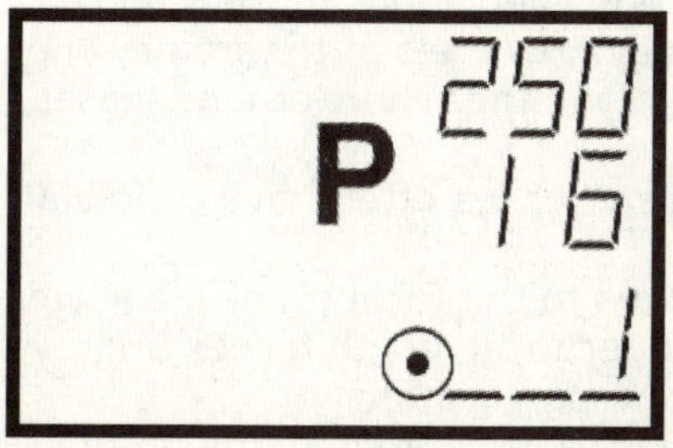

A data panel like this one might give you exposure readouts along with the current settings of shutter speed and aperture. This panel shows a program mode with current settings.

Is this your type of exposure readout?

Y❑ N❑

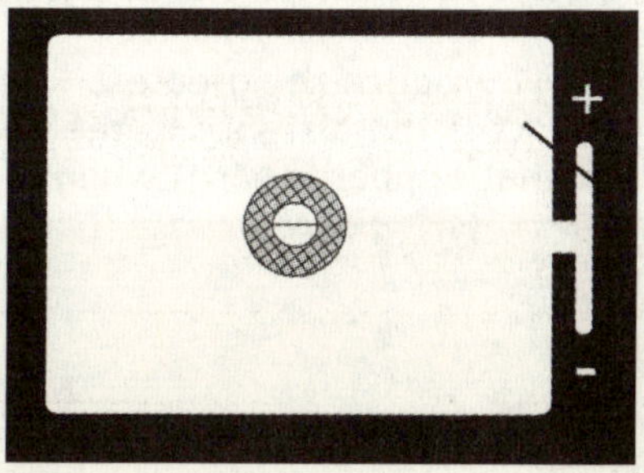

As you turn the shutter speed and aperture dials to different settings, the needle fluctuates between plus and minus. When it remains centered, the combination of shutter speed and aperture currently selected is the recommended exposure.

Is this your type of exposure readout?

Y❑ N❑

3 LENS

3.1 GLOSSARY

Aberration An optical defect in a lens causing a lack of sharpness and/or distortion.

Angle of view The outer edges of a scene seen through a lens or in the viewfinder form an angle of view from the camera position.

Aperture An adjustable opening within the lens used to control the intensity of the light falling on the film during exposure. The aperture, given by an f-number, refers to the size of this opening.

Automatic focus Also referred to as autofocus. Cameras with automatic focus select a part of the scene, most often located centrally in the frame, and focus automatically on this point.

Cable release A cable attached to the shutter release. Used to avoid touching and possibly moving the camera during exposure or to trigger the shutter from a distance.

Depth of field The area from near to far in a photograph that appears sharp.

Depth of field preview Manually stopping the lens down to various apertures by using a lever/button on the camera will allow the user to preview how depth of field (the degree of sharpness from near to far) will appear in the photograph.

Distortion Optical effects causing a photographed subject to appear strangely elongated, curved, or flattened. Lens aberrations in wide-angle lenses that curve straight objects at the edges of the frame, and the changes in perspective caused by either short or long lenses appear as distortions.

Fisheye lens An extreme wide-angle lens. Fisheye lenses often have a circular image.

Focal length The distance from a point in the lens to the focal (film) plane when the lens is focused on infinity. Longer focal length lenses bring you closer to the subject by increasing magnification.

Focus In focus refers to the point where rays of light converge on the film to form a sharp image. To focus involves adjusting the lens to film distance by turning the lens barrel until the desired subject in the scene appears sharp (in focus).

Hyperfocal distance Focusing on the hyperfocal distance will produce the greatest depth of field for a particular aperture. It is the distance to the nearest plane of depth of field (point that appears sharp) when the lens is focused on infinity.

3.2 SUMMARY

39 — **Lens**

All photographic lenses do the same basic job: They collect light rays and focus them in a sharp image on the film. This chapter explains how lens focal length, focus, aperture, and lens-to-subject distance can be controlled to produce the kind of pictures you want.

40 – 41 — **From pinhole to lens**

Although all the light rays reflected from an object cannot produce an image, a selection of rays can: If rays of light are filtered through a pinhole opening, only a few rays pass through in straight lines to render an image of the scene on the other side. The image is reversed both horizontally and vertically. **The trouble with a pinhole camera is its tiny opening:** It demands a very long exposure. **A pinhole, small as it is, actually admits a cluster of light rays:** A larger opening creates an image that is much less sharp, because each circle of confusion becomes larger and overlaps its neighbor to blur the image. **A lens creates a sharp image with a relatively short exposure:** A lens focuses the light through a larger opening to reduce the circles of confusion as much as possible. **Most modern photographic lenses are based on the convex lens:** Thicker in the middle, it focuses many rays of light emitted from the subject in one focal point at the focal plane, which is normally the film plane. **How does a lens refract (bend) light to form an image:** When light travels from one transparent medium into another, the rays of light are refracted. **For refraction to take place, light must strike the new medium at an angle:** If rays of light are perpendicular to the surface, they pass straight through. At other angles, the light is bent to a predictable degree. The further away from a straight angle, the more they are bent. **When light strikes a transparent medium with a curved surface, such as a lens:** The glass elements in a lens are carefully crafted to refract the light from a scene into a sharp image at the focal plane.

42 - 43 — **Lens focal length**

The most important way lenses differ is in their focal length: Focal length is technically the distance from the rear nodal point in the lens to the focal plane when the lens is focused on infinity. **Focal length controls magnification:** The longer the focal length, the greater the magnification, or size, of objects in the image. **Focal length also controls angle of view:** Longer lenses form a larger image, which include less of the scene. Please see page 43 in the textbook for an excellent illustration of these principles.

44 - 45 — **Normal-focal-length lenses**

A normal-focal-length lens, also called a standard-focal-length lens, approximates what the human eye sees: The relationship between objects in the scene appears as it does for the human eye. **A lens that is a normal focal length for one camera can be a long focal length for another camera:** Film size determines the "normal" focal length. As the film size increases, it requires a larger image circle to fit the negative format. Larger formats therefore use longer lenses as "normal" lenses. **A lens of normal focal length has certain advantages over lenses of longer or shorter focal length:** It is usually faster, cheaper, lighter, and more compact. **Choice of focal length is a matter of personal preference:** Most photographers use different focal lengths depending on the situation they are photographing in and the kind of photograph they want.

46 - 47 Long-focal-length lenses

A long-focal-length lens provides greater image magnification and a narrower angle of view than a normal lens: Longer lenses can be useful in many situations. **Long lenses are excellent when you cannot or do not want to get close to the subject:** Sports and wildlife photography usually require long lenses. Longer focal lengths are also used extensively for portraiture to avoid distortion of the subject's features. **There are subtle qualities that can be exploited when you use a long lens:** Extremely shallow depth of field and a compression of the image space into a flatter perspective are qualities of long lenses. **Long lenses have some disadvantages, and the longer the lens the more noticeable the disadvantages become:** Size, weight, and cost usually increase with the focal length of a lens. Shallow depth of field demands precise focusing. The risk of camera shake requires fast shutter speeds, which are hard to achieve without fast film due to the small maximum aperture of most long lenses. **Photographers commonly call any long lens a telephoto, or tele, although not all long lenses are actually of telephoto design:** Telephoto is a specific design used on a certain type of lens. It allows for an effective focal length that is longer than the physical length of the lens. A tele-converter can be placed between the lens and the camera body to increase the focal length of a lens.

48 - 49 Short-focal-length lenses

A short-focal-length lens increases the angle of view and shows more of a scene than a normal lens used from the same position: A short lens is also called a wide-angle lens. It is equally useful in confined spaces and expansive landscapes. **Wide-angle lenses have considerable depth of field:** This allows the photographer to keep photographing in fast moving situations without refocusing the lens between every shot. **Pictures taken with a wide-angle lens can show both real and apparent distortions:** Due to the extreme curvature of the glass elements in a wide-angle lens, it produces certain aberrations. Wide-angle lenses let you focus extremely close to the subject, altering the size relationship between objects in the scene. **A wide-angle lens can also show an apparent distortion of perspective:** The distorted perspective where objects close to the lens appear disproportionately larger than objects further away can be minimized or exploited by adjusting the lens-to-subject distance.

50 Zoom lenses

Zoom lenses are popular because they combine a range of focal lengths into one lens: By moving elements of the lens in relation to each other, a continuous range of focal lengths can be used. **A zoom has some disadvantages:** It is larger, heavier, and more expensive than fixed-focal-length lenses, but is does replace two or more of them. The best prices and fewest drawbacks are found with a modest zooming range. The greater the zooming range the more evident are the disadvantages of zoom lenses. **Some zoom lenses are best used where light is ample because they have a relatively small maximum aperture:** The small maximum aperture is perhaps their biggest drawback. The maximum aperture will change by as much as one stop over the focal length of the lens in many zoom lenses. Zoom lenses are generally not quite a sharp as fixed-focal-length lenses.

51 Special-purpose lenses

For the widest of wide-angle views, consider the fisheye lens: It can have a wide angle of view up to 180°. Barrel distortion is a feature of fisheye lenses that creates curvature towards the edges of the image. **A macro lens is useful for extremely close shots:** An extra long lens barrel allows for close focusing. It is corrected for aberrations at these distances. **Aberrations are deliberately introduced in a soft-focus lens, also called a portrait lens:** It diffuses the image for a soft-focus effect.

A perspective-control lens brings some view-camera adjustments to other types of cameras: The lens can be moved to control distorted perspective. **A catadioptric or mirror lens is similar in design to a reflecting telescope:** The use of reflecting mirrors inside the lens extends the focal length without increasing the length of the lens. Mirror lenses usually have only one fixed aperture.

52 - 53 **Focusing your lens – Manual focus**

With manual focusing, you select the part of the scene you want to be sharpest: Use focus to distribute attention to the most important parts of a photograph. In photographs of people, this is usually the eyes. **The nearer you are, the more important it is to focus critically:** Depth of field gets shallower at close distances. **Focus manually like you would tune a guitar:** Move back and forth on either side of perceived focus to determine the sharpest point. **Follow focus lets you keep a subject that is moving toward you well focused:** Turn the focusing ring on the lens at a rate that keeps a moving subject in constant focus. Practice to perfect this technique. **NOTE: Don't forget that shutter speed and aperture play an important role in making objects appear sharp in the final picture:** A slow shutter speed may blur your subject and a large aperture may cause important areas near the plane of critical focus to appear unsharp.

54 - 55 **Focusing your lens – Automatic focus**

Automatic focus (AF) does the focusing for you: By pressing the shutter-release button halfway, you activate the focusing mechanism. In most cases, the camera focuses on the subject in the center of your frame. More elaborate focusing mechanisms track the movement of the eye to determine a focusing point based upon your point of view. Advanced systems allow you to track a moving subject while keeping it in focus. **If your subject is not within the focusing brackets, you can use autofocus lock to make it sharp:** Depress the shutter-release button halfway while framing your subject and keep it down to maintain the same focusing distance. **Wide-area focus systems provide more elaborate electronics:** You select a focusing bracket that covers the subject from a menu on the camera. **Some wide-area autofocus systems use the light reflected off your eyeball to determine where you are looking in the viewfinder:** They focus where you look. **Your camera may let you select among manual, single shot, and continuous focus:** Single-shot autofocus prevents you from releasing the shutter until the picture is in focus. **With continuous focus, the camera constantly searches for the correct focus when you partially depress the shutter button:** It alters the focusing distance according to the subject found within the focusing brackets. Wait for focus to settle before taking the picture. **Once you lock onto a subject, some cameras predict where the subject is likely to be next:** Great for action shots. **Some cameras have two autofocus systems:** The two systems are active autofocus, a red beam of light measures the distance to the subject, and passive autofocus, which depends on contrast in the subject to determine when it is sharp. Both are prone to failure in certain circumstances, so many cameras feature both systems to ensure sharp pictures. **When photographing action, like a soccer game, an autofocus system can be fooled:** When several subjects move in and out of the frame at different distances, the focus might never settle on the subject you have in mind. **Read your camera's instructions:** Refer to your camera manual to make sure you know how your autofocus mechanism works and when manual focus is a better option.

56 - 57 **Focus and depth of field**

What exactly is sharpness, and how can it be controlled: A lens can only focus on a single distance at a time. This distance is called the plane of critical focus. Objects at all other distances in front of and behind this plane will gradually be rendered less sharp. **Depth of field is the part of a scene that appears acceptably sharp in a photograph:**

Depth of field can be shallow, showing only a small section of the image as sharp, or deep, with acceptable sharpness throughout the entire picture. **Images are composed of circles of confusion:** Each "point" in an image is actually made of tiny circles called circles of confusion. When they are small enough, the eye sees them as sharp "points". The farther a point is from the plane of critical focus, the larger its circle of confusion. As the circles grow in size, objects at distances progressively farther away will gradually lose sharpness and become blurred. Sharpness is also affected by the degree of print enlargement and viewing distance.

58 - 59 **Controlling depth of field**

Evaluating and controlling the depth of field is more important in some situations than in others: In subjects with little depth or when you are using short-focal-length lenses, it is less crucial to consider the depth-of-field effect**. You can use the aperture to control depth of field:** Reduce the size of the aperture to increase the depth of field. To reduce the depth of field, open up the aperture to a larger opening. **There are other ways to control depth of field:** To increase the depth of field, use a smaller aperture, a shorter-focal-length lens, or move further away from the subject. To reduce the depth of field, use a larger aperture, a longer-focal-length lens, or move closer to the subject. **Why does a lens of longer focal length produce less depth of field than a shorter lens used at the same f-stop:** The relative aperture opening is larger in longer lenses, producing a shallower depth of field for the same f-number. Please see the box on page 58.

61 **Zone focusing**

Two more techniques let you control the depth of field: Zone focusing and focusing on the hyperfocal distance. You need a camera with manual focusing and a depth-of-field scale on the lens. An automatic camera with automatic focus or a zoom lens is not likely to have these markings. **Zone focusing lets you set the depth of field in advance of shooting:** This is useful for fast moving subjects or when you want to work quickly in an unobtrusive fashion without looking through the viewfinder. **To zone focus, use a lens's depth of field scale to find the f-stop settings that will give you adequate depth of field:** Use the distance markings on the depth-of-field scale to select a zone that will appear sharp in the photograph. You can now photograph without focusing between shots. Everything within the designated depth-of-field zone will appear sharp.

61 **Focusing on the hyperfocal distance**

Focusing on the hyperfocal distance will give you maximum depth of field: You focus on the hyperfocal distance to increase the depth of field for a given aperture when infinity is your furthest limit. Align the infinity mark on the focusing ring with the selected aperture marking on the depth-of-field scale. The focusing distance opposite the focusing mark is the hyperfocal distance. **But for maximum depth of field in a scene that extends to a far distance, don't focus on infinity:** By focusing on the hyperfocal distance instead of infinity, you get more of the foreground in focus.

62 - 63 **Perspective**

The camera image can seem surprisingly different from reality: The telephoto effect compresses the impression of depth in a photograph. Wide-angle distortion affects the relative size and depth of objects in a scene. **Perspective is controlled by the lens-to-subject distance, not by lens focal length:** When the camera moves closer to a subject, objects in the foreground will gradually seem larger compared to objects in the background. This effect is responsible for an impression of increased depth. Please see page 62 for illustrations of this principle. **In one sense, the focal length of a lens does affect the perspective:** Short lenses focus closer than longer lenses, so they are more likely to be used at close lens-to-subject distances, where the impression of depth in a photograph is the greatest.

64 - 65 How to make a close-up photograph

A close-up subject must be focused closer then normal to the camera: To capture a larger than normal image on the negative, you can use a macro lens, a close-up filter on your regular lens, or extension tubes or bellows increasing the distance between camera and lens. **Working close up is somewhat different from working at normal distances:** Depth of field is minimal at small lens-to-subject distances, making focusing crucial. Camera movement is also exaggerated, so a tripod should be used. **Depth of field decreases as the subject is focused closer to the lens:** At close distances, the distribution of depth of field is also altered. At normal distances, it extends 1/3 in front of and 2/3 behind the plane of critical focus. In close-up work, the distribution of depth of field is roughly even on both sides of this plane. **A single-lens reflex or view camera is good for close-ups:** These cameras allow you to see how framing, focus, depth of field (through a preview), and composition will turn out before exposing the film. TTL metering is also great for close-up work. **A rangefinder or twin-lens reflex camera is less convenient for close-ups:** It is very difficult to frame and focus a close-up image properly when you are looking through a viewfinder or a viewing lens separate from the taking lens. What you see can get quite far removed from what you get. See the box on page 64 for an introduction to magnification ratios.

66 Close-up equipment

A macro lens is your best choice for sharp close-ups: It is specially designed to produce sharp results at close distances. Inserting extension tubes or bellows between the lens and the camera body will increase magnification further. One inconvenience is that macro lenses have a small maximum aperture. **A zoom lens with a macro feature:** These allow for close focusing, although not quite as close as a macro lens of fixed focal length. **Reversing a lens produces a sharper image when an ordinary lens is used very close to the subject:** An adapter ring allows you to reverse your lens for better results at close distances. **A close-up lens attaches to the front of an ordinary camera lens:** It magnifies the image further and allows for closer focusing. Close-up lenses come in different strengths or diopters. The diopter rating, +1, +2, +3 etc., denotes how many times the image is magnified and implicitly how close it is possible to focus. Lenses with longer focal lengths will produce a larger image with the same lens attachment compared to shorter lenses. Close-up lens attachments are cheap and easy to carry, but the sharpness of the images they produce is not the best. Usually used with very small apertures. **Extension tubes and bellows fit between the lens and the camera:** They increase the distance between camera and lens to allow for closer focusing. Tubes come in different sizes (can be combined), while flexible bellows cover a wider range. Both tubes and bellows may require an exposure increase, and separating the lens from the camera might disconnect the coupling between aperture and shutter speed used by the meter. If this is the case, stop down the lens manually to meter.

67 Close-up exposures

To get an accurate close-up exposure, you first need to get an accurate light reading: You have to meter correctly and then take the increased lens-to-film distance and/or the reciprocity effect into account. **The small size of a close-up subject can make metering difficult:** You may end up metering too much of the surroundings with a normal reflected-light meter. Use a spot meter, a substitute reading from a gray card, or an incident-light meter instead. **Increase the exposure with bellows or extension tubes:** The increased distance between lens and film reduces the amount of light striking the film. You must increase the exposure to compensate for this loss. **A camera that has a through-the-lens meter will read the light that actually reaches the film:** You should not add exposure manually with a TTL meter.

Manually set exposures: If the coupling between camera and lens is broken by an extension tube or bellows, stop down the lens manually to meter with your TTL meter. Otherwise, meter with a hand-held meter and set the increased exposure manually. See the table on page 67 for the amount of exposure increase needed. **Very long exposures need to be increased even more:** Account for the reciprocity effect in exposures longer than 1 second. **Bracket – to be sure:** Close-ups are most likely to be underexposed, so bracket towards overexposure to ensure excellent results. **Use electronic flash:** A fast shutter speed and small aperture will make focusing slightly less critical and diminish any problems with subject or camera movement.

68 **Guidelines for buying a lens**

Lenses with a wide maximum aperture are more expensive than similar lenses with a stop less on the aperture scale. They provide a brighter viewfinder image, have one more stop to play with in low-light conditions, but may not perform better in any other way. **These are some guidelines for buying camera lenses:**

1. Start with a normal lens or a moderate-focal-length zoom.
2. Get your lenses one at a time and think ahead to the assortment you may someday need.
3. Don't spend money on extra fast lenses unless you have special requirements.
4. Consider a second-hand lens.
5. Test the lens you intend to purchase.
6. A suitable lens shade is a desirable accessory.

69 **Getting the most from your camera and lens**

Cameras and lenses are rugged, considering what precision instruments they are: Care and cleaning will keep them in working order. **A clean lens performs better than a dirty one:** Dirty lenses scatter the light passing through them, causing a loss of contrast and sharpness. Clean your lens with care to avoid damaging the delicate lens coating. **Stopping down the lens aperture often improves the image:** By eliminating rays from the edges of the lens, the image is often crisper. But there is a limit to the improvements that comes with stopping down. Diffraction, the bending or light rays on the edges of the aperture diaphragm, becomes more noticeable at smaller apertures. It causes an overall loss of sharpness in the image.

69 **Protecting and cleaning your camera and lens**

Protect from dust and dirt: Use a padded camera bag to protect your equipment. Cover lens elements with caps when they are not in use. Consider placing an UV or Skylight filter on the lens at all times to protect it. See 3.4 Practical tips. **Protect from moisture:** Moisture and humidity are especially prone to damage or corrode both electronic and mechanical camera components. Keep the camera covered (a plastic bag with a hole for the lens will do) when it is used under wet conditions. **Protect from temperature extremes:** Excessive heat is more damaging than cold temperatures, but try to keep the camera from experiencing any rapid and extreme temperature changes. **Protect during storage:** Release the shutter, remove batteries, turn off the meter, and keep the camera in a dry, clean place during long-term storage. **Check the battery strength regularly:** Carry spare batteries and always replace them before they are completely empty. **Use professional care for all but basic maintenance:** Camera repair requires specialist tools and training. **Cleaning inside the camera:** Tilt the camera so dust falls out and gently blow or brush it away from all parts. Avoid touching or blowing hard on the fragile shutter curtains. Dust in the film path may scratch the film surface and ruin your photographs. **Cleaning the lens:** Hold the lens upside down and blow away all dust from the lens surface. Moisten lens tissue with a few drops of lens cleaner and wipe the lens in a circular motion. Finish with dry tissue.

3.3 TEST

FILL IN THE BLANKS

1 Lens focal length affects the ____________________ of view in a scene and the size of objects in the scene.

2 A normal lens closely resembles ____________________ vision.

3 Another name for a wide-angle lens is a ____________________ lens.

4 Depth of field is controlled by the ____________________ size, the lens ____________________, and the lens-to____________________ distance.

5 Focusing on the ____________________ distance for each aperture will produce the greatest depth field.

6 ____________________ lenses are designed for close-up work.

7 Zoom lenses combine a range of ____________________ in one lens design.

8 Perspective can be controlled in a photograph by altering the distance between lens and ____________________.

9 A lens can only focus on ____________________ distance at a time.

10 The sharp points in an image are in fact tiny ____________________ of confusion.

MULTIPLE CHOICE – CIRCLE ONE OR MORE

1 A normal lens for a 35mm camera is a:
- a. 150mm lens.
- b. 28mm lens.
- c. 50mm lens.

2 If you increase the distance to your subject, depth of field will:
- a. decrease.
- b. remain the same.
- c. increase.

3 At a normal (not extremely close) lens to subject distance, depth of field extends:
- a. from the point of focus to infinity.
- b. 1/3 in front of and 2/3 behind the plane of critical focus.
- c. from f/8 to f/16 in a normal scene.

4 A 150mm lens on a 4x5-inch view camera is considered a:
- a. normal lens.
- b. long lens.
- c. fisheye lens.

5 To increase the depth of field, an aperture of f/8 can be changed to:
- a. f/2.8
- b. f/16
- c. f/5.6

6 To increase the depth of field for a given aperture, you can change your 50mm lens to a:
- a. 150mm lens.
- b. 35mm lens.
- c. telephoto lens.

7	Wide-angle distortion refers to:	a.	the high viewpoint of these lenses.
		b.	the optical distortion of an image by the lens.
		c.	the strange perspective created by these lenses when used close to a subject.
8	A 50mm lens has a wider angle of view than a:	a.	85mm lens.
		b.	28mm lens.
		c.	17mm lens.
9	To increase the size of objects in a scene, you could:	a.	use a longer lens.
		b.	use a wider lens.
		c.	use a smaller aperture.
10	You focus for the greatest depth of field at a given aperture by:	a.	focusing on the aperture ring.
		b.	aligning the infinity mark on the focusing ring with this aperture on the depth of field scale.
		c.	focusing on the plane of critical focus.

3.4 PRACTICAL TIPS

Lens protection

Use an UV or Skylight filter to protect your lens.

Photographic lenses are coated with a thin layer of metallic fluoride to enhance the contrast and sharpness of the photographs they produce. This thin coating is very delicate, and any damage will result in an inferior image quality. Every time you accidentally touch the lens or clean it, the coating is corroded or worn. It is consequently always preferable to leave the lens surfaces alone, unless they have a fingerprint or dust particles on them. The best way to maintain the quality and value of your lens is to use an UV or Skylight filter on it at all times. These filters have a blue haze reducing and warming effect on color films, but they hardly affect black-and-white films at all. Instead of cleaning the lens whenever it gets dirty, you simply clean the filter in the same way. Good filters are also coated, but you can buy a new one for a fraction of the lens price when it gets worn or damaged.

Close-ups

Exposure compensation with bellows.

A common method for calculating exposure compensation with bellows is this formula:

$$\frac{\text{Bellows extension}^2}{\text{Focal length of the lens}^2} = \text{Exposure factor}$$

Once the camera is set up for the photograph, you measure the distance between an external point on the lens where the aperture can be found (actually the rear nodal point, which is close to the aperture in normal lens designs) and the film plane in the camera. Estimate these points as best you can. Apply this measurement to the formula above and translate the exposure factor (the same as for filters) into stops. Given the small measurements with 35mm equipment, the margin of error may be considerable. However, if you develop a certain way of measuring and stick to it, your results will soon become predictable. See 14.5 Journal also.

3.5 JOURNAL

3.5.1 LENS SPECIFICATIONS

Complete the tables below to identify the markings on your lenses. The various scales/marks on a lens contain important information for exposures (on the aperture ring), focusing (on the distance scale), and depth of field calculations (on the depth of field scale). If you have an autofocus camera, your lens might lack most of these scales. Fill out what you can from the information available on the lens. The 3.5.2 Lens specifications for zoom lenses section contains a table designed for zoom lenses.

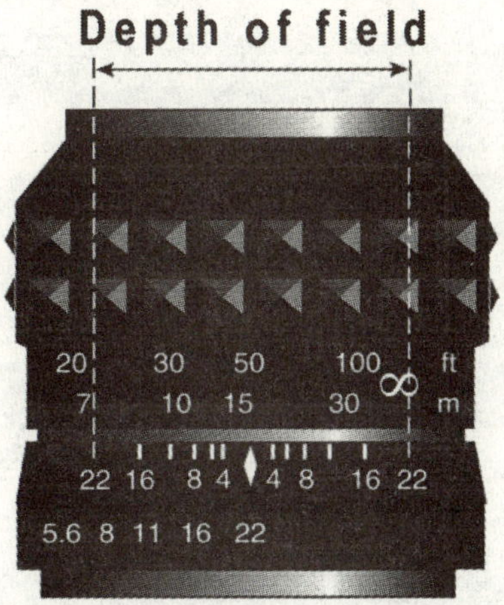

The depth of field scale is normally found in front of the aperture ring and behind the distance scale on the focusing ring. In this example, the lens is focused on the hyperfocal distance at 16m, and depth of field at f/22 extends from 7 meters to infinity. Use the markings on your lens to find the greatest depth of field for each aperture, and enter the near distance in the table below. You can of course also use the depth of field scale to find the depth of field at any focusing distance. Observe how depth of field increases as you use smaller apertures or move further away from your point of focus.

LENS MANUFACTURER ▾	LENS FOCAL LENGTH ▾	LENS SERIAL NUMBER ▾

LENS APERTURES – found on the aperture ring ▾									
Widest									Smallest

FOCUSING DISTANCES – found on the focusing ring ▾									
Closest									Infinity

DEPTH OF FIELD – found on the depth-of-field scale ▾			
Aperture	Closest sharp	Furthest sharp	Hyperfocal distance
		∞	
		∞	
f/2.8		∞	
f/4		∞	
f/5.6		∞	

▾

f/8		∞	
f/11		∞	
f/16		∞	
f/22		∞	
		∞	

LENS MANUFACTURER ▾	LENS FOCAL LENGTH ▾	LENS SERIAL NUMBER ▾

LENS APERTURES – found on the aperture ring ▾									
Widest									Smallest

FOCUSING DISTANCES – found on the focusing ring ▾									
Closest									Infinity

DEPTH OF FIELD – found on the depth-of-field scale ▾			
Aperture	Closest sharp	Furthest sharp	Hyperfocal distance
		∞	
		∞	
f/2.8		∞	
f/4		∞	
f/5.6		∞	
f/8		∞	
f/11		∞	
f/16		∞	
f/22		∞	
		∞	

3.5.2 LENS SPECIFICATIONS FOR ZOOM LENSES

Some lens markings are different on a zoom lens. As the focal length of the zoom lens increases, the f-stop of the widest aperture can change by as much as one stop. For instance, a 70-210mm zoom lens might have a maximum f-stop of f/4 at 70mm and only f/5.6 at 210mm. The actual aperture opening remains the same, but the f-stop changes because it is dependent upon the focal length of the lens. The depth of field scale also changes with the focal length of the lens. If you have a tapering graph running along the lens barrel, this will be your depth of field scale. It works the same way as the scale for fixed-focal-length lenses (see above).

LENS MANUFACTURER ▾	ZOOM RANGE ▾	LENS SERIAL NUMBER ▾

LENS APERTURES – found on the aperture ring ▾

Widest									Smallest

Maximum aperture at shortest focal length ▸	
Maximum aperture at longest focal length ▸	

FOCUSING DISTANCES – found on the focusing ring ▾

Closest									Infinity

DEPTH OF FIELD – found on the depth of field scale running along the lens barrel ▾

Shortest focal length ▸

Aperture	Closest sharp	Furthest sharp	Hyperfocal distance
		∞	
		∞	
f/2.8		∞	
f/4		∞	
f/5.6		∞	
f/8		∞	
f/11		∞	
f/16		∞	
f/22		∞	
		∞	
		∞	

Longest focal length ▸

		∞	
		∞	
f/2.8		∞	
f/4		∞	
f/5.6		∞	
f/8		∞	
f/11		∞	
f/16		∞	
f/22		∞	
		∞	
		∞	

LENS MANUFACTURER ▾	ZOOM RANGE ▾	LENS SERIAL NUMBER ▾

LENS APERTURES – found on the aperture ring ▾

Widest									Smallest

Maximum aperture at shortest focal length ▸	
Maximum aperture at longest focal length ▸	

FOCUSING DISTANCES – found on the focusing ring ▾

Closest									Infinity

DEPTH OF FIELD – found on the depth of field scale running along the lens barrel ▾

Shortest focal length ▸

Aperture	Closest sharp	Furthest sharp	Hyperfocal distance
		∞	
		∞	
f/2.8		∞	
f/4		∞	
f/5.6		∞	
f/8		∞	
f/11		∞	
f/16		∞	
f/22		∞	
		∞	
		∞	

Longest focal length ▸

		∞	
		∞	
f/2.8		∞	
f/4		∞	
f/5.6		∞	
f/8		∞	
f/11		∞	
f/16		∞	
f/22		∞	
		∞	
		∞	

3.5.3 EXPOSURE INCREASE FOR CLOSE-UPS

These tables will help you determine the exposure increase needed when you use extension tubes or bellows with your 35mm camera. Don't forget that a TTL meter measures the light that strikes the film, so no manual increase is needed. Enter the measurements you make and read off the required increase from the tables provided. You might want to try both methods and compare results.

1 Measure the long side of the subject in your viewfinder.

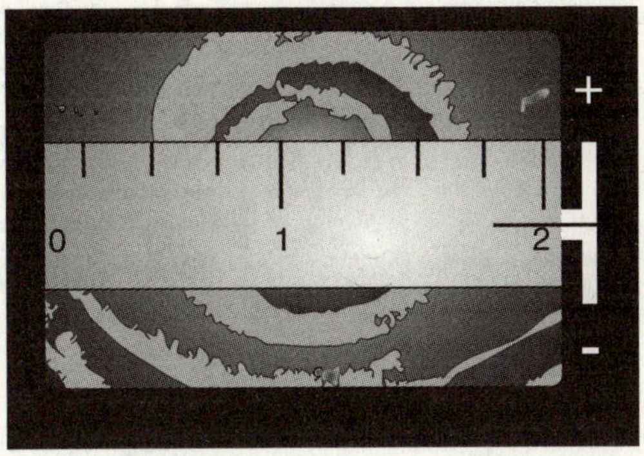

2 Note the measurement.

Subject length (in inches) ▸	2 1/8				

3 Find the exposure increase. Open the lens aperture OR multiply the exposure time.

Subject length (in inches)	11	5 1/8	3 1/4	2 1/4	2	1 3/4	1 3/8	1
Open lens aperture by (stops)	1/3	2/3	1	1 1/3	1 1/2	1 2/3	2	2 1/2
Multiply the exposure time by	1.3	1.6	2	2.5	2.8	3.2	4	5.7

Notes

1 Measure the distance from the rear nodal point in the lens to the film plane.

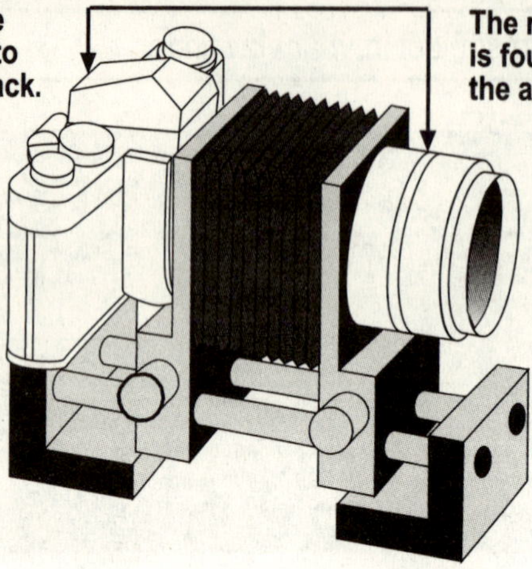

2 Note the measurement.

Distance (in mm) ▸	41					

3 Find the exposure increase. Open the lens aperture OR multiply the exposure time.

Open the lens aperture (stops)	1/3	1/2	1	1 1/3	1 1/2	1 2/3	2	2 1/2
Multiply the exposure time by	1.3	1.6	2	2.5	2.8	3.2	4	5.7
28mm lens								
Bellows extension	31.92	35.42	39.60	44.27	46.85	50.09	56	66.85
35mm lens								
Bellows extension	39.91	44.27	49.50	55.34	58.57	62.61	70	83.56
50mm lens								
Bellows extension	57.01	63.25	70.71	79.06	83.67	89.44	100	119.37

Notes

4 LIGHT AND FILM

4.1 GLOSSARY

Anti-halation coating This bottom layer of film prevents light from bouncing back after passing through the emulsion.

ASA (American Standards Association) Another measure for film speed. The numerical ratings used with ASA are the same as ISO and EI ratings.

Color balanced Different color films are color balanced for use under different light sources. The term also applies to the accurate color rendition of a color print or a color transparency.

Color temperature A numerical measure for the color of light given in degrees of Kelvin (K).

Daylight balanced film A color film balanced to produce accurate color renditions when it is used in normal daylight or with an electronic flash (5000°K).

DIN (Deutsche Industrie Norm) A measure for film speed. The numerical ratings used with DIN are different from ISO, EI, and ASA ratings.

EI (Exposure Index) A measure for film speed often used in conjunction with ISO. The numerical ratings used with EI are the same as ISO and ASA ratings.

Emulsion Silver halide crystals are contained in a thin gelatin layer with other chemicals to form this light sensitive component of film.

Film speed A measure for the light sensitivity of film. The most common ratings are ISO, EI, ASA, and DIN. The numerical ratings attached to these units increase as a film's sensitivity to light increases.

Fluorescent light Light emitting from fluorescent light tubes. Green in color on daylight film. Filters must be used to color balance fluorescent light.

Graininess Prints made from fast negative films and/or large enlargements display a coarse, mottled effect caused by large silver particles in the negative. This effect is referred to as graininess.

High contrast film A film that reduces all tones in the subject to either black or white to produce a very high contrast image.

Infrared film A film that is sensitive to and records the infrared bands of the spectrum.

ISO (International Standards Organization)The most common measure for film speed. Used with a numerical rating to describe a film's sensitivity to light.

Negative film A film that produces a negative image (tones are reversed from the original subject). Used when prints are desired.

Orthochromatic A film that is sensitive to the blue and green but not the red wavelengths of the spectrum.

Panchromatic Film that is sensitive to all colors (wavelengths) of the spectrum.

Reversal film A film that produces a positive image (a transparency).

Silver halide — The light sensitive element of common photographic emulsions. Usually one of these silver halide compounds: silver bromide, silver chloride, or silver iodide.

Slide — The term most accurately describes a 35mm transparency mounted for projection. Reversal film is sometimes referred to as transparency film or slide film.

Spectrum — The visible spectrum, seen as the colors from red to violet at different wavelengths, is only a small part of the electromagnetic spectrum.

Transparency film — Another term used for reversal film. A transparency is a positive image suitable for projection when it is placed in a slide mount.

Tungsten balanced film — A color film balanced to produce accurate color renditions under tungsten (incandescent) light sources (3200°K).

Wavelength — Light is a form of electromagnetic radiation found at a certain band of wavelengths.

4.2 SUMMARY

71

Light and film

Film is sensitive to light: Silver-halide crystals in the film emulsion undergo a change when exposed to light. Light is a form of electromagnetic energy, and only a small part of the electromagnetic spectrum is visible to the human eye. **The human eye is sensitive to a very small group of waves near the middle of the spectrum:** Most films are sensitive to a similar range, but some are also sensitive to the UV or infrared wavelengths.

72 - 73

Selecting and using film

Manufacturers provide many types of film: You select a film based upon the final use for the negatives or positives and the conditions you will be photographing in. **Color balance is one basic choice concerning only color film:** Daylight-balanced color films are for use outdoors or with electronic flash. Tungsten-balanced color films are for use with artificial light sources, such as incandescent lamps. **Do you want a print:** Choose negative films. Tones are reversed from the original scene in a negative - dark areas become light and vice versa. When the image is printed, the tones are reversed to a positive image once more. **Do you want a transparency:** Choose reversal films. Transparency films produce a positive image. A slide is a 35mm transparency mounted in a frame for projection. **What film speed do you need:** Fast films need less light to form an image, but they produce prints with reduced sharpness and more grain compared to slower films. **What film size should you buy:** Your camera determines the film size you can use. **35mm films:** These come packaged in film cassettes with either 24 or 36 exposures. For avid photographers, there is also bulk film in large rolls available. **Roll films:** Packaged on a spool with a light proof backing paper. The actual negative formats of roll-film cameras vary. **Sheet film or cut films:** Sheets are loaded in special holders before use. Sizes include 4x5 inches and 8x10 inches. **Do you want a film for a special purpose:** Instant films allow you to view your results immediately. High-contrast films produce only two tones – black and white. Infrared films respond to the infrared wavelengths of the spectrum. The results are often enshrined in a ghostly haze. **Chromogenic black-and-white films:** These films produce and image of dye instead of silver. The grain is exceptionally fine for the film speed. They require processing in C-41 color chemistry.

Professional films: Professional black and white films do not differ significantly from what might be considered amateur alternatives. Most films are actually labeled "Professional" as a marketing strategy. With color films, where the color balance of the film is affected by the age of the emulsion, professional films are matured and stored to ensure predictable and repeatable results with extreme accuracy. **Advanced Photo System films:** The negative format is slightly smaller than 35mm. They contain a magnetic layer that stores user information for the processing lab.

73

Storing and handling film

Store film away from heat: Heat causes film to deteriorate very rapidly. **For longer storage, refrigerate film:** Cold storage extends the life of a film emulsion by slowing down the aging process. Do not freeze Polaroid instant film. Infrared film and professional color film should be kept refrigerated at all times, even in the shop. **Protect film from moisture:** Wrap the film packaging in waterproof materials, such as a plastic bag, when you store film in a moist or humid environment. Let the film warm up to room temperature before using it to avoid condensation. **Load and unload your camera out of strong light:** Block the sun with your body when loading film outdoors to prevent unwanted exposure. **Check the film's expiration date before buying:** Some retailers might have outdated film on their shelves. This is more critical for color films, so do not hesitate to buy slightly out-of-date black-and-white films at a discount. **Consider protecting your film from airport security X-ray machines:** Only a concern with high-speed films - ISO 1600 and ISO 3200. However, be aware that X-ray exposures are cumulative.

74

Film speed

The faster the film speed, the less light required to produce an image: Faster films can therefore be used in less light or with smaller apertures and/or faster shutter speeds. **What film speed should you use:** Faster films are less sharp and they produce larger grain in a print. Use the slowest film the conditions you photograph under allow, unless you prefer the gritty aesthetic of fast films.

74

Film speed rating systems

A film speed number tells how sensitive that film is to light: The rating systems currently in use are: ISO, ASA, EI, and sometimes DIN. ISO and ASA have the same numerical scale, so they are the same for all practical purposes. One thing they all have in common is that the film speed is doubled or halved for each step on the scale. **The higher the number in a given system, the faster the film – and the less light you need for a correct exposure:** The relationship between film speeds is the same as it is for apertures and shutter speeds. A film's sensitivity to light is doubled or halved for each step on the film-speed scale. For example, an ISO 200 film is twice as sensitive to light as an ISO 100 film. The difference between the two ratings is the same as the difference between two apertures and two shutter speeds – a stop. **Some typical film speeds and their uses are:** Slow films (ISO 50 or less) are suitable for very bright conditions and for still subjects photographed with the use of a tripod. They produce sharp negatives with fine grain. Medium-speed films (around ISO 100) are often a good compromise between fast and slow. They allow for a wider use than slow films and they produce better results than fast films. Fast films (around ISO 400) are for use under low light conditions and with fast moving subjects. Extra fast films (ISO 1600 or ISO 3200) are for use in extremely low light.

75

Film speed and grain

The faster a film, the more visible its grain: Fast films have larger light-sensitive crystals, and they produce larger grains of silver when the film is developed. These grains will give the print a speckled rather than smooth appearance in areas with a uniform tone.

The relationship between speed and graininess: Enlargements of the same subject shot with different speed films clearly show how grain increases with film speed. **Some newer films have reduced graininess:** T-grain technology exposes more of a silver-halide crystal's surface to light. This grain structure allows for smaller grain at a given film speed compared to traditional films. **Standard films continue to be popular, however:** There are other characteristics besides grain that you might find appealing or technically superior in standard films. **Other factors also affect grain:** These factors increase grain in a negative and print: degree of enlargement, type of printing paper, type of enlarger, overdevelopment, overexposure, temperature changes in developing solutions, and type of developer used. **Certain film and developer combinations enhance fine grain:** Slow films and developers formulated to produce fine grain can render excellent result with small negative sizes.

76 - 77 **Fast film – when speed is essential**

A fast film, ISO 400 or higher, is useful for stopping motion: Fast films require less light, so they can be used with faster shutter speeds capable of stopping motion. **A fast film is an asset in dim light:** The high sensitivity to light allows for photography in situations where slower films would have been a victim of camera shake due to slower shutter speeds. You can also "push" a fast film by deliberately underexposing and overdeveloping it. **How fast is fast:** Any film rated above ISO 400 is considered a fast film. Kodak's T-Max P3200 film is the fastest choice available.

78 - 79 **Medium-speed and slow films – for maximum detail**

A medium-speed film, around ISO 100, delivers better sharpness and detail than faster films: For fine detail, excellent sharpness, and high degrees of enlargement, choose a slow or medium-speed film. **If light is moderately bright:** Medium-speed films will give you more flexibility due to their increased speed, but you sacrifice some print quality. **Slow speeds, ISO 50 or less:** With slow color films, you get better color saturation along with the usual benefits of fine detail and outstanding sharpness. There is often very little difference between an ISO 25, ISO 50, and ISO 100 or 125 black-and-white film.

80 - 81 **Instant films**

Instant films give you a visible image almost at once: Film, paper, and chemicals come in the same sealed package with Polaroid films to facilitate immediate development. Some films do not provide a film negative, only a print. Sheet-film sizes require special holders that also facilitate the development process. **Polaroid makes instant materials in many formats:** These include the small instant prints from cheap amateur cameras to professional materials for use in large 8x10-inch view cameras. **Instant film is popular with professional photographers, who use it to make a quick check of a setup:** Polaroid film is often used to proof the composition, lighting, and exposure of a setup or scene before the final exposures are shot on transparency or negative materials.

81 - 83 **How film responds to light**

Recording an image on film involves a reaction between light and silver halide crystals: The silver-halide crystals found in the emulsion are a compound of silver and a halogen (such as bromine, iodine, or chlorine). Please refer to pages 81 - 83 for a breakdown of the strata in film and an illustrated journey of film's response to light. **A chromogenic film is somewhat different from conventional silver halide film:** These films contain dye couplers in addition to silver-halide crystals. After development, where the reduction of silver leads to a similar build-up of dyes, the silver is bleached out to leave an image made of dye.

84 - 85 **Characteristic curves**

The more light that reaches film, the denser with silver (or dyes) the developed negative will be: As the negative becomes denser (darker), the tones in the corresponding print will become lighter. **The response of a particular film to light can be diagrammed as its characteristic curve:** It shows exactly how the density of the negative increases with exposure to light. **The curve and photos show that density does not increase in exact proportion to the amount of light reaching the film:** Density builds slowly at the toe of the curve, gathers momentum in the middle part, only to taper off again toward the shoulder. In the central straight-line portion of the curve, the relationship between exposure and density is proportional, while much more exposure is needed in the toe and shoulder parts to produce a change in density. **When film is underexposed and receives too little light, the tones move toward the toe of the curve:** Only small deposits of density can be found in the developed negative. Tonal separation is bad and dark areas in the scene have not even registered. The print will be too dark. **When film is considerably overexposed and receives too much light, the tones move toward the shoulder of the curve:** Bright values in the scene are so dense that they show no separation of values, and they may actually prevent any light at all from passing through during printing. The print will be too light. **Exposure is not the only process that affects the density of a negative:** Development affects the density of the highlight areas more than the shadow areas. Adjustments in exposure and development are used to gain fine control over the density and contrast of a negative. The photographer Ansel Adams developed the Zone System for this purpose.

86 - 87 **How black-and-white film records color**

Different types of black-and-white films react differently to colors in a scene: All colors are reproduced as shades of gray. Dyes added to a film affect the wavelengths it responds to. **Panchromatic film is the most commonly used black-and-white film:** By far the most used black-and-white film, with the largest range of products. These films are sensitive to all the colors of the visible spectrum and ultraviolet radiation. **Orthochromatic film is sensitive to ultraviolet, blue, and green:** Used in copy and graphic arts work. **Blue-sensitive film is much like orthochromatic film:** Sensitive to UV and blue. Early photographic emulsions were blue sensitive. Used in copy work. **Infrared film:** Sensitive to infrared wavelengths in addition to the visible spectrum. Mostly fine art and scientific applications.

88 - 89 **Infrared film**

Infrared film can produce unusual photographs, particularly in black and white: Changes in gray tones can render striking results, while color distortions are usually less desirable. **How infrared film works:** Infrared waves are not absorbed and reflected in the same way as visible wavelengths, creating unexpected tonal relationships. By using a red filter on the lens, most of the visible light is blocked, and the image is formed by infrared waves. **Uses for infrared film:** Landscapes photographed on infrared film will reduce the blue haze often obscuring the distant parts of a scene. Other uses utilize its infrared sensitivity to reveal things beyond the visible spectrum not readily apparent to the human eye. **Some films are not true infrared but have extended red sensitivity:** These films, including Ilford SFX 2000, are marginally easier to handle and use since they do not require complete darkness for loading. Please see page 88 for instructions on how to use infrared film.

90 - 91 **Using filters**

Attach a filter to the front of a lens, and you can change the light that reaches the film: Filters absorb some of the wavelengths of a scene and thereby change the way it will look in a photograph. With the use of filters, the exposure must be increased to compensate for the loss of light. **Gelatin or plastic filters are taped to the front of the lens or placed in a filter holder:** They are not optically perfect and easily damaged. **Glass filters screw or clamp onto the front of the lens:** These are the best choice. Each filter only fits a certain lens diameter, but this can be remedied by using a selection of cheap step-up or step-down rings to make it fit any lens.

90 **Types of filters**

Colored filters let you control the relative lightness and darkness of tones in a black-and-white photograph: They absorb light of certain colors to render objects of those colors a darker tone in the photograph. **A colored filter absorbs its complementary color:** Red filters absorb green, yellow filters absorb blue, and so on, to make those colors appear darker in the photograph. It does not lighten its own color, although this is obviously the impression it creates by making the other colors/tones darker. **Contrast filters are colored filters that change the relative brightness of colors:** When complementary colors are found in the same scene, a colored filter in one of these colors will darken the opposite tone to increase the contrast. **Correction filters are colored filters designed to correct the response of film:** By using a filter to adjust the tones in a scene to correspond with human perception, you create a more "natural" looking photograph. **Neutral density filters absorb a quantity of all wavelengths of light:** They have no effect on the relationship between tones. The purpose of using them is to increase the exposure of the scene to allow for other combinations of shutter speed and aperture. **A polarizing filter affects only light vibrating at certain angles:** It is used to remove reflections, darken skies, and intensify colors. **Some filters or lens attachments produce special effects:** These are numerous and often somewhat extravagant in their transformation of a scene. The less intrusive are used to create a hazy soft-focus effect for portraits, but you may also add your own rainbow with the right filter.

92 **Filters for black-and-white film**

You need to increase the exposure when using a filter: Since filters absorb some of the light passing through them, the exposure must be increased to compensate. **In manual exposure operation:** Change the exposure manually as required by the filter. **In automatic exposure operation:** You can not simply meter through the lens and filter as usual. **You can meter through a filter if you run a simple test first:** Meter a scene containing a good range of colors with and without the filter. Note the difference in exposure recommended by the meter. Refer to the filter factor for the filter and add the exposure difference between the two readings and the filter's recommendation to your exposure when you use it. **Some sources list the exposure increase as a filter factor, not directly in stops:** The factor indicates how many times the exposure should be increased – a factor of 2 stands for a doubling of the exposure, which means 1 stop. The increase for tungsten light (from light bulbs) is different from the increase for daylight. This is due to the color difference between these sources. Please see page 92 for a comprehensive listing of filters, their effect, use, and the amount of exposure increase they usually require.

93 ______ **A polarizing filter to reduce reflections**

A polarizing filter can remove or reduce reflections from water, or any smooth surface except metal: Bright reflections are polarized – the light they reflect only vibrates in one plane. Light normally vibrates in all directions perpendicular to its direction of travel. **A polarizing filter:** The filter consists of parallel slats that can be turned to block light vibrating in a single plane. Best results are achieved by photographing at a slight angle, about 35°, to the reflective surface. **The filter can also decrease reflections:** Light is often reflected off dust and water particles in the atmosphere. A polarizing filter can remove these to darken the sky and increase color saturation. Best results are achieved by keeping the sun at a right angle to the scene. **To use a polarizing filter:** Look through it and rotate it until the unwanted reflection is reduced. Once satisfied, place the filter on the lens in the same position. With a single-lens reflex camera or a view camera, you can observe the changes through the viewfinder or on the ground glass as you turn the filter. Expect to increase the exposure by about 1 1/3 stops.

4.3 TEST

FILL IN THE BLANKS

1 The light-sensitive layer of film contains silver-halide crystals and is referred to as the ____________________.

2 A ____________________ film is sensitive to all colors.

3 A fast film is more sensitive to light than a ____________________ film.

4 Film speed is most commonly rated on the ____________________ scale.

5 Infrared film is sensitive to the ____________________ wavelengths of the spectrum.

6 Reversal film is also referred to as slide film or ____________________ film.

7 ____________________ films have fine grain and excellent sharpness.

8 ____________________ films have coarse grain and reduced sharpness.

9 The filter ____________________ is an indication of how much the exposure must be increased with a particular filter.

10 Colored filters darken their ____________________ color.

Notes

MULTIPLE CHOICE – CIRCLE ONE OR MORE

1	Store film:	a.	in its original packaging.
		b.	in direct sunlight.
		c.	away from humidity and heat.
2	A fast film is rated at:	a.	ISO 25.
		b.	ISO 125.
		c.	ISO 400.
3	Choose a film according to:	a.	the light conditions you are likely to encounter.
		b.	the quality and size of enlargements you want.
		c.	the kind if subject you will be photographing.
4	To get a negative suitable for large enlargements, choose a:	a.	fast film.
		b.	infrared film.
		c.	slow film.
5	A reversal film produces a:	a.	positive image.
		b.	negative image.
		c.	slide.
6	T-grain films have smaller grain compared to traditional films with:	a.	the same ISO rating.
		b.	the same film speed.
		c.	orthochromatic characteristics.
7	A yellow filter used in black-and-white photography makes the blue sky:	a.	lighter.
		b.	darker.
		c.	white.
8	The "toe" on a characteristic curve describes the:	a.	first effects of exposure on negative density.
		b.	highlight areas of a normally exposed negative.
		c.	shadow areas of a normally exposed negative.
9	The difference between ISO 200 and ISO 100 is equal to:	a.	a stop.
		b.	the difference between two aperture settings.
		c.	the difference between two shutter-speed settings.
10	A filter factor of 1.5 demands an exposure increase of:	a.	1.5 stops.
		b.	1 stop.
		c.	2/3 stops.

4.4 PRACTICAL TIPS

Film economy

Bulk loading film.

If you plan to use a lot of film, you might consider buying your film in bulk to save money. Most of the standard films are available in rolls of 100 feet at considerable savings compared to the same length bought in individual 24 or 36 exposure film cassettes. However, you need some specialist equipment to load your film, which will be an initial expense that you can recover on the savings from your first rolls of bulk-loaded film. The investment you have to make consists of a bulk-film loader and reusable film cassettes. Once the entire roll of 100 feet is inserted in the loader, you can load each cassette in daylight. The loader counts the frames. If you make sure to keep all the equipment clean and dust-free to avoid scratches, bulk-loaded film is as good as film loaded into cassettes by the manufacturer. 100 feet will give you about 18 rolls of 36 exposures.

Travel with film

Protect your film and stay organized.

It is best not to expose film to excessive heat or high humidity. For long term storage, the fridge or freezer is an ideal place to store film in its unopened packaging to protect it from moisture. On travels, make sure to keep your film as far away from direct sunlight as possible. Take the rolls you need for a day of photographing, and leave the rest protected from the heat or humidity that will ruin it. It is a good idea to label your film for identification later. Place strips of masking tape on the film boxes and write down details of the content, along with any instructions for development. Develop your film as soon as you can after exposure. The latent image formed on the film will gradually lose quality, and it is of course preferable to avoid any deterioration at all.

Filters

Test the exposure increase for a filter with your SLR.

Most filters require an increase in exposure. Normally this increase is given by a factor for the filter, and it can be useful to compare this recommended exposure increase with the through-the-lens (TTL) meter reading you get when the filter is placed on your camera. Find an average scene with a range of colors and meter the scene with the filter on the camera. Remove the filter and meter the exact same scene again. Write down the two readings and compare results. Ideally the difference in exposure should match the recommended exposure increase. If the results do not match, you need to make up for the difference manually. Do not trust the meter, but the exposure increase given by the filter factor. Use the results you get from such a test to adjust the entries in the 4.5.5 Filter factors section of this chapter.

Notes

4.5 JOURNAL

There are many brands and types of film on the market, and these journal entries will help you identify the main choices. You need to consult a resource, such as a manufacturer's website, a mail-order catalog, or a local retailer. You can also enlist the help of your instructor to complete the table. It will give you an idea of what is available, and once you have tried a few films, you can start to argue the merits of one film over another with other photographers. You might find that there are as many opinions as there are products. Please be aware that there are several black-and-white films intended for processing in C-41 color chemistry.

4.5.1 BLACK-AND-WHITE NEGATIVE FILMS

SLOW FILMS ▸
ISO 25
ISO 50

Slow films have very fine grain and relatively high contrast. They maintain fine detail and are suitable for large prints with subtle tonal gradations.

Manufacturer ▾	Film name ▾	Speed ▾	Comments ▾
Agfa	Agfapan APX 25	ISO 25	An ultra-fine grain film.

MEDIUM-SPEED FILMS ▸
ISO 100
ISO 125

Medium-speed films are a good compromise between fine image quality and versatility in use under a wider variety of conditions.

Manufacturer ▾	Film name ▾	Speed ▾	Comments ▾

FAST FILMS ▸
ISO 400
ISO 3200

Fast films have large grain, decreased contrast, and appear less sharp compared to slow films. Their increased sensitivity to light allows for photography in very dim light.

Manufacturer ▾	Film name ▾	Speed ▾	Comments ▾

4.5.2 COLOR NEGATIVE FILMS

SLOW FILMS ▸
ISO 50

Slow color films have very fine grain. They maintain fine detail and are suitable for large prints with subtle tonal gradations and vibrant colors.

Manufacturer ▾	Film name ▾	Speed ▾	Color balance ▾	Comments ▾

MEDIUM-SPEED FILMS ▸
ISO 100
ISO 160

Medium-speed color films are a good compromise between fine image quality, good color saturation, and versatility in use under a wider variety of conditions.

Manufacturer ▾	Film name ▾	Speed ▾	Color balance ▾	Comments ▾

FAST FILMS ▸
ISO 400
ISO 800

Fast color films have large grain, decreased contrast, duller colors, and they also appear less sharp compared to slow films. Speed is their main attraction.

Manufacturer ▾	Film name ▾	Speed ▾	Color balance ▾	Comments ▾

4.5.3 COLOR REVERSAL FILMS

SLOW FILMS ▸
ISO 25
ISO 50
ISO 64

Slow reversal films have very fine grain and truly amazing colors. They can be printed with outstanding results and projected very large without losing quality.

Manufacturer ▾	Film name ▾	Speed ▾	Color balance ▾	Comments ▾

MEDIUM-SPEED FILMS ▸
ISO 100
ISO 160

Medium-speed reversal films have an image quality that rivals the slower films. The colors can look more natural due to a slight loss in saturation.

Manufacturer ▾	Film name ▾	Speed ▾	Color balance ▾	Comments ▾

FAST FILMS ▸
ISO 400
ISO 800

Fast reversal films have a loss of sharpness and less saturated colors. As with all fast films, they are primarily chosen for conditions with very little available light.

Manufacturer ▾	Film name ▾	Speed ▾	Color balance ▾	Comments ▾

4.5.4 SPECIAL-PURPOSE FILMS

SPECIAL-PURPOSE ▸ FILMS	List any special-purpose film you may want to use. These could include infrared film, orthochromatic film, inter-negative film, black-and-white slide film, and slide-duplicating film.		
Manufacturer ▾	Film name ▾	Speed ▾	Use / Comments ▾

4.5.5 FILTER FACTORS

Find the filter factors for the filters you have and enter them in the table provided. Consult the reference below and include the actual exposure increase in stops. If you use your filters on a SLR camera with through-the-lens metering, you must perform a simple metering test to determine the actual exposure increase needed. See 4.4 Practical tips above for a description of the procedure.

FILTER FACTOR ▾									
1	1.2	1.5	2	2.5	3	4	5	6	8
0	1/3	2/3	1	1 1/3	1 2/3	2	2 1/3	2 2/3	3
EXPOSURE INCREASE IN STOPS ▴									

FILTERS FOR B&W PHOTOGRAPHY ▾	Filter factor ▾	Exposure increase ▾	Metered exposure + ▾
#8 Yellow filter	2	1 stop	Not tested

5 EXPOSURE

5.1 GLOSSARY

Aperture	An adjustable opening within the lens used to control the intensity of the light falling on the film during exposure. The aperture, given by an f-number, refers to the size of this opening.
Bracketing	The common practice of making several exposures on either side of what is perceived of as the correct exposure. Bracketing leaves room for slight error and gives more choice at the printing stage.
Exposure	An exposure describes the amount of light falling on the light sensitive film after the shutter is released. The exposure is controlled by a combination of aperture and shutter speed.
Exposure compensation	An automatic feature on cameras used to overexpose or underexpose the film by the number of stops set on the exposure compensation dial.
Exposure latitude	Overexposure or underexposure can produce usable negatives or transparencies. Latitude refers to the margin of error for acceptable results.
Exposure lock	A memory button on cameras used to maintain a light reading and exposure setting for the subject in order to use it for another composition.
Exposure meter	Also referred to as a light meter. An instrument that measures the light falling on it (incident) or the light reflected from a subject towards it (reflected). The light measurement is most often given as an exposure combination of shutter speed and aperture. Exposure meters are either built into the camera or used hand held.
Film speed	A measure for the light sensitivity of film. The most common ratings are ISO, EI, ASA, and DIN. The numerical ratings attached to these units increase as the film sensitivity increases.
f-stop/ f-number	The relative size of an aperture opening is given by the f-stop. A common sequence of f-stops for a 35mm lens: f/2.8, f/4, f/5.6, f/8, f/11, f/16, and f/22. A lens might have larger (smaller f-number) or smaller (larger f-number) aperture openings. The f-number = The focal length of the lens divided by the diameter of the lens opening. The intensity of light given by one particular f-number is the same for all lenses.
Gray card	A gray card that reflects 18 percent of the light falling on it. Used to determine exposure settings by taking a reflected reading of the card under the same light conditions as the subject.
Highlight	The darkest area in a negative and the lightest area in a print.
Incident light	Light falling on a subject.
Meter weighting	Term describing the emphasis a reflected-light meter gives to particular areas of the frame.

Middle gray — Every light meter presumes that the tonal values of a given subject average out to a middle-gray tone. A subject with 18 percent reflectance defines middle gray.

Negative — The tones in a negative image recorded on film are reversed in relation to the original subject. Light becomes dark and vice versa.

Normal exposure — An exposure that produces a negative ideally suited for the desired print.

Overexposure — An exposure that produces a dense (dark) negative, which prints too light.

Reflected light — Light emitted or reflected from a subject.

Shadow area — The most transparent areas in the negative and the darkest areas in a print.

Shutter speed — The actual time that the shutter remains open to expose the film.

Stop — The unit of light described by one step on the aperture ring, one step on the shutter speed dial, or a doubling/halving of the film speed. Apertures, shutter speeds, and film speeds all involve either a halving or doubling of values between full steps. The amount of light either halved or doubled by moving up or down in full steps on any of these scales is a stop. Moving either the aperture ring or the shutter speed dial one step consequently changes the exposure by one stop.

TTL-meter — Through-The-Lens exposure meter common in most 35mm SLR cameras.

Underexposure — An exposure that produces a thin (almost transparent) negative, which prints too dark.

5.2 SUMMARY

97

Exposure

To get a rich image with realistic tones, dark but detailed shadows, and bright, delicate highlights, you need to expose your film correctly: Films have an exposure latitude that allows for acceptable results within a certain range of exposures, but a correct exposure always gives you superior results. Overexposed negatives will produce grainy and unsharp prints, while underexposed negatives will have no detail in the shadows and bad tonal separation. To expose your film correctly, you use the combination of aperture and shutter speed best suited to produce a negative that will easily print the way you want the photograph to look. **Personal judgment is important even if your camera can set the exposure automatically:** These features are programmed for average results that can always be improved by manual adjustments of the exposure based on your interpretation of the scene. **One of the best cures for exposure problems is experience:** By learning how the light meter and film respond, you develop a technical vocabulary for decisions that will improve on your exposures.

98

Summary addendum: Photography in a nutshell

Shutter speeds: The doubling or halving difference between two shutter speed settings is 1 stop. **Aperture settings:** The doubling or halving difference between two aperture settings is 1 stop. **Film speed:** The doubling or halving difference between two film speed ratings is 1 stop. The common unit of a stop allows for equivalent exposures.

98

Equivalent exposures

Exposure = Intensity (aperture) x Time (shutter speed): Exposure is a combination of the intensity of the light reaching the film and the time this light is allowed to strike the film. The aperture controls the intensity of the light and the duration of the exposure is controlled by the shutter speed. **An exposure calculated by a light meter provides a combination of aperture and shutter speed that will expose your picture correctly:** An exposure meter gives you a recommended exposure combination of shutter speed and aperture based upon an average distribution of light and dark tones in your subject. **But you are not limited by this one combination:** For each combination of shutter speed and aperture, there is a series of equivalent exposures that will expose the film with the same amount of light. **Which combination you choose is one key to creative photography:** Your choice of aperture and shutter speed will affect depth of field and motion blur. Please see page 98 for an excellent illustration of how choices of aperture and shutter speed combinations affect the picture.

99

How exposure meters work

You will need an exposure meter in order to consistently expose your film correctly, so that it is neither too light or too dark: Exposure meters measure the light and recommend a combination of aperture and shutter speed based on a subject with an average distribution of light and dark tones. **Exposure meters are designed to measure middle gray:** Meters presume that all the tones in a scene always average out to be a specific middle-gray tone appropriately referred to as middle gray. This tone is based upon a surface with 18 percent reflectance. The exposures it recommends aims to reproduce the combined tones of the subject as a middle-gray tone in the final photograph. **Reflected-light meters measure the light reflected from a subject:** Meters built into SLR-cameras measure reflected light. **Reflected-light spot meters read light from a very small area of the subject:** This allows you to read the individual values of a scene accurately and carefully calculate an exposure. **Incident-light meters measure light falling on a subject:** These are hand-held meters pointed away from the subject towards the camera position to measure the intensity of the light. **Some meters can make either reflected or incident readings:** When the cell is directly exposed to light, it measures reflected light, and when a white translucent dome covers it, the meter reads incident light. Advanced meters can actually take spot readings in addition to reflected and incident light measurements. **Flash meters:** These meter the brief burst of light emitted from an electronic flash. **Color temperature meters:** These measure the color temperature of light for filter use or color correction.

100

In-camera exposure meters

Meters built into cameras measure the light reflected or produced by the objects in their view and then calculate an exposure setting: Built-in meters measure reflected light from the objects seen through the viewfinder. The exposure readout, either in the viewfinder or a data panel, gives you the recommended exposure setting. **Many built-in meters are averaging meters and are center-weighted:** Center-weighted meters give emphasis to the area defined by the central circle in the viewfinder. They assume that the most important part of a subject is always placed right in the middle of the frame. With subjects placed towards the edges of the frame or with areas around the subject being much darker or lighter, the reading given by the meter does not produce a very accurate exposure. **Some cameras have multi-segment meters:** They read from several defined areas in the viewfinder and use programs to alleviate potential exposure problems. **A camera may offer several different metering modes:**

Advanced cameras give you several metering options, such as center-weighted, multi-segment, and spot-metering, so you can choose the one best suited to the subject at hand. **Certain scenes can cause a meter to produce the wrong exposure:** In fact, most scenes will cause a meter to calculate a less than ideal exposure. The meter always averages the dark and light tones of a subject to recommend an exposure where these add up to a middle-gray tone. When a subject is lighter or darker than middle gray, this recommendation will obviously produce a negative where the resulting print will be either too dark or too light. A light subject exposed for middle gray will be too dark, and a dark subject exposed for middle gray will be too light.

101 **Automatic exposure**

Many cameras incorporate automatic exposure: They determine the exposure setting based upon an average meter reading. The most common modes are (see box on page 101): **Aperture-priority automatic:** You set the aperture and the camera sets the shutter speed. **Shutter-priority automatic:** You set the shutter speed and the camera sets the aperture. **Programmed automatic:** The camera sets both aperture and shutter speed. **Manual:** You set both aperture and shutter speed. **Sometimes automatic exposure can underexpose or overexpose your subject:** All scenes that do not meet the average criteria determined by the meter will be exposed wrongly to a degree proportional to how much they differ from the average middle-gray scene.

101 **Overriding automatic exposure**

Automatic exposure works well much of the time, but for some scenes you will want to alter the exposure set by the automatic circuitry: You will want to overexpose or underexpose your negatives to depart from the middle-gray exposure recommendation when your subject is lighter or darker than average. There are several ways to do this. **Manual mode:** Allows you to adjust the exposure settings as you see fit. Often an option on automatic cameras. **Exposure compensation dial:** Allows you to underexpose or overexpose your film in relation to the meter reading in a number of stops. **Backlight button:** This button adds a fixed amount of exposure to bring out detail in a subject silhouetted against a light background. **Exposure lock:** You can meter a select part of a scene and lock this reading for use with another framing of the scene. **Film speed dial:** By resetting the film speed dial, your meter will fool the camera to alter the automatic exposure. For example, changing the film speed from ISO 400 to ISO 200 will overexpose the film by 1 stop.

102 **An overall reading for an average scene**

How do you get a good exposure: The first step is always to accurately meter the scene. **An overall reading works well for metering average scenes:** When the scene has an even distribution of light and dark tones, it will fit the meter's exposure recommendation for an average scene. This is especially true for scenes with diffuse and even illumination, while contrasty scenes can pose some problems, even if the range of tones matches middle gray. In most cases, however, you will probably want to make some adjustments to the exposure. **A reflected-light meter (built into the camera or hand held) typically acts as if the scene it is metering is middle gray:** It averages all the tones in a scene seen through the viewfinder and assumes that they will add up to middle gray. The exposure recommendation is based upon this presumption. A hand-held reflected-light meter reads an angle of view similar to a normal-focal-length lens. **An overall reading may not work well for contrasty scenes:** If a scene contains very bright values, the meter will lean towards underexposure of the negative and the print will be too dark. If there is a predominance of dark areas around the subject, the meter will lean towards overexposure of the negative and the print will be too light.

An incident-light meter reads only the light falling on a subject: It does not take the reflected values of the subject into account, but measures the intensity of the light falling directly on it. You photograph the reflected light, so it can be less accurate for fine exposure calculations. It is difficult to use for objects that emit light themselves. However, an incident-light meter used correctly is a great source of exposure information in most situations.

104 - 105 **Metering high-contrast scenes**

The most common situation in which overall metering does not work is one with a subject against a much lighter background: The meter will use the background in its middle-gray calculation, and the average value of the negative will become too dark for the subject. It will most likely end up as a dark silhouette against a gray background. **Meter up close to prevent problems with contrasty scenes:** Meter only the subject up close and use this exposure to prevent underexposure problems. Always exclude strong light sources, such as a lamp, from a meter reading. **If you are metering a landscape, cityscape, or other distant scene, tilt the camera or meter down:** For expansive landscapes with high contrast, tilt the camera downwards, away from a bright sky, to meter the ground. Reframe your scene and expose with the previous meter reading. **Less common, but sometimes a problem, is a subject against a much darker background:** Follow the same procedure – move in close to meter. **How do you use an automatic camera to expose a picture with a background much lighter or darker than the subject:** You must adjust the exposure manually or use one of the tricks described on page 101 (see summary above). **If you are using an incident-light meter:** Decide if the dark or light areas of your subject are the most important, and then place your meter either in direct light or in the shadows to get the most accurate reading for the value of your choice. Please see pages 104 - 105 for illustrations of these methods in action. **What do you do if you can't get close:** You use a substitution reading. You read a similar subject or a subject with a known tonal value in the same light as your intended subject. **One subject always with you that can be metered is the palm of your hand:** Meter your hand and adjust the exposure according to the value of your hand in relation to middle gray. **Another useful substitution reading is from a gray card:** The gray card is a piece of plain card manufactured to exacting standards. It reflects 18 percent of the light falling on it, and thereby qualifies as the ideal middle-gray subject for any reflected-light exposure meter. By making a substitution reading of the card in the exact same light as your subject, you get an exposure recommendation that will reproduce a middle-gray card as a middle-gray value in the print. If you use this exposure setting on your real subject, the values of that subject will also be reproduced accurately in the print. A gray card can be used in color photography to discern the color balance of a print.

106 - 107 **Exposing for specific tones**

You can decide in advance the tonal value of an important area in your final photograph: Since you know that an exposure reading of a uniform tone will always produce a middle-gray print of that tone, you can change the exposure to lighten or darken the print according to the value of your subject. **You can choose how light or dark an area will appear by adjusting the exposure indicated by the meter:** By adding exposure, you get a denser negative and a lighter print. By reducing exposure, you get a thinner negative and a darker print. Determine how light or dark your subject is in relation to middle gray and add or subtract exposure accordingly. **One area often metered when calculating exposure for a portrait is skin tone:** Skin tones may vary from two stops of overexposure to one stop of underexposure in relation to a middle-gray tone. **The other area often metered to determine exposure is the darkest shadow area in which it is important to retain texture and detail:**

It is important to retain detail in the shadow areas during exposure. Otherwise they will print as blocks of black that give little information about your subject. Meter the shadow areas and give two stops less exposure to make sure that they are reproduced in the print with a dark tone and detail. **Changing the exposure affects all the values in the print, not just the tone you meter:** The entire range of tones in a print is moved up and down on the tonal scale according to your exposure decisions. **When shooting negative film, it is better to overexpose the film than to underexpose it:** Detail missing from underexposed shadow areas in the negative can never be recovered, while overexposed highlights can usually be made darker in the printing process.

108 **Hard-to-meter scenes**

Some scenes can't be metered in the usual way: Meters have a working limit when used in near darkness. Most will indicate permanent underexposure (asking for more light). Try metering the brightest surface you can find and give two stops more exposure. **If metering is not practical at all:** Refer to a general exposure table, such as the one on page 108, or bracket your exposures to ensure a usable result. Experience and record keeping are your best guides. **Very long exposures can cause underexposure:** This is due to the reciprocity effect, where the reciprocal relationship between a doubling and halving of the exposure for each stop ceases to be valid. **Depending on the film, reciprocity effect occurs at exposures of one second or longer and at exposures shorter than 1/1000 second:** As the exposure time indicated by the meter increases beyond one second, the effective exposure time must be adjusted. There are general tables for this (see page 108), but the best results can only be achieved through testing. Always bracket long exposures. **Very long exposures cause an increase in contrast:** Highlights build faster than shadows in dark scenes that require long exposures, leading to an increase in contrast. Contrast can to some degree be controlled through film development. More about this in chapter 6. The individual layers of color film respond differently to long exposures to produce quite strange results.

109 **Bracketing exposures**

Bracketing produces lighter and darker versions of the same scene: Changing the exposure by altering the aperture, the shutter speed, or both, will ensure that you get either optimal or usable results. Bracketing is therefore not just a beginner tactic – professional photographers use it extensively to meet their very exacting standards. **Bracketing is easy if you set the exposure manually:** Simply change the exposure controls to bracket on either side of what you perceive to be the best combination. **Bracketing is not always simple with an automatic exposure camera:** See the box on page 101 or the summary above for methods used to override exposures with an automatic camera.

110 - 111 **Using exposure**

Before making an exposure, stop for a moment to visualize how you want the final print or slide to look: Use this visualization to make exposure adjustments in relation to the meter reading. **When using black-and-white film:** Expose for the shadows and develop for the highlights. If shadow detail is lost in exposure, the negative will be blank in these areas and it can not be corrected. Bright highlights on the other hand can usually be printed down. **The reverse is true for transparency film:** Make sure that your highlights are not overly bright. If they are bleached out in exposure, there will be nothing in these areas on your slide. Sometimes, however, you will want an out-of-the-ordinary interpretation. Many striking photographs are based upon a creative visualization of the scene and corresponding exposure decisions.

5.3 TEST

FILL IN THE BLANKS

1 A correct exposure is made by an ideal combination of ____________________ and ____________________.

2 Changes in ____________________ alter the overall lightness or darkness of an image.

3 Exposure ____________________ refers to a margin of error in exposure for usable negatives.

4 A light meter built into the camera measures ____________________ light.

5 The light meter assumes that any scene in front of the camera averages out to be the equivalent of a uniform ____________________ value.

6 Changing the aperture from f/5.6 to f/8 results in an exposure change of ____________________ stop(s).

7 The ____________________ mode on a camera allows you to make exposure adjustments using both aperture and shutter speed controls.

8 ____________________ describes the practice of making several over- and underexposures on either side of what is presumed to be a correct exposure.

9 The ____________________ must always be set on the camera to get a correct exposure reading for the film used.

10 Only an ____________________ scene can be exposed according to the recommended meter reading with good results.

Notes

MULTIPLE CHOICE – CIRCLE ONE OR MORE

1	An incident-light meter measures:	a.	light reflecting off the subject.
		b.	light falling on the subject or the meter.
		c.	only artificial light.
2	If your camera has a center-weighted light meter,:	a.	it measures light within a small central circle.
		b.	it measures light in the entire frame, but with an emphasis on the center.
		c.	it is not a meter for SLR cameras.
3	Deliberate overexposure of the negative in relation to the meter reading will give you a:	a.	lighter print.
		b.	darker print.
		c.	middle-gray print.
4	To change an exposure you can:	a.	manually adjust the aperture and shutter speed.
		b.	use an exposure compensation dial.
		c.	adjust focus by at least 3 feet.
5	You set the aperture and the camera automatically sets the shutter speed in:	a.	shutter-priority mode.
		b.	aperture-priority mode.
		c.	manual mode.
6	A gray card is:	a.	black on one side and white on the other.
		b.	a card with 18 percent reflectance.
		c.	a middle-gray card used for metering and exposure calculation.
7	A backlit subject in a high-contrast scene:	a.	must be overexposed to bring out detail in the subject.
		b.	should be metered close to the subject for a better exposure.
		c.	can be underexposed to exaggerate a silhouette effect.
8	If the tones in a scene average out to be middle gray, the film should be:	a.	overexposed in relation to the meter reading.
		b.	exposed according to the meter reading.
		c.	underexposed in relation to the meter reading.
9	If the tones in a scene average out to be lighter than middle gray, the film should be:	a.	overexposed in relation to the meter reading.
		b.	exposed according to the meter reading.
		c.	underexposed in relation to the meter reading.
10	If the tones in a scene average out to be darker than middle gray, the film should be:	a.	overexposed in relation to the meter reading.
		b.	exposed according to the meter reading.
		c.	underexposed in relation to the meter reading.

5.4 PRACTICAL TIPS

Exposure

Overexposure and underdevelopment in high-contrast situations.

If you photograph on a clear and sunny day, the scenes you are photographing can have a contrast range that is too extensive for the film to record. In very high-contrast scenes, it is simply impossible for the film to capture both shadows with details and highlights with tone at the right negative densities for an acceptable print, unless you carefully expose and develop your film to accommodate the conditions. A golden rule in photography is to expose for the shadows and develop for the highlights. With this procedure in mind, you can use the following method to get better results. Overexpose your entire roll of film by one stop and then underdevelop it. For instance, if you are using ISO 400 film, change the ISO setting to 200, expose the entire roll as if it was rated at this speed, and then underdevelop it by 20-30 percent of the normal development time (more about contrast control through development in chapter 6). These actions will give you negatives with one stop more exposure, which means more detail in the shadow areas, and a loss of density in the highlights due to underdevelopment, which means a darker tone in the print. By making a decision to overexpose and underdevelop before you start photographing in high-contrast conditions, you will compress the contrast range to produce much better negatives.

5.5 JOURNAL

5.5.1 EXPOSURE EXERCISES

As you have learned in this chapter, the metering and automatic exposure capabilities of any camera have certain limitations. To make the necessary manual changes on the occasions when they are needed, you need to understand how these shortcomings of your equipment work and how to correct them based on your own creative and technical decisions. This section will give you an opportunity to practice the theory of equivalent exposures and deliberate underexposure or overexposure through some simple exercises. Familiarize yourself with the sequences of apertures and shutter speeds below and refer to them if you are in doubt.

SHUTTER SPEEDS ▾										
More light										Less light
1	1/2	1/4	1/8	1/15	1/30	1/60	1/125	1/250	1/500	1/1000

APERTURES ▾						
More light						Less light
f/2.8	f/4	f/5.6	f/8	f/11	f/16	f/22

EQUIVALENT EXPOSURES

The amount of light required for an exposure can be given as a series of aperture and shutter speed combinations. Your camera gives you one combination in the exposure readout. This recommendation is usually dependent upon current aperture and shutter speed settings. You can change this combination for an equivalent exposure to accommodate a fast-moving subject with a faster shutter speed or increase the depth of field in a scene with a smaller aperture. However, if you change one setting, you have to change the other in the opposite direction to retain an equivalent exposure. Below is an example of what would happen to a series of negatives and their resulting prints in a series of equivalent exposures. The metered reading was f/11 and 1/30 with ISO 100 film. Even though every exposure is the same, the appearance of the subject in the photograph will of course change according to the combination of shutter speed and aperture used. You choose one particular combination of the equivalent exposures based on your visualization of the photograph.

EQUIVALENT EXPOSURES ▾									
f/2.8 1/500	f/4 1/250	f/5.6 1/125	f/8 1/60	f/11 1/30	f/16 1/15	f/22 1/8	f/22 1/4	f/22 1/2	f/22 1
Negative density scale ▾									
Print value scale ▴									

As you can see from the table, the relationship between negative density and print value remains the same for every exposure. Since the metered reading was used throughout, it remains middle gray for every equivalent exposure combination. Now, complete a series of equivalent exposures for the table below. Your metered reading was f/5.6 and 1/30 with ISO 100 film. If the series offer few combinations for hand-held photography (1/60 or faster with a 50mm lens), you should change your film to a faster speed or put the camera on a tripod.

EQUIVALENT EXPOSURES ▾									
				f/5.6 1/30					
Negative density scale ▾									
Print value scale ▴									

OVEREXPOSURE

Overexposure in this context refers to a photographer's deliberate decision to manually depart from the meter's exposure recommendation to get a better negative for the print she or he has in mind. The term "overexposed", on the other hand, is often used to describe an exposure mistake. If a negative is too dense and consequently prints too light in relation to what the photographer actually wanted, it is usually referred to as "overexposed". Do not confuse overexposure as a method of exposure compensation with "overexposed" used in the sense of a poor result. Purposeful overexposure is done to improve on your negative, while a badly "overexposed" negative is usually the result of exposing a darker than middle gray subject according to the meter reading. If the combined tones of a subject average out to be lighter than middle gray, it is necessary to deliberately overexpose the film in relation to the meter reading. Increased exposure will increase the density of the negative, which results in a print more aligned with the lighter tonal values of the subject. In the example below, the shutter speed or aperture was changed in one-stop increments to gradually overexpose the film. As the negative density increases, the tonal value of the print becomes lighter. Page 107 in the textbook has a better reproduction of the photographic grayscale simulated below. The metered exposure reading was f/8 and 1/250 with ISO 400 film.

OVEREXPOSURE ▾									
Overexposure in stops ▸					+1	+2	+3	+4	+5
X	X	X	X	f/8 1/250	f/8 1/125	f/5.6 1/125	f/5.6 1/60	f/4 1/60	f/4 1/30
Negative density scale ▾									
Print value scale ▴									

The table above seeks to illustrate how the print value gets lighter as the negative density increases. To make an exposure compensation for a lighter than average subject, you have to determine how much lighter than middle gray your subject is. The amount of exposure correction is determined by this decision. If it is only marginally lighter, one stop of overexposure in relation to the recommended reading will ensure a better negative. A bright snow scene, for instance, might require as much as three stops of overexposure. In the example below, your meter reading is f/11 and 1/500 with ISO 400 film. Complete the series of overexposures.

OVEREXPOSURE ▾									
Overexposure in stops ▸					+1	+2	+3	+4	+5
X	X	X	X	f/11 1/500					
Negative density scale ▾									
Print value scale ▴									

UNDEREXPOSURE

Once more, underexposure in this context refers to a photographer's deliberate decision to manually depart from the meter's exposure recommendation to get a better negative for the print she or he has in mind. The term "underexposed", on the other hand, is used to describe an exposure mistake. If a negative is lacking density and consequently prints too dark in relation to what the photographer actually wanted, it is usually referred to as "underexposed" or "thin". An "underexposed" negative is often the result of a exposing a lighter than average subject according to the meter reading, so do not confuse it with intentional underexposure, which is intended to create a less dense negative for a dark subject. If the combined tones of a subject average out to be darker than middle gray, it is necessary to deliberately underexpose the film in relation to the meter reading. Reduced exposure will decrease the density of the negative, which results in a darker print. The table below shows a series of deliberate underexposures. Take a quick look at page 107 in your textbook to get a better idea of how the photographic grayscale will be reproduced in a print. The metered exposure reading was f/8 and 1/250 with ISO 100 film.

UNDEREXPOSURE ▾									
- 4	- 3	- 2	- 1	◂ Underexposure in stops					
f/22 1/500	f/16 1/500	f/11 1/500	f/11 1/250	f/8 1/250	X	X	X	X	X
Negative density scale ▾									
Print value scale ▴									

As the negative density is reduced due to underexposure, the print value gets progressively darker. With underexposure, you also have to determine how much darker than middle gray the overall value of your subject is to decide on the amount of exposure correction. However, since you must be careful to maintain texture and detail in your darkest shadow areas, it is best not to underexpose any subject with more than two stops. If you fail to record adequate shadow detail in your negative, these areas are lost forever, and a print from such a negative is seldom satisfactory. Complete the series of underexposures below, using your metered reading of f/4 and 1/60 with ISO 64 film as your staring point.

UNDEREXPOSURE ▾									
- 4	- 3	- 2	- 1	◂ Underexposure in stops					
				f/4 1/60	X	X	X	X	X
Negative density scale ▾									
Print value scale ▴									

5.5.2 EXPOSURE RECORDS

Use these exposure records to keep track of your exposures for a few rolls of film. The records will help you understand how your exposure decisions translate into negatives. After exposing and developing these rolls, you will be in a better position to predict your results based on the references below and the experience you have gained. Assign a number to each roll of film in your negative file, and use the same numbers for the entries in 6.5.5 Development records. In combination, the records for exposure and development will help you master these fundamental aspects of photography very quickly, and they will also help your instructor to sort out any problems that you might be having. The first table below explains the record entries.

Film type ▸	**Enter the type of film used.**
Film speed ▸	**Enter the film speed you actually set on the camera.**
Exposure reading ▸	**Enter the recommended meter reading for the scene you photographed.**
Exposure ▸	**Enter the actual exposure that you used.**
Comments ▸	**Enter comments on your exposure correction and the developed negative.**

This example shows how the exposure records may be filled out. Please note the space for comments both at the time of exposure and after the negatives have been developed. It might be helpful to consider the exposure comments before you make departures from the recommended exposure reading. After all, it is this visualization of the photograph that determines what changes should be made to the metered exposure. Although exposure is mainly about negative density and the corresponding tonal values in a print, don't forget to use equivalent exposures to control the appearance of your subject (as in exposure 4 and 6 below).

FILM 1	Film type ▸	KODAK TRI-X			Film speed ▸	400
	Exposure reading ▾		Exposure ▾		Comments ▾	
#	Shutter	f/	Shutter	f/	Exposure	Negative
1	125	8	125	5.6	Light subject, +1	Still not dense enough
2	60	11	250	11	Very dark subject, -2	Dark with detail, perfect
3	250	11	250	11	Average subject	Middle gray OK
4	250	11	125	16	+ Depth of field	Better sharpness
5	125	16	1000	5.6	Fast moving subject	Stopped Motion OK
6	125	16	60	22	Blur motion more	60 did not blur enough
7	125	16	125	11	Light subject, +1	Not the best, 9 below
8	125	16	125	8	Bracketed, +2	Print exposure 9
9	125	16	60	8	Bracketed, +3	Better interpretation
10	125	11	125	8	Lighten skin tone, +1	Good tone on contacts

FILM 1	Film type ▸					Film speed ▸
	Exposure reading ▾		Exposure ▾		Comments ▾	
#	Shutter	f/	Shutter	f/	Exposure	Negative
1						
2						
3						
4						
5						
6						
7						
8						
9						
10						
11						
12						
13						
14						
15						
16						
17						
18						
19						
20						
21						
22						
23						
24						
25						
26						
27						
28						
29						
30						
31						
32						
33						
34						
35						
36						

FILM 2	Film type ▸				Film speed ▸	
	Exposure reading ▾		Exposure ▾		Comments ▾	
#	Shutter	f/	Shutter	f/	Exposure	Negative
1						
2						
3						
4						
5						
6						
7						
8						
9						
10						
11						
12						
13						
14						
15						
16						
17						
18						
19						
20						
21						
22						
23						
24						
25						
26						
27						
28						
29						
30						
31						
32						
33						
34						
35						
36						

FILM 3 Film type ▸ Film speed ▸

	Exposure reading ▾		Exposure ▾		Comments ▾	
#	Shutter	f/	Shutter	f/	Exposure	Negative
1						
2						
3						
4						
5						
6						
7						
8						
9						
10						
11						
12						
13						
14						
15						
16						
17						
18						
19						
20						
21						
22						
23						
24						
25						
26						
27						
28						
29						
30						
31						
32						
33						
34						
35						
36						

FILM 4	Film type ▸				Film speed ▸	
	Exposure reading ▾		Exposure ▾		Comments ▾	
#	Shutter	f/	Shutter	f/	Exposure	Negative
1						
2						
3						
4						
5						
6						
7						
8						
9						
10						
11						
12						
13						
14						
15						
16						
17						
18						
19						
20						
21						
22						
23						
24						
25						
26						
27						
28						
29						
30						
31						
32						
33						
34						
35						
36						

FILM 5	Film type ▸				Film speed ▸	
	Exposure reading ▾		Exposure ▾		Comments ▾	
#	Shutter	f/	Shutter	f/	Exposure	Negative
1						
2						
3						
4						
5						
6						
7						
8						
9						
10						
11						
12						
13						
14						
15						
16						
17						
18						
19						
20						
21						
22						
23						
24						
25						
26						
27						
28						
29						
30						
31						
32						
33						
34						
35						
36						

6 DEVELOPING THE NEGATIVE

6.1 GLOSSARY

Agitation	A movement pattern of the developing tank performed at set intervals during the developing process to ensure even development.
Contamination	The spread of chemicals into areas where the do not belong. The result of contamination is ruined negatives and prints.
Contrast	The difference in density between two areas on the negative image or two tones in the corresponding print. Normally used in photography to describe the difference between the darkest shadow areas and the brightest highlights.
Density	The degree of exposed and developed silver in a particular area of the negative. A full-tonal-range negative contains a range of densities, from almost transparent shadow areas to near opaque highlights.
Development	A process that transforms a latent image into a visible and permanent one on your film.
Highlight area	The darkest area in a negative and the lightest area in a print.
Hypo	Short for sodium hyposulfite. Another term used for fixer.
Manufacturer's instructions	The recommendations for dilution and use at various times and temperatures supplied with the product.
Normal	A negative with good separation of values - shadows, mid-tones, and highlights - which prints easily on normal-contrast-grade paper.
Overdeveloped	The shadow areas in the negative are fine, but the highlights are too dense.
Overexposed	The shadow areas in the negative are too dense.
Oxidation	Chemical contact with oxygen leading to exhaustion.
Push processing	A procedure of underexposure and overdevelopment used under low-light situations.
Reticulation	A textured pattern on the film caused by rapid temperature changes during development.
Shadow area	The most transparent area in a negative and the darkest area in a print.
Stock solution	Concentrated chemistry.
Underdeveloped	The shadow areas are fine, but the negative lacks density in the highlights.
Underexposed	The negative lacks detail in the shadow areas.
Working solution	The stock solution is diluted with water to produce a working solution.

6.2 SUMMARY

113 **Developing the negative**

Once your image has been exposed, your next step is to make it visible: The latent or invisible image formed by exposing the film is made visible through development. **There are many opportunities in developing and printing to control the quality of the final photograph:** Precision, care, and control during development will ensure that your exposures are transformed into the kind of photographs you envisioned.

114 **Equipment and supplies you'll need**

Equipment to load film: Developing reels (plastic or stainless steel), developing tank, bottle-cap opener, scissors, a completely dark room. **Equipment to process film:** Manufacturer's instructions, containers for working solutions, tray or pan for temperature control, timer. Please see page 114 for a full description of each item. **Equipment to mix and store chemicals:** Source of water (distilled water may improve on your results in some areas), photographic thermometer, graduated containers, mixing containers, storage containers, stirring rod, funnel, safety equipment (mask, goggles, gloves, etc.). Please see page 114 for a full description of each item. Other equipment you may need includes: Film washer, film clips, photo-sponge (or chamois leather), negative storage pages, negative folder.

115 **Processing chemicals and how to handle them**

Chemicals to process film: There are three basic solutions in the development process – developer, stop bath, and fixer. **Developer:** Converts the latent or invisible image into a visible and stable silver image. There are many different types of developer, and each has special characteristics suitable for a specific purpose. **Stop bath:** A mild acid bath, which stops the action of the alkaline developer. Some have an indicator that changes color when the solution is exhausted. **Fixer:** Removes the unexposed and undeveloped silver-halide crystals in the emulsion. After fixing, the film is no longer sensitive to light. **Fixer check or hypo check:** Like all chemicals, the fixer is exhausted through use. The fixer check makes sure that the fixer is actually working. **Washing aid:** Removes chemical residue from the film during washing much faster than ordinary water. Used to ensure the archival properties of the negatives, save water, and speed up the development process. **Wetting agent:** Ensures that water runs off the surface of the film evenly to promote uniform and fast drying. **How to mix and handle chemicals:** Follow mixing instructions for best results and handle all chemicals with care to protect your health. **Record keeping:** Chemicals are exhausted through use, storage, and in some cases, exposure to air. Keep a record of how many rolls of film have been developed and fixed by your working solutions to determine when they are nearing exhaustion. **Replenishing developers:** After each use, you add a certain amount of stock solution to the working solution in order to maintain its strength. **One-shot developers:** Mixed immediately before use and discarded once development is complete. Same strength each time and no worries about exhaustion. **Mixing dry chemicals:** Add dry chemicals to water and stir until the solution is dissolved. Use a mask to avoid breathing in chemical particles. **Diluting a stock solution to a working solution:** Chemicals are usually mixed up to a stock solution first. The stock solution is then diluted with water to make a working solution. The proportion of stock solution to water is often given as a ratio, for example 1:4, where the stock solution is listed first. **Adjusting temperature:** Use water baths or tap water to alter and control the temperature of your working solutions. **Avoid unnecessary oxidation:** Exposure to air (oxygen) will exhaust most chemicals.

Developers are also sensitive to light, so store them in dark and airtight bottles. **Contamination – chemicals where they don't belong – can result in many darkroom ills:** If chemicals come into contact with each other when they are not supposed to, the result is contamination. This can take many shapes, but the outcome is always the same – ruined negatives or prints. You can take some basic precautions to avoid contamination; rinse and dry your hands frequently to avoid transferring one chemical to another, keep all work surfaces clean, and keep all equipment clean by washing it after each use. Your clothes may also be a victim of contamination, so an apron or lab coat might be a worthwhile investment.

116

Chemical safety

Photographic chemicals should be handled with reasonable care, like all chemicals: Prevention is better than cure, so avoid exposing yourself to potentially damaging chemicals. **Know what you are handling:** Read labels on the chemical packaging or refer to the Material Safety Data Sheet (MSDS) for a particular substance. **Avoid skin contact:** Use rubber gloves or tongs when handling chemicals or developing films/prints. If you get chemicals on your skin, wash the affected area thoroughly with soap and water. **Avoid getting chemicals in your eyes:** Wear protective goggles or a face shield. If you get chemicals in your eyes, wash with running water for a minimum of 15 minutes. **Avoid getting chemicals in your mouth:** Avoid any activity (eating, drinking, or smoking) that may cause you to ingest chemicals in the darkroom. **Avoid inhaling chemicals:** Use a mask or respirator to cover your nose and mouth when mixing dry chemicals. Look for liquid alternatives. **Clean up chemical spills promptly, safely, and thoroughly:** Take care of minor accidents yourself by washing the affected areas, but do not hesitate to call for professional assistance if the spill is serious, and you are unable to clean it up without exposing yourself to the hazard it poses. **Be cautious when using any acid, particularly in concentrated form:** Add water to acid, never acid to water. Rinse with plenty of running water in case of an accident and seek medical help. The acetic acid used in stop baths is very mild. **Take extra precautions with certain chemicals:** Refer to the MSDS for proper handling and risks associated with exposure. **Store chemicals safely and out of the reach of children:** Label containers and lock them away. **If you do have a problem, do not try to self-medicate:** Be aware that repeated exposure is the most likely cause of serious responses to chemical substances. Treat any developing symptom, such as a minor skin rash, with respect and seek advice on how to remedy it. **Dispose of chemicals properly:** Small amounts of developer and stop bath can be mixed together to neutralize the solutions and discarded through the sewer system. Fixer should ideally be delivered for silver recovery. Large users of photo-chemistry (schools, universities, or commercial labs) have waste collection programs that take care of the discarded solutions.

118 - 123

Processing black-and-white roll film step by step

A more extensive summary of the development process can be found on page 118 in the textbook. Please refer to 6.5.4 Developing guide to fill out your own customized guide to developing. **How to develop film successfully:** Simple attention to detail will ensure excellent results. **Orderliness:** Arrange equipment and solutions in an orderly way to avoid mistakes. **Consistency:** Follow the same procedure each time you develop film to make the results repeatable (if they are good) and easy to change (if they turn out to be bad). This includes mixing the solutions to the same strength each time, developing at the same temperature, agitating the film according to the same pattern, and keeping track of the development time. **Cleanliness:** Avoid contamination by keeping your equipment and hands meticulously clean.

A brief summary of the developing process for 35mm film:

Preparation
1. Select a time and temperature for your film and developer combination.
2. Mix the developer, stop bath, and fixer to their working strength and adjust their temperatures.
3. Set out the materials for loading the film.
4. Lock the door and turn out all the lights. Remove the film from the 35mm cassette.
5. Use the scissors to cut off the half-width strip at the beginning of a roll of 35mm film.
6. Align the film to the reel and insert.
7. Hold the reel in both hands and turn the two halves of the reel back and forth.
8. When you reach the end of the roll, cut off the film spool.
9. Assemble the tank and reel.

Development
10. Check the solution temperatures. Pour the developer solution into the tank and start the timer immediately.
11. Start agitation immediately.
12. Begin the regular agitation pattern to be followed throughout the development.
13. Remove only the tank cap so you can pour out the developer.

Stop bath
14. Quickly pour the stop bath into the tank through the funnel opening in the cover.
15. Remove the tank cap, leaving the funnel/cover in place, and pour out the stop bath.

Fixer
16. Pour fixer into the tank through the funnel opening in the cover.
17. Check that the film is clearing.
18. Pour out the fixer.

Washing and drying
19. Treat the film with a washing-aid solution before washing.
20. Wash the film.
21. After washing, treat the film with a wetting agent.
22. Unwind the film from the reel and hang it up to dry.
23. If water spots are a problem, try wiping the film with photo-sponge or damp chamois leather (see 6.4 Practical tips).
24. Protect the dry negatives and clean up the darkroom.

124 - 125 **How developer and fixer affect a negative**

A general knowledge of developer chemicals is useful background information: You may want to mix your own chemistry from a formula instead of always relying upon standard packages. **The most important ingredient in any developer formula is the reducing agent, also called the developing agent:** It reduces the exposed silver-halide crystals in the emulsion to metallic silver. **Some reducing agents are used alone, but often two together assist each other:** The effects of individual reducing agents are mixed to find the best possible blend of negative characteristics. For example, tonal gradation and contrast. **Most reducing agents work only in an alkaline solution:** The alkaline solution works as an accelerator, so most developers also contain a restrainer to slow down the process, as well as a preservative to prevent rapid oxidation.

After development, fixer sets the image permanently on the film: The fixer removes the unexposed and undeveloped silver-halide crystals from the emulsion. **The active ingredient in fixer is sodium thiosulfate:** Fixers used for film often contain a hardener to protect the fragile film emulsion from scratches during washing. Rapid fixers are what their name suggests – they fix films faster than standard solutions. **Follow the fixer instructions carefully:** Fix for the recommended time in properly diluted, fresh fixer to prevent irreversible damage to an unfixed film exposed to light or a depletion of the metallic silver due to excessive fixing. As a rule of thumb, fix for twice the clearing time.

126 - 127

How time and temperature affect development

The longer the developing time, the darker and more contrasty the negative becomes: The density of the negative increases with development time. The rate of conversion to metallic silver is uneven – highlights develop faster than shadow areas as the time increases. This effect is used to control negative contrast, the relationship between dark and light tones. **Development time controls contrast and density:** Increase the development time to increase the contrast in your negatives. **The rate of development changes during the process:** It starts off slow, peaks, and then tapers off. **Developer temperature also affects development:** An increased solution temperature will speed up the development process considerably. However, the emulsion is very easily damaged at higher temperatures. **Time-and-temperature charts:** Manufacturers of developing solutions or films provide these. The times and temperatures are initial recommendations that normally need some adjustments. Film is usually developed at 68°F, which is a practical temperature to maintain for developing solutions in most darkrooms. Please see page 126 for an example of a time-and-temperature chart.

128

The importance of proper agitation and fresh solutions

The purpose of agitation is to supply fresh chemicals to the emulsion at regular intervals: Agitation is important for all solutions, but absolutely crucial during development. **Too much or too little agitation can create problems:** Inadequate agitation exhausts the solution close to the surface of the film, leading to a suspension of the process until fresh solution is brought to the area. Too little agitation shows up as a mottled appearance, easily seen in areas with a uniform value. **Too much agitation creates problems more often than too little agitation:** Excessive agitation leads to overdeveloped negatives and frequently lighter streaks along the edges of the film. **To avoid these problems, agitate gently at regular intervals:** The normal sequence consists of 5 seconds of agitation every 30 seconds. Try to agitate (move the tank) in a random pattern. If you are developing fewer films than the tank can hold, fill up your developing tank with empty reels to avoid excessive movement. **Always use fresh solutions:** Exhausted solutions will in the best case scenario lead to mediocre results and in the worst case scenario completely ruin your negatives. Keep track of the number of films developed or fixed in the various solutions and their storage time. Do not let these numbers and times exceed the manufacturer's recommendation.

129

The need for careful washing and drying

Film can fade or turn yellow if it is not thoroughly washed after fixing: Residue of fixer left on the film causes these reactions. **Careless drying also damages negatives and shows immediately:** Dust sticks to wet film and can become embedded in the film emulsion during drying. Rough handling easily scratches wet negatives. **Proper washing and drying is relatively easy:** Use a hypo-clearing agent and wash the film in running water. Handle the film as little as possible while it is wet and hang the film in a dust-free area to dry.

130 - 131 **Exposure and development: Under, normal, over**

A correctly exposed and properly developed negative will make your next step – printing - much easier: A negative with a range of densities that correspond with the tonal range of the print you want will print very easily. **Expose for the shadows, develop for the highlights:** Exposure and development both affect the negative, but in different ways. **Changing the development time has little effect on shadow areas, but it has a strong effect on highlight areas:** Increase development time to increase negative contrast. Reduce development time to decrease the contrast. **Changing the exposure affects both highlight and shadow areas:** The greater the exposure, the denser they both will be. Expose to make sure that your shadow areas have adequate detail and develop to control the highlight areas. **The practical application of these relationships lets you alter exposure or development if you have persistent difficulty printing your negatives:** Evaluate your results and change exposure and/or development to improve on them. Page 131 shows how negatives should be evaluated for density and contrast.

132 - 133 **Push processing**

What do you do when the light is too dim for a fast enough shutter speed, even when you are using a fast film: You push process through underexpose and overdevelopment. **Pushing film lets you shoot at a higher-than-normal speed if you increase the film development:** Set the film speed one or more stops (depending on the film you are using) faster than normal and expose your entire roll at this speed. Overdevelop your film to bring out as much detail as possible from the negative. **Rather than truly increasing film speed, push processing simply underexposes and overdevelops the film:** Push processing produces a negative with larger grain and more contrast compared to a normally exposed and developed negative. Due to underexposure, the shadow areas are usually very dark. **To develop pushed film:** Increase the development time, about 25-50 percent per stop, or use a special-purpose film developer. See the table on page 133 for some suggestions. **There are limits to the amount that film can be pushed:** One or two stops is the practical limit before image quality starts to seriously deteriorate. Seek out faster films rather than pushing slower ones if possible. Some films tolerate one stop of underexposure without overdevelopment. **Pushing color films is also possible:** You will get color shifts along with the usual increase in contrast and grain. Commercial labs usually offer this service.

Notes

6.3 TEST

FILL IN THE BLANKS

1 Development transforms the ____________________ image into a visible one.

2 The development process involves three chemical solutions in this order: ____________________, ____________________, and ____________________.

3 When a developer is mixed at a ratio of 1:4, it contains 4 parts of ____________________.

4 Development is affected by time and ____________________.

5 The highlights, not the shadows, of an ____________________ negative are too dense.

6 Push processing involves ____________________ and overdevelopment.

7 Agitation is important for ____________________ development.

8 The ____________________ removes the unexposed and undeveloped silver halide crystals from the film.

9 A stock solution is diluted to make a ____________________ solution.

10 A final rinse in a bath with ____________________ ensures that water runs off the negatives evenly for uniform drying without spots or water marks.

MULTIPLE CHOICE – CIRCLE ONE OR MORE

1 An underexposed negative has:
- a. not been fixed long enough.
- b. inadequate shadow detail.
- c. dense highlights.

2 An increased development time will result in:
- a. more visible grain in your negative.
- b. higher contrast in your negative.
- c. a faster film speed.

3 Underdeveloped negatives look:
- a. flat.
- b. milky in appearance.
- c. like they would need more density.

4 Exposure determines overall negative density, while contrast is largely affected by:
- a. the shutter speed.
- b. development.
- c. film speed.

5	Stop bath is:	a.	the step in development between developer and fixer.
		b.	a mild alkaline.
		c.	a weak dilution of acetic acid.
6	Less development time for a negative will result in:	a.	more shadow detail.
		b.	a longer fixing time.
		c.	darker highlights in the print.
7	Contamination is:	a.	damaging to negatives and prints.
		b.	caused by chemistry traces in places where they do not belong.
		c.	usually caused by dirty equipment and a lack of care during the developing process.
8	The negatives must be washed to:	a.	reduce the grain.
		b.	remove all chemical traces.
		c.	adjust their density.
9	Fix for:	a.	twice the clearing time.
		b.	the same time as the development time.
		c.	the same time as the stop bath.
10	You tap your development tank on the working surface during development to:	a.	secure the lid.
		b.	dislodge air bubbles from the film.
		c.	give the film more exposure.

Notes

6.4 PRACTICAL TIPS

Film rewind

Keep the film leader for easy loading of developing reels.

If you have a camera with manual rewind, you can stop rewinding before the film leader disappears into the film cassette. Listen for a tiny click as the film is released from the take-up spool, feel for the loss of tension, and stop immediately. Open the back at this point, and about 3-4 inches of your film leader will be left. You exposed this part when you loaded your camera, so no frames are ruined. Trim the leader square, insert this exposed end into the developing reel in daylight, and turn off the lights to load the rest in darkness. Pull film out of the film cassette as you proceed. This simple trick makes loading the film onto the developing reel quick and easy. You avoid opening the cassette in the dark, trimming the film in the dark, and getting started on the reel in the dark. Practice with a scrap roll first to get used to the click and tension loss telling you to stop rewinding. It is good practice to tear off a small strip of the leader, so you do not mistake it for an unexposed roll and put it through the camera again for double exposures.

Pre-soak

Pre-soak your film in water for even development.

You agitate during development to let fresh developer flow over the surface of your film. This ensures even development of the negative and even tones in the resulting print. Large areas with uniform density, such as a clear sky, can sometimes show marks of uneven development despite your best efforts to keep the same agitation pattern of set intervals and randomized movements. One solution to uneven development might be to change the agitation time along with the actual movements of the tank. Another method that could alleviate problems of this kind involves a pre-soaking of your film in water. Prepare a water bath at the same temperature as the developing solutions (68ºF). Pour this into the loaded developing tank prior to the developer, and let it soak for 1 minute without any agitation before pouring it out. Expect the water to be colored. By pre-soaking your film this way, the emulsion is softened by the water and the developer works equally well on all areas of the negative from the moment it is poured in.

Watermarks

Wipe the film carefully with a pad of chamois leather.

You use a wetting agent such as Kodak Photo-Flo to prevent watermarks on your film, and to promote uniform drying. But sometimes, even with Photo-Flo diluted in distilled water, these watermarks are hard to avoid. If they persist, you might want to try wiping the film while it is wet with a chamois leather. By removing all excess water from the surface, there is no chance of marks forming, but you run the risk of scratching your film. To prevent this, buy a good quality chamois leather and cut it up into smaller squares of about 5 inches by 5 inches. Just before you hang your film to dry, wet the leather thoroughly until it is very soft, and wring out all excess water. Hang your film, and form the chamois leather into a small pad. Gently wipe both sides of the film once with this soft and absorbent pad to remove all water. Dry the leather and keep it clean in a plastic bag. This trick works wonders against watermarks, and it is not likely to scratch your film if you are careful.

6.5 JOURNAL

6.5.1 LAB FILM-CHEMISTRY CHART

Complete a chart for the film-development chemistry used in your lab. Add any entries that you may have purchased yourself at the bottom. You may need to consult your instructor, notices in the lab, product packaging and literature, or Material Safety Data Sheets to complete all the entries.

LAB CHEMISTRY	Product name	Dilution	Safety / Handling / Comments
Developer			Avoid prolonged skin contact. Rinse off immediately. Wash skin with soap and water. Do not inhale or ingest.
Developer			
Stop bath			
Stop bath			
Fixer			
Fixer			
Clearing bath			
Clearing bath			
Wetting agent			
Wetting agent			
OTHER PRODUCTS			
Developer			
Developer			
Developer			
Stop bath			
Stop bath			
Stop bath			
Fixer			
Fixer			
Fixer			
Clearing bath			
Clearing bath			
Clearing bath			
Wetting agent			
Wetting agent			
Wetting agent			

6.5.2 FILM TEMPERATURE-AND-TIME PROCESSING CHARTS

Film development is temperature and time dependent. Use these tables to compile a selection of temperature-and-time development charts for the films you use most often. You can find these combinations either in your lab, packaged with the product, or in special data sheets available from the manufacturer. The Internet is a great resource for researching this kind of information. Recommendations are often highlighted in bold type.

FILM ▸	Kodak T-Max 400	Temperature ▾				
Exposure index ▾	Developer ▾	65°F	68°F	70°F	72°F	75°F
ISO 400	Kodak D-76	14.5	12.5	11	10	9
ISO 200	Microdol-X	12	10.5	9	8.5	7.5
ISO 400	T-Max	–	7	6.5	6.5	6

FILM ▸		Temperature ▾				
Exposure index ▾	Developer ▾	65°F	68°F	70°F	72°F	75°F

FILM ▸		Temperature ▾				
Exposure index ▾	Developer ▾	65°F	68°F	70°F	72°F	75°F

FILM ▸		Temperature ▾				
Exposure index ▾	Developer ▾	65°F	68°F	70°F	72°F	75°F

FILM ▸		Temperature ▾				
Exposure index ▾	Developer ▾	65°F	68°F	70°F	72°F	75°F

FILM ▸		Temperature ▾				
Exposure index ▾	Developer ▾	65°F	68°F	70°F	72°F	75°F

6.5.3 MEASURING GUIDE

There are many different types of developing tanks. You need to establish how much chemistry your tank needs to cover one roll of film in development. Look at the packaging or underneath your tank to see if this information is listed there. If it is not, you can put one empty developing reel in the tank, fill it with water until the reel is covered, and measure how much water you pour out. This measurement is the total amount of chemistry you need for one reel. Keep in mind that the chemistry is exhausted through use and oxidation. Label your storage containers and keep a record of how many films you have put through it. Tables for these records are provided in 6.5.6 Chemistry records. See the examples below for ratio calculation and the rest of the measuring guide. Fill it out once, and refer to the exact dilutions for each solution every time you develop film. Use the metric system for calculation, and keep all units in milliliters.

Ratio calculation example

❶ Take the total amount of chemistry required for the number of reels you intend to use and divide it by the total number of units in the ratio: 300ml (for one reel) divided by 10 (for a developer ratio of 1:9) = 30.

❷ Multiply each unit of the ratio with this number to get the proportion of chemistry to water: 30 x 1 = 30ml. and 30 x 9 = 270ml.

❸ The working solution of developer you need to mix for the development of one reel in this type of tank contains 30ml. of stock solution and 270ml. of water.

DEVELOPING TANK ▸		*Paterson tank, 5 reels.*					Chemistry per reel ▸			*300 ml.*	
	Dilution	1		2		3		4		5	
Developer	1:9	30	270	60	540	90	810	120	1080	140	1350
Stop bath	1:5	50	250	100	500	150	750	200	1000	250	1250
Fixer	1:4	60	240	120	480	180	720	240	960	300	1200
Clearing bath	1:3	75	225	150	450	225	675	300	800	375	1125
Wetting agent	1:200	1.5	300	3	600	4.5	900	6	1200	7.5	1500

DEVELOPING TANK ▸							Chemistry per reel ▸				
	Dilution	1		2		3		4		5	
Developer											
Stop bath											
Fixer											
Clearing bath											
Wetting agent											

DEVELOPING TANK ▸							Chemistry per reel ▸				
	Dilution	1		2		3		4		5	
Developer											
Stop bath											
Fixer											
Clearing bath											
Wetting agent											

DEVELOPING TANK ▸							Chemistry per reel ▸				
	Dilution	1		2		3		4		5	
Developer											
Stop bath											
Fixer											
Clearing bath											
Wetting agent											

6.5.4 DEVELOPING GUIDE

Fill out this guide before developing your first roll of film and refer to it during development. Get the exact times for fixer, clearing bath, and wash from your instructor. The rest of the information required can be found in the previous parts of this 6.5 Journal. Use the suggested agitation pattern at first. If you are in the slightest doubt about the procedure, the numbers in the left-hand column correspond with the steps covered in the textbook. Refer to any section you are unclear about before starting to develop your film.

1	Select a time and temperature for your film and developer combination.
	Refer to Journal 6.5.2.
	Film ▸
	Temperature ▸
	Time ▸
2	Mix the developer, stop bath, and fixer to their working strength and adjust their temperatures.
	Refer to Journal 6.5.1, 6.5.2, and 6.5.3 for handling and mixing.

	Dilution ▾	Temperature ▾	Time in solution ▾
Developer			
Stop bath			
Fixer			
Clearing bath			
Wetting agent			

Materials check list
- ❑ Chemistry
- ❑ Water source
- ❑ Graduated cylinders
- ❑ Stirring rod
- ❑ Photographic thermometer
- ❑ Containers

3	Set out the materials for loading film.

Materials check list
- ❑ Film to develop
- ❑ Bottle opener (if you have no film leader)
- ❑ Scissors
- ❑ Developing tank
- ❑ Developing reels

4	Lock the door and turn out all the lights. COMPLETE DARKNESS FROM NOW ON.
	DARKNESS
5	Open the 35mm film cassette. Cut off the half-width strip at the beginning of a roll of film.
	DARKNESS
6	Align the film to the reel and insert.
	DARKNESS
7	Hold the reel in both hands and turn the two halves of the reel back and forth.
	DARKNESS
8	When you reach the end of the roll, cut off the film spool.
	DARKNESS
9	Assemble the tank and reel. DAYLIGHT FROM NOW ON.

10	Check the solution temperatures. Start the timer and quickly pour the developer into the tank.
	Development time ▸ — START → TIMER
11	Start agitation immediately.
	Agitate continuously for the first minute.
12	Begin the regular agitation pattern to be followed throughout the development time.
	After the first minute, agitate 5 seconds every 30 seconds.
13	Remove only the tank cap so you can pour out the developer.
	Pour the developer out 10 seconds before the development is finished. — RESET ← TIMER
14	Quickly pour the stop bath into the tank through the funnel opening in the cover.
	Agitate continuously. Stop bath time ▸ — START → TIMER
15	Remove the tank cap, leaving the funnel/cover in place, and pour out the stop bath.
	Pour the stop bath out after 30 seconds. — RESET ← TIMER
16	Pour fixer into the tank through the funnel opening in the cover.
	Follow the same agitation pattern as you did for the developer. Fixer time ▸ — START → TIMER
17	Check that the film is clearing.
	After half the fixing time, remove the film briefly from the tank to check that it is clearing. If you have hypo-checked your fixer, or just mixed it, there is no need to perform this step.
18	Pour out the fixer.
	Pour the fixer out 10 seconds before the fixing time is finished. — RESET ← TIMER
19	Treat the film with a washing aid solution before washing.
	Agitate at 30-second intervals. First rinse in water ▸ 30 seconds to 2 minutes. Clearing bath time ▸ — START → TIMER

20	Wash the film.
	Wash in running water around 68ºF.
	Washing time ▸ START → TIMER
21	After washing, treat the film with a wetting agent.
	Do not agitate to prevent foam from forming.
	Wetting agent time ▸ START → TIMER
22	Unwind the film from the reel and hang it up to dry.
	Be careful when you handle the wet film. It is easily damaged. The film should be dry in 2-4 hours, depending on the climate.
23	If water spots are a problem...
	Consider wiping the film with a chamois leather or a photo sponge if you are consistently plagued by residue on your film. See 6.4 Practical tips above.
24	Protect the dry negatives and clean up the darkroom.
	Adjust these entries with your instructor after evaluating the results in combination with your exposure records.

6.5.5 DEVELOPMENT RECORDS

Keep a record of your development to get consistent results. Mark each film in your negative folder with a number from the tables below. Try increased development for low-contrast scenes and reduced development for high-contrast scenes. As an initial guideline, use a 25-40 percent increase or a 20-30 percent reduction in the normal development time to adjust the contrast. These records will help you to predict your results with accuracy after a few rolls. Ask your instructor to evaluate your negatives with you if you are in doubt.

FILM Example ▾	EI ▾	Developer ▾	ºF ▾	Normal	N + 1	N -1
Kodak T-Max 400	400	D-76	68		16	
Comments						
The scenes on this film were all very low-contrast. I gave increased development to increase the contrast, but the negatives were still somewhat flat. Try 18 minutes next time for N + 1 increased development.						

FILM Example ▾	EI ▾	Developer ▾	ºF ▾	Normal	N + 1	N -1
Agfapan APX 25	400	Rodinal 1:50	68			8
Comments						
Very sharp negatives. Easy to print. 8 minutes for N-1, reduced contrast, seems to be about right for this particular roll.						

FILM 1 ▾	EI ▾	Developer ▾	°F ▾	Normal	N + 1	N -1
Comments						

FILM 2 ▾	EI ▾	Developer ▾	°F ▾	Normal	N + 1	N -1
Comments						

FILM 3 ▾	EI ▾	Developer ▾	°F ▾	Normal	N + 1	N -1
Comments						

FILM 4 ▾	EI ▾	Developer ▾	°F ▾	Normal	N + 1	N -1
Comments						

FILM 5 ▾	EI ▾	Developer ▾	°F ▾	Normal	N + 1	N -1
Comments						

FILM 6	EI	Developer	°F	Normal	N + 1	N -1
Comments						

FILM 7	EI	Developer	°F	Normal	N + 1	N -1
Comments						

FILM 8	EI	Developer	°F	Normal	N + 1	N -1
Comments						

FILM 9	EI	Developer	°F	Normal	N + 1	N -1
Comments						

FILM 10	EI	Developer	°F	Normal	N + 1	N -1
Comments						

FILM 11 ▾	EI ▾	Developer ▾	°F ▾	Normal	N + 1	N -1
Comments						

FILM 12 ▾	EI ▾	Developer ▾	°F ▾	Normal	N + 1	N -1
Comments						

FILM 13 ▾	EI ▾	Developer ▾	°F ▾	Normal	N + 1	N -1
Comments						

FILM 14 ▾	EI ▾	Developer ▾	°F ▾	Normal	N + 1	N -1
Comments						

FILM 15 ▾	EI ▾	Developer ▾	°F ▾	Normal	N + 1	N -1
Comments						

FILM 16	EI	Developer	°F	Normal	N + 1	N -1
Comments						

FILM 17	EI	Developer	°F	Normal	N + 1	N -1
Comments						

FILM 18	EI	Developer	°F	Normal	N + 1	N -1
Comments						

FILM 19	EI	Developer	°F	Normal	N + 1	N -1
Comments						

FILM 20	EI	Developer	°F	Normal	N + 1	N -1
Comments						

6.5.6 CHEMISTRY RECORDS

Use these records to keep track of how many rolls of film you put through your developer and fixer. Once the capacity is exhausted or the recommended storage time is exceeded, dispose of the chemicals in the proper manner. Resist the temptation to put one last roll through chemistry that you believe to be nearing exhaustion. The results are seldom satisfactory, and some photographs can of course never be repeated. To link your storage containers to the records, place a numbered piece of masking tape on the bottle and enter the number in the designated space below. Most stop baths have an indicator that changes color when it should be discarded. Each number in these tables represents a roll of film. Cross them out as you develop and fix.

DEVELOPER ▸	Kodak D-76											
Container # ▸	1	~~1~~	~~2~~	~~3~~	~~4~~	~~5~~	Container # ▸		1	2	3	4	5
Mixing date ▸	1/1	~~6~~	~~7~~	8	9	10	Mixing date ▸		6	7	8	9	10
Exhausted date ▸	3/1	11	12	13	14	15	Exhausted date ▸		11	12	13	14	15
Capacity (35mm) ▸	12	16	17	18	19	20	Capacity (35mm) ▸		16	17	18	19	20

DEVELOPER ▸												
Container # ▸		1	2	3	4	5	Container # ▸		1	2	3	4	5
Mixing date ▸		6	7	8	9	10	Mixing date ▸		6	7	8	9	10
Exhausted date ▸		11	12	13	14	15	Exhausted date ▸		11	12	13	14	15
Capacity (35mm) ▸		16	17	18	19	20	Capacity (35mm) ▸		16	17	18	19	20

FIXER ▸												
Container # ▸		1	2	3	4	5	Container # ▸		1	2	3	4	5
Mixing date ▸		6	7	8	9	10	Mixing date ▸		6	7	8	9	10
Exhausted date ▸		11	12	13	14	15	Exhausted date ▸		11	12	13	14	15
Capacity (35mm) ▸		16	17	18	19	20	Capacity (35mm) ▸		16	17	18	19	20

DEVELOPER ▸												
Container # ▸		1	2	3	4	5	Container # ▸		1	2	3	4	5
Mixing date ▸		6	7	8	9	10	Mixing date ▸		6	7	8	9	10
Exhausted date ▸		11	12	13	14	15	Exhausted date ▸		11	12	13	14	15
Capacity (35mm) ▸		16	17	18	19	20	Capacity (35mm) ▸		16	17	18	19	20

FIXER ▸													
Container # ▸		1	2	3	4	5	Container # ▸		1	2	3	4	5
Mixing date ▸		6	7	8	9	10	Mixing date ▸		6	7	8	9	10
Exhausted date ▸		11	12	13	14	15	Exhausted date ▸		11	12	13	14	15
Capacity (35mm) ▸		16	17	18	19	20	Capacity (35mm) ▸		16	17	18	19	20

DEVELOPER ▸													
Container # ▸		1	2	3	4	5	Container # ▸		1	2	3	4	5
Mixing date ▸		6	7	8	9	10	Mixing date ▸		6	7	8	9	10
Exhausted date ▸		11	12	13	14	15	Exhausted date ▸		11	12	13	14	15
Capacity (35mm) ▸		16	17	18	19	20	Capacity (35mm) ▸		16	17	18	19	20

FIXER ▸													
Container # ▸		1	2	3	4	5	Container # ▸		1	2	3	4	5
Mixing date ▸		6	7	8	9	10	Mixing date ▸		6	7	8	9	10
Exhausted date ▸		11	12	13	14	15	Exhausted date ▸		11	12	13	14	15
Capacity (35mm) ▸		16	17	18	19	20	Capacity (35mm) ▸		16	17	18	19	20

DEVELOPER ▸													
Container # ▸		1	2	3	4	5	Container # ▸		1	2	3	4	5
Mixing date ▸		6	7	8	9	10	Mixing date ▸		6	7	8	9	10
Exhausted date ▸		11	12	13	14	15	Exhausted date ▸		11	12	13	14	15
Capacity (35mm) ▸		16	17	18	19	20	Capacity (35mm) ▸		16	17	18	19	20

FIXER ▸													
Container # ▸		1	2	3	4	5	Container # ▸		1	2	3	4	5
Mixing date ▸		6	7	8	9	10	Mixing date ▸		6	7	8	9	10
Exhausted date ▸		11	12	13	14	15	Exhausted date ▸		11	12	13	14	15
Capacity (35mm) ▸		16	17	18	19	20	Capacity (35mm) ▸		16	17	18	19	20

7 PRINTING THE POSITIVE

7.1 GLOSSARY

Agitation — Term used in printing to describe the gentle rocking of the developing trays. Agitation constantly refreshes the liquid in contact with the print to ensure even development and fixing.

Burning in — Adding light after the initial print exposure to darken an area of the print.

Contact print — A print made by placing negatives directly on the surface of the printing paper. The negatives are covered with a sheet of glass to keep them in contact with the paper.

Contamination — The spread of chemicals into areas where they do not belong. Prints are very easily ruined by traces of chemistry left on hands or other implements used to handle prints.

Contrast — The difference in density between two areas on the negative image or two tones in the corresponding print. Normally used in photography to describe the difference between the darkest shadow areas and the brightest highlights.

Contrast filters — A set of colored filters used with variable contrast papers to change the color of the enlarger light and thereby the contrast grade.

Contrast grade — The contrast of the printing paper on a scale of 0 to 5. Low numbers have low contrast and high numbers have high contrast.

Cropping — The practice of printing only select areas of the negative.

Density — The lightness or darkness of a print determined by exposure time.

Dodging — Shading light during the exposure to lighten an area of the print.

Easel — An easel is placed on the baseboard of the enlarger to hold the printing paper flat and frame/crop the projected image with adjustable blades.

Enlarger — The enlarger projects a negative image onto sensitized printing paper to make a positive print.

Fiber based (FB) — A type of printing paper. FB papers produce fine prints, but they demand longer processing times than RC papers.

Focusing magnifier — Enlarges the projected image so grain in the negative is visible for accurate focusing.

Highlights — The darkest areas of the negative and the lightest areas of the print.

Printing frame — A holder designed to keep negatives in firm contact with the printing paper during contact printing.

Resin coated (RC) — A type of printing paper. RC papers are convenient to use due to their shorter processing times.

Shadow areas — The most transparent areas of the negative and the darkest areas of the print.

Spotting — The careful application of photographic dyes to the unwanted white specks on a print usually caused by dust on the negative during printing.

Variable contrast — Variable contrast papers contain all the contrast grades. Changing the color of the enlarging light with contrast filters changes the contrast.

7.2 SUMMARY

135

Printing the positive

Printmaking is one of the most pleasurable parts of photography: Printing offers you the chance to further enhance and interpret your negative images. **Like film, printing paper is coated with an emulsion containing light-sensitive silver compounds:** Light passes through the negative to create a positive image in the printing process. The exposed printing paper is then developed and fixed before it is washed and dried. **The negative is a reversal of the tones in the original scene:** The densities of the negative are proportionally reversed to the values of the print – dense areas become light and vice versa.

136 - 137

Black and white printing: Equipment and supplies for printing

Darkrooms for printing are set up with a dry side and wet side: The paper is exposed on the dry side and processed on the wet side. **Dust is a common problem on the dry side:** Dust or fingerprints on negatives or lenses show up in your prints. Keep the equipment clean and handle negatives with care. **Contamination can cause a plague of spots, stains, and weakened chemicals:** Avoid transferring excessive amounts of chemicals from one solution to the next. Keep the dry side dry and free of chemical residue at all times. Carry wet prints in clean trays for viewing. **Equipment and supplies for printing:** Enlarger, enlarger timer, printing paper, printing frame, easel, safelight, means of cleaning the negative (brush, blower), focusing magnifier, and paper cutter or scissors. Please see page 137 for a full description of each item. **Equipment to process the print:** Trays, tongs, timer or clock, print washer or washing siphon, sponge or squeegee, and drying racks. Please see page 137 for a full description of each item. **Chemicals for printing:** Developer, stop bath, fixer, and washing aid. **Developer:** Converts the exposed silver-halide crystals in the paper emulsion into metallic silver. There are special developers for use with papers (not the same as film developers). They affect print tone and contrast in different ways. Developers have a certain capacity measured in the number of prints they can develop per quantity of working solution. **Stop bath:** A weak acid bath stops the action of the alkaline developer. Indicator stop-baths change color when they are exhausted. **Fixer:** Removes the unexposed and undeveloped silver-halide crystals in the emulsion. The fixer can only process a certain amount of prints before it is exhausted. Test the strength with hypo-check. **Washing aid:** For use with fiber-base prints only. Removes the fixer residue faster and better than plain water.

138 - 139

The enlarger

An enlarger can produce a print of any size: However, it is usually used to make the image larger, to enlarge it. A light source in the enlarger head shines light through the negative, which is focused on the baseboard by a lens, and onto the printing paper.

Moving the enlarger column up and down controls the size of the image, which is focused by altering the distance between the negative and the lens. A separate timer controls the exposure. Please see page 139 for an illustration of a standard enlarger design. **An enlarger should spread light rays uniformly over the negative:** Diffuser enlargers have a piece of cloudy translucent material inserted between the light source and negative. This diffuses the light sufficiently to make it uniform over the entire negative area. Condenser enlargers have a series of glass elements that gathers the light from the light source so it passes straight through the negative. **The most noticeable difference between diffusion and condenser enlargers is in contrast:** Diffuser enlargers produce prints with less contrast. Dust or other blemishes on the negative are also less noticeable when printed on a diffuser enlarger. **The focal length of the enlarger lens must be matched to the size of the negative:** 35mm negative - lenses 50-63mm, 2 1/4 x 2 1/4 negative - lenses 75-80mm, 2 1/4 x 2 3/4 negative - lenses 90-105, 4x5-inch negative - lenses 135-165, 8x10-inch negative - lenses 240-360. **Condensers must be matched to the negative and lens for even illumination:** Changing the glass elements in the condenser unit or altering the distance between them secures even illumination. **The light source in an enlarger is usually a tungsten or quartz-halogen bulb:** Cold-light enlargers use special fluorescent tubes. **A stable and correctly aligned enlarger is a vital link in the printing process:** The negative stage and the baseboard where the printing paper is placed must be in perfect alignment to produce a sharp print. Please see page 139 for a breakdown of the enlarger parts and their function.

140 **Printing papers**

Black-and-white printing papers vary in texture, color, contrast, and other characteristics: Your choice of paper and developer can drastically alter the way your print will look. **Variable-contrast paper is more economical than graded-contrast papers because you have to purchase only one package of paper:** VC papers come with all the contrast grades in one package. You change contrast by altering the color of the enlarging through the use of colored contrast filters. **Many photographers prefer a glossy surface, smooth-textured paper because it has the greatest tonal range and brilliance:** Glossy papers produce the greatest tonal range and the sharpest image. **Resin-coated (RC) papers require much less washing time than fiber-base papers:** The chemicals do not penetrate the paper-base to the same extent. Fiber-base papers, however, produce better prints and they are the only choice for archival fine-art applications. **Paper storage is important because stray light fogs unprocessed paper, giving it an overall gray tinge:** Do not expose your paper to light. Open the packaging only in the darkroom under safelights. Old or improperly stored paper may become fogged. It will have an overall gray tone in the unexposed margins when you process your prints.

141 **Black and white paper characteristics**

Texture: The surface pattern of the paper. Smoother surfaces render sharper images, but they also accentuate grain. **Gloss:** The actual surface sheen, or coating, of the paper. The glossiest is the sharpest with the greatest tonal range. Glossy RC paper is so shiny that it usually causes unwanted reflections. **Paper base tint:** The color of the paper stock. Affects the color of the print. **Image tone:** The color of the silver deposits in the final print. Your choice of developer can emphasize the tone of the paper, from blue-black to brown-black. **Weight:** The actual thickness of the paper stock. From single- to double- and even museum weight. RC papers are usually medium weight, between single and double. **Size:** Papers come in a range of standard sizes. **Resin coating:** A plastic coating protects the paper from chemical saturation, and thereby speeds up all processing times. Easier to handle and work with than FB papers. **Printing grade:** The contrast grade of the paper.

On a scale from 0 to 5, 0 is low contrast and 5 is high contrast. Grade 2 or 3 is considered a normal contrast grade. VC papers use colored filters in the path of the enlarger light to change contrast. **Speed:** The sensitivity of the emulsion to light. Contact printing papers very are slow, but apart from that actual paper speed is not very important to the printing process. **Color sensitivity:** Black-and-white printing papers are sensitive to the blue end of the spectrum, which makes it possible to work with them under yellowish safelights. **Latitude:** The degree an exposure time or development time can vary from the ideal and still produce acceptable results. There is very little latitude in printing. Test-strips for the exposure time and set development times are used to keep results consistent. **Premium papers:** These more expensive papers contain extra silver in the emulsion to produce a richer image.

142 - 143 **A contact sheet: A whole roll at once**

A contact sheet or proof is useful when you want to choose a negative to enlarge: The negatives are sandwiched between a piece of glass and the printing paper to produce positive images of the same size as the negatives. **Contact sheets are easy to make:** One 35mm or medium-format roll fits one 8x10-inch piece of paper perfectly. The contact print is a useful reference in your negative archives. **Making a test strip will help you determine the correct exposure for your first contact print:** The test strip contains several exposures on one piece of paper for evaluation purposes. Start with a normal contrast grade. **Making a black-and-white contact print step by step:**

1. Prepare the developing solutions.
2. Prepare the enlarger.
3. Identify the emulsion side of the film.
4. Identify the emulsion side of the paper.
5. Place negatives and test strip under glass.
6. Expose the test strip.
7. Process the test strip.
8. Evaluate the test strip in room light to select a printing time.
9. Make a complete contact print.

144 - 145 **Setting up an enlargement**

Personal judgments are important when selecting negatives for enlargement when you have many shots of the same scene: When viewed through a loupe, the positive images on the contact sheet makes it easy to choose the best image. **Consider technical points as well. For example, is the negative sharp:** Evaluate your negatives for exposure and sharpness. **Standardized exposure and development of your contact sheets will help you evaluate the individual frames:** On a correctly exposed contact sheet (the film base should blend into the maximum black of the paper), underexposed negatives will be dark, overexposed negatives will be light, and correctly exposed negatives will look almost exactly like the prints you would like to make from them. You may also be able to determine the correct contrast grade for a particular negative from the contact sheet. **Setting up an enlargement step by step:**

1. Select a negative for printing.
2. Insert the negative in the enlarger's carrier.
3. Clean the negative.
4. Insert the negative carrier in the enlarger.
5. Open the enlarger's aperture.
6. Insert a piece of white paper in the easel.
7. Adjust the masking blades of the easel.
8. Arrange the picture.
9. Focus the image.
10. A magnifier helps make the final adjustments in focus.

146 **A test strip for your print**

A test strip will give you some exposure choices for your final print: It will show your negative exposed at different times on the same piece of paper. **For a medium-contrast print:** Start on contrast-grade 2. **Stop down the enlarger lens a few stops from its widest aperture:** This provides the best lens performance and increases the depth of field to compensate for errors in enlarger alignment. **Due to the intermittency effect:** The test strip exposure might be somewhat inaccurate if 5x5 seconds is used instead of 25 seconds.
Making a test strip step by step:
1. Insert paper for a test strip.
2. Expose the test strip.
3. Process the test strip.
4. Evaluate the test strip in room light to select a printing time.

147 **A trial print – and eventually a final print**

Now you are ready to make a full-size print: Your first print will be a test print you will most likely improve on. **Evaluate the print under ordinary room light:** View your print under the same lighting conditions that it will normally be viewed. Allow for the dry-down effect (a print will be 5-10 percent darker when dry) in your exposure evaluation. You may need to change the exposure time if you change contrast grade. **Dodging and burning:** You can lighten (dodge) or darken (burn) local areas during or after the basic exposure time. **When you are satisfied with a print, complete the fixing, washing, and drying:** Fix, wash, and dry it for the recommended times to complete processing. **A trial print and final print step by step:**
1. Expose a full-size trial print.
2. Process the print.
3. Look at the highlights to confirm the exposure time. When highlights are right, look at the shadows to evaluate the contrast.

148 - 151 **Processing a black-and-white print**

1. Set out trays and tongs.
2. Prepare the solutions.
3. Begin development.
4. Agitate the print gently in the developer.
5. Drain developer from the print.
6. Transfer the print to the stop bath.
7. Agitate the print in the stop bath.
8. Drain stop bath from the print.
9. Transfer the print to the fixer.
10. Agitate the print.
11. Remove the print from the fixer.
12. Treat a fiber-base print in a washing aid.
13. Wash the print.
14. Remove surface water from the print.
15. Dry the print – drying racks or blotter roll.

Please see page 148 in the textbook for a more comprehensive summary of print processing.

152 – 153 **Evaluating density and contrast in a print**

Prints are judged – and adjusted – for density and contrast: Evaluate your prints under ordinary viewing conditions. Aim for a full-tonal range print, with dark detailed blacks, many shades of gray, and highlights with tone and texture. **Density refers to the overall darkness or lightness of the print:** Density is controlled by the exposure. With more light, more silver is exposed, and an area in the print will appear darker.

Contrast is the difference in brightness between light and dark areas within the print: Contrast is controlled in printing by the contrast grade of the paper. The correct contrast will have dark detailed shadows and highlights with tone and texture. **How to proceed:** Judge density first and then contrast. **Judge the density:** Determine the best exposure time for your most important highlight areas. **Judge the contrast:** If the shadow areas are too dark for this exposure time, reduce the contrast grade (to a lower number). If the shadow areas are too light, increase the contrast grade (to a higher number). **Evaluate the print overall:** Once density and contrast (exposure time and contrast grade) have been determined at the test-strip stage, make a full-size test print to see how the whole image will look. Make any changes you find necessary, and carefully examine the print for areas you may want to darken or lighten through local controls - dodging and burning. Don't forget the dry-down effect, which is quite minimal for RC papers but considerable for FB papers. **If you are printing a portrait:** The skin tone is the most important print value in a portrait.

154 **Controlling contrast: Graded-contrast and variable-contrast papers**

Contrast – the relative lightness and darkness of areas in a scene – is important in any photograph: You can use contrast creatively to interpret your subject in the print. However, at the printing stage, the contrast is already determined by the subject itself, the type of film used, and the way it was developed. **You can adjust the contrast of the final print:** You can change the contrast of the printing paper to match the contrast of the negative with the contrast of the paper, or use it to increase or reduce the contrast in a print. **Suppose you shot a scene in very contrasty light:** Print on low-contrast paper to reduce the contrast in the negative. **If you shot in flat, dull light:** You should increase the paper grade to increase the contrast. There are two ways to change paper contrast. With variable-contrast papers, you change the contrast of the paper by altering the color of the enlarger light. Colored contrast-filters are used for this purpose. VC papers consequently contain all the contrast grades in one box. Alternatively, you can use graded-contrast papers, which come in one grade per box. The contrast-grade rating, from 0 to 5, is the same for both types, but individual differences exist between papers. **Other factors besides the printing paper affect contrast:** To a lesser degree, the enlarger, the surface finish of the paper, and the developer used also affect print contrast.

154 **Graded-contrast papers**

Many photographers prefer to work with graded-contrast papers: These papers are usually made in more surface finishes than variable-contrast papers. If you are printing with a cold-light enlarger, you are usually better off with graded-contrast papers instead of filtering the enlarger light for VC papers. Available in the usual range of contrast grades.

154 **Variable-contrast papers**

With variable-contrast paper, you produce different degrees of contrast by filtering the enlarger light: It contains two emulsions, one for low and one for high contrast, which are sensitive to different parts of the spectrum. By changing the enlarger light, you determine the amount of exposure given each emulsion and thereby the contrast. Dichroic color enlarger heads can also be used for variable-contrast printing by dialing in a different color filtration for each contrast grade. Variable-contrast paper is very convenient and economical because you buy only one kind of paper. You can print on all contrast grades from 0 to 5 with 1/2-grade increments (determined by the filter set) with one box of VC paper. They also allow for split-filter printing, where a print is exposed with more than one contrast grade for fine control of values.

Change the exposure if you switch between certain filters: You can usually use the same exposure time with filters 0 through to 3 or 3 1/2. Higher grades need a longer exposure time due to the increased density of the contrast filter. Make test strips to determine exposure changes between filters.

156 - 157 **Dodging and burning**

You can give different exposures to different parts of a print by dodging and burning: Control the local tonal values of a print by dodging and burning. **Dodging lightens an area that prints too dark:** By masking light from the enlarger to the print with a shaped object on a thin wire during the basic exposure time, you can lighten the areas obscured by this tool. If you are trying to lighten a dark shadow area with no negative detail, the result will be an undesirable gray tone with no black and no real improvement. In most cases, only dodge shadows when they have detail in the negative. **Burning adds exposure when part of a print is too light:** By masking off all areas of the print except the one you would like to darken with a piece of card or your hands, you can expose the area further to darken it after the basic exposure time. **If you want to darken an area considerably, try flashing it – exposing it to white light directly from a small penlight flashlight:** You can add a light gray tone, or any tone, to the print overall (using white enlarger light without a negative inserted) or locally (with the aid of a small flashlight) to improve on the print. Keep in mind that these techniques do not produce any texture or detail from a negative, only a tone. Use flashing as a rescue mission, and avoid it if you can. **Keep the dodging and burning tool, your hands, or the penlight moving:** The goal is to make dodging and burning invisible in the final print. Movement and random patterns are the best ways to achieve this. Control the penumbra (the sharpness of the shadows cast by your tools) by altering the distance from the print. **Many prints are both dodged and burned:** Evaluate your prints critically to look for possible improvements in local tonal values.

158 **Cropping**

Eventually you must decide on cropping – what to leave out and what to include along the edges of a photograph: You always crop your subject with the viewfinder frame when photographing. It is also possible to crop the negative during printing to improve on the composition. **Cropping by enlarging a very small part of a negative can create problems:** Grain becomes more visible as smaller parts of a negative are enlarged to a greater degree. **Two L-shaped guides will help you decide how to crop a picture:** Use them to form a central square over the photograph, or the image formed on the enlarger baseboard, and then visualize cropping decisions through this window.

159 **Archival processing for maximum permanence**

How long does a photograph last: The question is most important to museums or individuals that collect photographs, and the answer depends on the type of photograph and the way it was processed. **Archival processing provides maximum permanence for fiber-base silver prints:** RC papers ate not archival. You process your FB prints the same way, but with some additional steps and to more exacting standards. **Archival processing eliminates residual chemicals, those that washing alone cannot remove entirely:** Proper fixing, which removes unexposed silver-halide crystals, and washing with a wash-aid to remove the fixer, which may tarnish the silver image, are the most crucial steps of archival processing. **Protective toning converts the silver in the image to a more stable compound:** Toning with selenium toner, a popular choice for archival processing, converts the silver in the image into a more stable silver selenide. Please see page 159 for archival processing suggestions.

160 - 161 **Toning for color and other effects**

Toning can make a significant change in print color: By toning the print in different chemical solutions after processing, you can alter the print color from warm sepia to cold blue. Masking the print for selective toning is also an option. **Toning for intensification changes the print color only a little:** Short toning times or weak dilutions of selenium toner will increase the density of the shadow areas slightly to increase the contrast and give an impression of enhanced sharpness. Longer toning times and/or stronger dilutions will actually change the image tone quite drastically with most papers. **Most toners help increase the life of a print:** Some toners convert the silver in an image into a more stable compound. Please see pages 160 and 161 for toning information.

7.3 TEST

FILL IN THE BLANKS

1 A print where each image is the exact same size as the negative is called a ____________________ print.

2 Processing a print involves three initial steps: ____________________, ____________________, and ____________________.

3 ____________________ refers to the overall lightness and darkness of a print.

4 To ensure that the negative is properly focused on the baseboard of the enlarger, you can use a focusing ____________________.

5 ____________________ is a technique used to lighten a print locally, and ____________________ is a technique used to darken a print locally.

6 A ____________________ is used to determined the correct exposure and contrast grade of a print.

7 Two L-shaped pieces of card are useful for the visualization of ____________________ decisions.

8 A correctly ____________________ enlarger ensures that the negative stage is exactly parallel to the enlarger's baseboard.

9 Papers with a ____________________ surface finish display the greatest tonal range and the best sharpness in a print.

10 ____________________ processing is necessary to secure the longevity of a photographic print.

MULTIPLE CHOICE – CIRCLE ONE OR MORE

1 The following are characteristics associated with printing papers:

a. shutter speed, aperture, focusing ring.
b. contrast grade, weight, surface finish.
c. focus control, negative carrier, filter drawer.

2	Variable-contrast printing papers contain:	a.	only one contrast grade.
		b.	all the contrast grades.
		c.	two emulsions sensitive to different parts of the spectrum.
3	A correctly color-balanced darkroom safelight is safe for:	a.	printing papers.
		b.	panchromatic films and some printing papers.
		c.	stop bath and fixer, but not developer.
4	Contrast grade 2 is considered a:	a.	less contrasty grade than grade 3.
		b.	a more contrasty grade than then grade 3.
		c.	normal contrast grade.
5	A fine print normally has:	a.	no white spots or hairs left by dust on the negative.
		b.	detail and texture in both highlights and shadows.
		c.	a full tonal range, from bright highlights to dark shadows, with good separation in the midtones.
6	Purple or brown stains on your prints are most likely caused by:	a.	overexposure of the print.
		b.	safelight exposure.
		c.	chemical contamination on your printing or drying equipment.
7	When focusing a negative on the baseboard, your aperture should be:	a.	at its widest opening.
		b.	at its smallest opening.
		c.	in the middle of the aperture range.
8	To increase the contrast in a print, you need to:	a.	change the fixer.
		b.	change the contrast filter/paper grade to a higher number.
		c.	develop your prints longer.
9	The correct procedure for judging a test strip or test print is to:	a.	evaluate it under safelights.
		b.	find the desirable highlight value and then adjust the shadow areas through contrast changes.
		c.	consider density first and then contrast.
10	Toning a print can:	a.	deepen the blacks to enhance the contrast.
		b.	alter the surface finish from glossy to matte.
		c.	enhance the archival properties of a print.

7.4 PRACTICAL TIPS

Dodging

The DIY dodger kit.

The dodger is an essential tool in every photographer's darkroom kit. There are many prefabricated versions available for sale, but there is no need to spend money on a dodger when you can design better tools yourself than what is on the market. All you need to make a dodger tool is a stiff wire (thin enough to avoid obscuring light) and a piece of card or tape at the end of it to shade the area you would like to lighten. Make sure that the card is black on one side and white on the other. Keep the black side facing down to prevent light from reflecting back onto the print, and the white side facing up so you can see what part of the image is obscured and consequently lightened. It is best to make the shape of the card somewhat uneven, since the eye is more easily attracted to regular signs of your dodging actions than random patterns. The goal, of course, is to make all evidence of dodging invisible in the final print. Make several shapes and sizes in a kit, or bring some card with you to customize the dodging tool for a particular job. By adding a piece of card to both ends of the wire, you can dodge different shapes and sizes by a flick of the wrist during the same basic exposure time.

Burning

Burning in highlights with a different contrast grade.

The most common areas for burning in are no doubt highlights. They can sometimes fall outside the contrast scale of the print and leave no desirable tone to distinguish them from the paper itself. If the negative is significantly denser in certain areas, you may find yourself burning in to little or no avail. The elusive tone will just not appear. In some cases, the highlights might be what is termed "blocked", which means that the negative is so dense in these areas that no light will *ever* pass through it. No matter how long you burn in highlights with such a negative, light will never reach the paper. It is a lost cause (but you may try flashing the paper to rescue it). When a highlight area is dense, but there is some evidence of light coming through to add tone, you can speed up the burning process by changing to another contrast filter. If you are printing on grade 2, and then change to grade 0 after the initial exposure, you will burn in with a contrast grade that prints darker highlights for the same negative. You will effectively be adding exposure with a contrast grade that matches the tone you would like to see in those highlights more closely.

Even light

Make sure your enlarger light is even for contact prints.

The image projected by the enlarger lens is circular, and on condenser enlargers in particular, you will find that the intensity of the light drops off towards the edges of the circle. When you make a contact print, you do not necessarily need a negative carrier, but insert one anyway before framing your contact prints on the baseboard with enlarger light. Without the carrier, you could place and print your contact prints under light with a gradual change in intensity, which would result in a gradual exposure change and an unreliable record for negative evaluation. The carrier gives you an area of light that is guaranteed even.

7.5 JOURNAL

7.5.1 LAB PRINT-CHEMISTRY CHART

Complete a chart for the print-development chemistry used in your lab. Add any entries, such as developers, that you may have purchased yourself at the bottom. You may need to consult your instructor, notices in the lab, product packaging and literature, or Material Safety Data Sheets to complete all the entries.

LAB CHEMISTRY	Product name	Dilution	Safety / Handling / Comments
Developer			Avoid prolonged skin contact. Rinse off immediately. Wash skin with soap and water. Do not inhale or ingest.
Developer			
Stop bath			
Stop bath			
Fixer			
Fixer			
Clearing bath			For fiber-base prints only.
Clearing bath			For fiber-base prints only.
OTHER PRODUCTS			
Developer			
Developer			
Developer			
Stop bath			
Stop bath			
Stop bath			
Fixer			
Fixer			
Fixer			
Clearing bath			
Clearing bath			For fiber-base prints only.
Clearing bath			For fiber-base prints only.

7.5.2 PRINT TEMPERATURE-AND-TIME PROCESSING CHARTS

Print development is temperature and time dependent. Some paper developers may also be diluted and used at different strengths to control either the contrast or the image tone of a print. The temperature of the paper chemistry may be difficult to control because the trays are often used for several hours in darkroom temperature. Let the solutions adjust to the temperature of the room and change the development time slightly if it is 7-8°F warmer (less time) or colder (more time) than 68°F. You can also keep the trays in water baths to control the temperature. Use these tables to compile a selection of temperature-and-time processing charts for the papers and developers you use most often. You can find the recommended combinations either in your lab, packaged with the products (open that box in the darkroom), or in special data sheets available from the manufacturer. The Internet is a great resource for researching this kind of information. Recommendations are often highlighted in bold type.

PAPER ▸ Ilford Multigrade IV, RC paper, medium weight, glossy.

Developer ▾	Dilution ▾	Temperature ▾	Time ▾
Agfa WA	1:7	68 F	1 minute

PAPER ▸

Developer ▾	Dilution ▾	Temperature ▾	Time ▾

PAPER ▸

Developer ▾	Dilution ▾	Temperature ▾	Time ▾

PAPER ▸

Developer ▾	Dilution ▾	Temperature ▾	Time ▾

7.5.3 MEASURING GUIDE

Paper developers are different from film developers, but you normally use the same stop bath and fixer chemicals for film and paper processing. The fixer will most likely require a different dilution. The amount of chemistry required for print processing depends on the size of trays you are using and the number of prints you plan to process. The processing solutions are exhausted after a certain number of prints, and their capacity is almost always listed with the manufacturer's recommendations. Do not mix up more chemistry than you need for a printing session. Each tray should always have enough chemistry to generously cover a sheet of paper during constant agitation. Use the table below to enter the information you need to mix the processing solutions, and include their capacity as an indication of when they will be exhausted. Keep all units in milliliters to make calculation easy.

Ratio calculation example

1. Take the total amount of chemistry required for the tray you intend to use and divide it by the total number of units in the ratio: 1000ml (for one 8x10 tray) divided by 5 (for a developer ratio of 1:4) = 200.

2. Multiply each unit of the ratio with this number to get the proportion of chemistry to water: 200 x 1 = 200ml. and 200 x 4 = 800ml.

3. The working solution of developer you need to mix for an 8x10 tray contains 200ml. of stock solution and 800ml. of water.

TRAY SIZE ▸	8 x 10	Amount of chemistry ▸		1000 ml.	
	Name ▾	Dilution ▾	Stock ▾	Water ▾	Capacity ▾
Developer	Agfa WA	1:11	83	917	30 8x10 prints
Stop bath	Kodak Indicator	16/1000	16	1000	Indicator
Fixer	Kodak Rapid	1:7	125	875	50 8x10 prints
Clearing bath	Wash-aid	1:5	167	833	50 8x10 prints

TRAY SIZE ▸	20 x 24	Amount of chemistry ▸		3000 ml.	
	Name ▾	Dilution ▾	Stock ▾	Water ▾	Capacity ▾
Developer	LPD	1:4	600	2400	20 20x24 prints
Stop bath	Kodak Indicator	16/1000	48	3000	Indicator
Fixer	Kodak Rapid	1:7	375	2625	30 20x24 prints
Clearing bath	Wash -aid	1:5	500	2500	30 20x24 prints

TRAY SIZE ▸		Amount of chemistry ▸			
	Name ▾	Dilution ▾	Stock ▾	Water ▾	Capacity ▾
Developer					
Stop bath					
Fixer					
Clearing bath					

TRAY SIZE ▸		Amount of chemistry ▸			
	Name ▾	Dilution ▾	Stock ▾	Water ▾	Capacity ▾
Developer					
Stop bath					
Fixer					
Clearing bath					

TRAY SIZE ▸		Amount of chemistry ▸			
	Name ▾	Dilution ▾	Stock ▾	Water ▾	Capacity ▾
Developer					
Stop bath					
Fixer					
Clearing bath					

TRAY SIZE ▸		Amount of chemistry ▸			
	Name ▾	Dilution ▾	Stock ▾	Water ▾	Capacity ▾
Developer					
Stop bath					
Fixer					
Clearing bath					

TRAY SIZE ▸		Amount of chemistry ▸			
	Name ▾	Dilution ▾	Stock ▾	Water ▾	Capacity ▾
Developer					
Stop bath					
Fixer					
Clearing bath					

7.5.4 PRINT PROCESSING GUIDE

Fill out this guide before developing your first prints, and refer to it during processing. Get the exact times for fixer, wash, and the optional clearing bath (not necessary for RC prints but strongly recommended for FB prints) from your instructor. The rest of the information required can be found in the previous parts of this 7.5 Journal. If you are in the slightest doubt about the procedure, the numbers in the left-hand column correspond to the steps covered in the textbook. Refer to any section you are unclear about before starting to process your prints.

1 Set out trays and tongs.

Materials check list

- ❑ Chemistry (see 2 below)
- ❑ Water source (use distilled water for best results)
- ❑ Graduated cylinders
- ❑ Stirring rod
- ❑ Photographic thermometer
- ❑ Mixing and storage containers
- ❑ Processing trays
- ❑ Tongs or rubber gloves to handle prints

2 Prepare the solutions.

Please see Journal 7.5.1, 7.5.2, and 7.5.3 for mixing and handling.

	Dilution ▾	Temperature ▾	Time ▾
Developer		68 F	
Stop bath		68 F	30 seconds.
Fixer		68 F	
Clearing bath		68 F	

3 Begin development.

Development time RC ▸		Development time FB ▸		START → TIMER

4 Agitate the print gently in the developer.

Agitate the print continuously for the duration of the development time.

5 Drain developer from the print.

RESET ← TIMER

6 Transfer the print to the stop bath.

Stop bath time ▸	30 seconds.	START → TIMER

7 Agitate the print in the stop bath.

Agitate the print continuously in the stop bath.

8	Drain the stop bath from the print.	
		RESET ← TIMER
9	Transfer the print to the fixer.	
	Fixing time ▸	START → TIMER
10	Agitate the print in the fixer.	
	Agitate the print continuously in the fixer to ensure fast and even fixing.	
11	Remove the print from the fixer.	
		RESET ← TIMER
12	Treat a fiber-base print in a washing aid.	
	Clearing bath time for FB prints ▸	START → TIMER
13	Wash the print.	
	Wash time RC ▸ Wash time FB ▸	START → TIMER
14	Remove surface water from the print.	
	Wipe the back and front of the print to ensure that it dries evenly.	
15	Dry the print.	
	Make sure that any surfaces or racks you use to dry your prints on are completely free of chemical contamination.	

Notes

7.5.5 BLACK-AND-WHITE TEST PATCHES

Printing papers have a maximum black and a maximum white. Maximum black is reached when all the silver in the paper has been exposed and it can not turn darker. The equivalent maximum white is the unexposed base of the printing paper. A print is made in the tonal range between maximum black and maximum white. Dark shadows emerge from maximum black with subtle details and bright highlights are seen as a textured tone against the maximum white of the paper. Make a maximum black and a maximum white square from the instructions below and use them as references during printing to make sure that your shadow areas are dark with detail and that highlights are set apart from the paper itself. When your developer is unable to produce a maximum black in the print, it is a sign that it is exhausted.

MAXIMUM BLACK ▾		MAXIMUM WHITE ▾	
Take a small square of paper out of the darkroom and expose it to light for a minute. Process the piece of paper as normal, and glue or tape the maximum black square into the space on the right.		Process a small square of paper as normal without any exposure to light. Glue or tape the maximum white square into the space on the right.	

7.5.6 THE TEST STRIP

Make your first test strip in increments of one stop. For example, 2, 4, 8, 16, and 32 seconds. Make a second test strip in smaller increments between the stops closest to the correct exposure time. For example, 8, 10, 12, 14, and 16 seconds. The test strip should ideally cover the darkest and lightest area of a print so you can evaluate density and contrast for each exposure time. Use this method to evaluate your test strip:

1. Find the exposure time with the right density for your highlights. Remember to allow for the dry-down effect, which is significant for FB papers.

2. Evaluate the shadows for the same exposure time and adjust contrast if necessary. If the shadows are too light and border on gray, increase the contrast grade to a higher number. If the shadows are too dark and show no detail that is present in the negative, reduce the contrast grade to a lower number.

3. Make another test strip with the new contrast grade or proceed to make a test print with the exposure time determined in step 1. Once you have made a test print, evaluate it for any changes in local value. See 7.5.8 Dodging and burning records below.

Consult with your instructor and glue in a series of test strips where the placement of the paper, the exposure times, and the contrast adjustment are exemplary. Add any comments about the times, choices, and changes in the spaces provided. Use these strips for reference until you are comfortable with the principles of test strip placement and evaluation.

Notes

TEST STRIP EXAMPLE

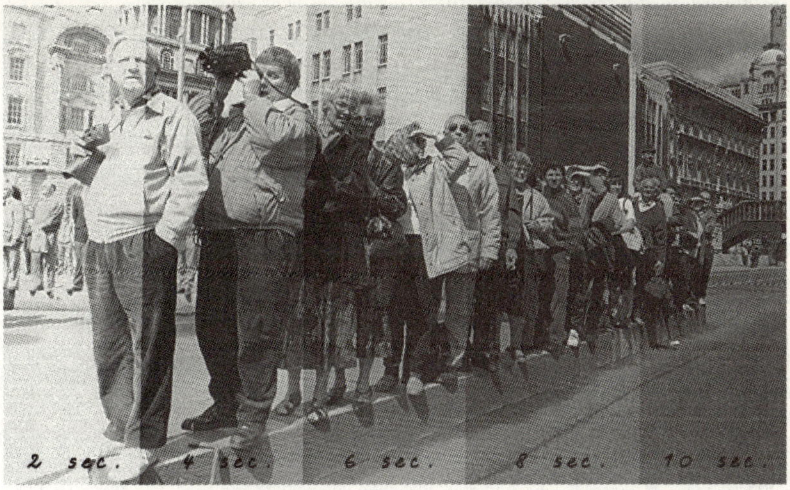

Comments

The test strip was placed to cover both shadows and highlights for each exposure time. 6 seconds has the right highlight density. I will now increase the contrast and make another test strip on grade 3 paper.

TEST STRIP 1

Comments

TEST STRIP 2

Comments

TEST STRIP 3

Comments

7.5.7 THE CONTACT PRINT

The contact print must be made correctly to give accurate information about film exposures. Expose the contact print so the paper just reaches maximum black and the density of the clear film base blends into the maximum-black paper. The paper has reached maximum black at the first step on your test strip where the black does not change. Consult with your instructor and include exemplary strips of contact prints in the spaces provided. Use them for reference until you are comfortable with the principles of contact-print exposure.

EXEMPLARY CONTACT PRINT EXPOSURE ▾

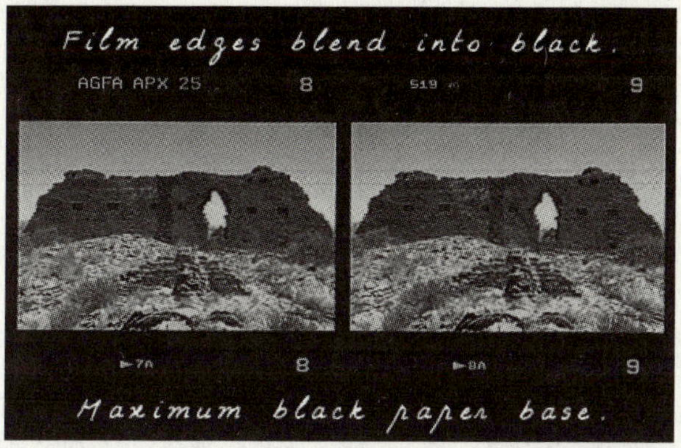

EXEMPLARY CONTACT PRINT EXPOSURE ▾

EXEMPLARY CONTACT PRINT EXPOSURE ▾

7.5.8 DODGING AND BURNING RECORDS

Dodging and burning are invaluable techniques for local control of values in a print. Upon close evaluation, every print can be improved by employing dodging and burning to lighten a shadow or darken a highlight, or to adjust any value in the print during (dodging) or after (burning) the basic print exposure. Work in percentages of the basic exposure to make the changes more predictable. Burning in for 50% of the time with a basic exposure of 10 seconds and burning in for 50% of the time with a basic exposure of 20 seconds will give different times (5 and 10 seconds respectively), but the burning results will be roughly the same. Once you have made your first print from a negative, evaluate it critically for any local changes in print value that will improve it. Note these changes with a marker on the print itself, or use a simple rectangle to represent the outline of the print and mark the areas you would like to dodge and/or burn in the appropriate places. Take these notes into the darkroom and work from them to make your improved print. If you decide to print the negative again later, records of dodging and burning will also save you both time and paper. The example below illustrates how the entries provided with this journal should be used.

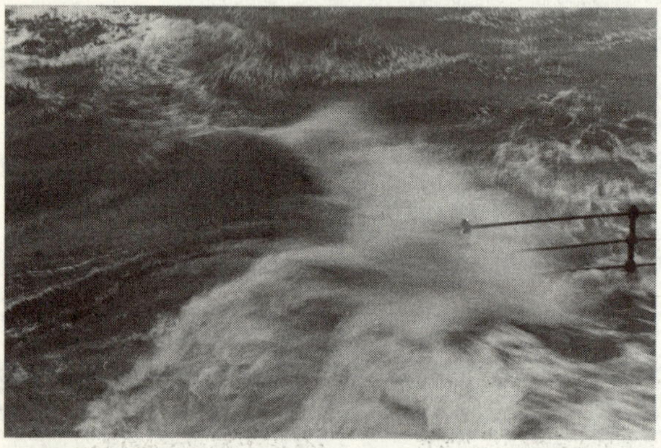

The straight print from this negative did not display the desired values in all areas. The overall exposure time and contrast is acceptable, but some values can be improved locally through dodging and burning. The edge of the wave breaking onto the fence would benefit from a lighter tone, and the dark areas of the sea should be deeper. The print corners can be burned in to focus the attention more towards the center of the frame. All notes below are in percentages of the basic exposure time.

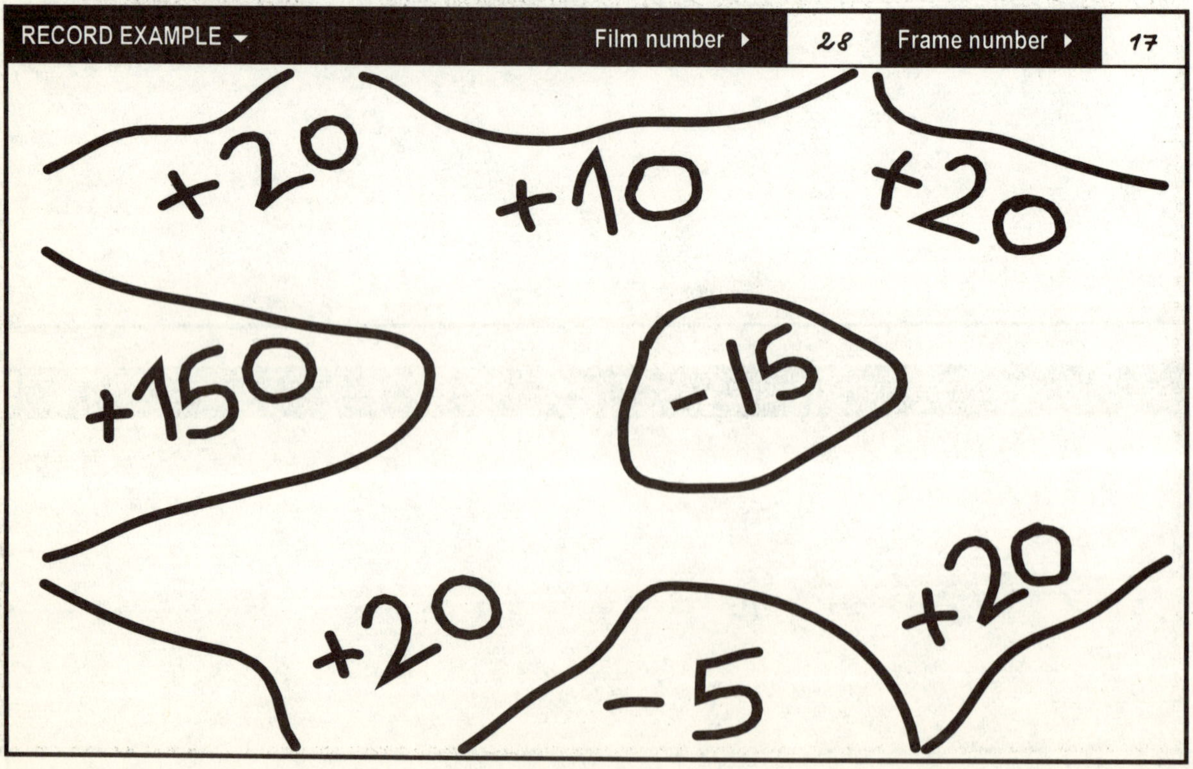

RECORD 1	Film number ▸		Frame number ▸	

RECORD 2 ▾	Film number ▸		Frame number ▸	

RECORD 3 ▾ Film number ▸ Frame number ▸

RECORD 4 ▾ Film number ▸ Frame number ▸

RECORD 5	Film number		Frame number	

RECORD 6	Film number		Frame number	

7.5.9 THE FIRST PHOTOGRAPH

The first photograph you developed and printed yourself will not be your best, but it is certainly worth remembering. Use this page to keep it both as a memento and as a measure of your technical progress.

8 FINISHING AND MOUNTING

8.1 GLOSSARY

Cropping The practice of printing only select areas of the negative or masking parts of an image with an overmat.

Dry-mounting The practice of attaching a photograph to a mount board by inserting a sheet of dry-mount tissue between them and heating this in a mounting press until the adhesive in the tissue melts.

Mat cutter Instrument used to cut straight or beveled windows in a mount board for overmatting.

Mount board Usually refers to an archival (acid free) board intended for the long term display and protection of photographs.

Mounting press A heated press used for dry mounting. Also used to flatten fiber-based prints after drying.

Museum board An archival mount board of premium quality.

Overmatting A common presentation method for photographs. The photograph is mounted on one board and then covered by another board with an image-sized window.

Photo corner A triangular sleeve used to attach a photograph to the backing board in overmatting.

Ply The thickness of mount board. 2-ply is single weight, and 4-ply is double weight.

Spotone The most common photographic dye used for spotting.

Spotting The careful application of photographic dyes to the unwanted white specks on a print usually caused by dust on the negative during printing.

Tacking iron Instrument used to attach dry-mount tissue to the back of a photograph and the front of a mount board before inserting it in the mounting press.

8.2 SUMMARY

163 **Finishing and mounting**

Much pleasure lies in taking pictures, but the real reward is in displaying and viewing the results: A finished and mounted print lends a certain aura to your photographs. **Your choice of mounting materials depends on the degree of permanence you want for a print:** Archival processing and archival mounting materials are a necessity if you want your photographs to last as long as possible. **The gelatin, silver, and paper in a photographic print can be seriously damaged:** Keep archival prints away from all materials that deteriorate relatively rapidly, such as masking tape and ordinary card and paper. Use less expensive materials when archival properties are less of an issue.

164 **Spotting to remove minor flaws**

Spotting corrects small imperfections in a print: White specks caused by dust on the negative or paper during printing are removed by spotting the print with special photographic dyes. Spotting is done on the final dry print. **Practice is essential with all these techniques:** Work with a scrap print first to determine the correct tonal value, and stop before the tone gets too dark.

164 **Spotting**

Remove white spots with dyes: Special dyes are added to the white spot until its tonal value matches the surrounding area. Dyes such as Spotone come in several shades to match the image tone of a print. You also need a very fine brush, #000 or smaller. **Spotting:**

1. **Match the dye to the color of your print:** Mix the dyes and try them in the margin of a scrap print until you get a tone that is slightly lighter than the final value.
2. **Spot the darkest areas first:** Apply the dyes with a dotting motion. Do not "paint". Start light and build up gradually, allowing the dyes to dry between applications.
3. **Now work in the lighter areas:** Dilute your dyes further before starting to work on the lighter areas. Keep in mind that the dyes dry darker so always err on the light side when you mix the tone.

164 **Etching**

Etching can remove a small or thin black mark: Use a scalpel or a sharp knife to scrape away layers of the emulsion until the tone matches the surrounding area. Do not cut into the paper or remove all the silver down to the paper base. It is possible to correct excessive etching through spotting, but it is virtually impossible to restore the surface finish. To be honest, etching seldom works very well.

164 **Local reduction**

Local reduction or bleaching lightens larger areas: Apply bleach or Farmer's Reducer to a wet print and wash it off when the process is complete. Be aware that a bleached print requires re-fixing and washing to be permanent. Selective bleaching is sometimes used to brighten highlights.

165 **Mounting a print: Equipment and materials you'll need**

Mounting materials: Mount board, dry-mount tissue, cover sheet, release paper, and tape. If you are mounting prints from digital imaging output, avoid heat mounting (use cold-mount tissue or overmatting) to prevent print damage or shortened print life. **Mounting equipment:** Mounting press, tacking iron, utility knife with sharp blade, mat cutter, a cutting surface, metal ruler, miscellaneous items: pencil, soft eraser, razor blade, T square, and cotton gloves. Please see page 165 for a comprehensive description of each item.

166 **Dry mounting: Bleed mounting**

1. Heat the press to 200ºF or as instructed, make sure the materials are clean, and predry FB prints and the mount board.
2. Tack the dry-mount tissue to the print, and trim off any mounting tissue that extends beyond the print.
3. Tack the dry-mount tissue and print to the board.
4. Mount the print.
5. Trim the mounted print.
6. The finished print.

167 **Dry mounting: Mounting with a border**

1. Heat the press to 200ºF or as instructed, make sure the materials are clean, and predry FB prints and the mount board.
2. Tack the dry-mount tissue to the print.
3. Trim the print and dry-mount tissue.
4. Position the print on the mount board.
5. Tack the dry-mount tissue and print to the board.
6. Mount the print.
7. The finished print.

168 **Cutting an overmat**

An overmat provides a raised border around a print: It protects the print surface and separates it from the glass in a frame. Handle all photographs by the edges to avoid damaging the print surface. **Practice cutting the inner corners:** The inner window can be cut straight, but beveled edges will add a more professional finish to your mounting efforts. Hand held mat cutters are very difficult to use without the occasional mishap. These mistakes can get costly with expensive mat board, so consider buying one of the budget cutters with a fixed metal straight-edge if you anticipate cutting a lot of overmats. **Cutting an overmat:**

1. Measure the image area.
2. Plan the mount dimensions.
3. Mark the cuts on the mat board.
4. Cut the overmat.
5. Position and attach the print.
6. Attach the overmat to the backing board.

8.3 TEST

FILL IN THE BLANKS

1 In dry mounting, a ____________________ is inserted between the photograph and the mounting board.

2 Mounting materials used for long term storage should be ____________________.

3 White specks in the print caused by dust on the negative or the paper during printing are removed by ____________________.

4 An ____________________ separates the image from the glass in a frame.

5 The dyes used in spotting are applied with a very small ____________________.

6 Large dark specks in a print can be reduced through selective ____________________.

7 The thickness of mount board is stated as its ____________________.

8 A ____________________ is used to attach the dry-mount tissue to the print and the board before insertion in the mounting press.

9 Avoid mounting RC prints at temperatures above ____________________ºF.

10 Spot the ____________________ areas first.

MULTIPLE CHOICE – CIRCLE ONE OR MORE

1	Spotting:	a.	is a slow process that requires patience.
		b.	removes black spots and specks in the print.
		c.	is done with special photographic dyes.
2	Digital-imaging software:	a.	makes spotting flaws in a negative very easy.
		b.	allows you to save your corrections in an image file.
		c.	can make changes to an image permanent, so you avoid repeating the corrections for every print.
3	A bleed-mounted print is preferably trimmed:	a.	before insertion in the mounting press.
		b.	after the print has been mounted.
		c.	in the mounting press.
4	When overmatting a photograph, it is important to:	a.	get all the print and mount measurements right.
		b.	cut the print down to the size of the window.
		c.	spot the print after is has been mounted.
5	An easy and safe way to attach a print to the backing board of an archival overmat is to use:	a.	masking tape hidden by the board.
		b.	a spray adhesive for an even and strong bond.
		c.	photo corners.
6	When spotting a print:	a.	always start with a lighter tone than the surrounding image area.
		b.	try to match the desired tone as closely as possible with your first application of dye.
		c.	apply the dyes with a dotting motion.
7	The dry-mount tissue bonds at a temperature of about:	a.	10 °F.
		b.	100 °F.
		c.	200 °F.
8	A dry mounted fiber-base print will bond in:	a.	10 seconds.
		b.	35-40 seconds.
		c.	3-4 minutes.
9	A bleached fiber-base print must be:	a.	developed for 30 seconds after bleaching.
		b.	fixed and washed again after bleaching.
		c.	dried face up.
10	Prints from digital output, such as dye-sublimation and thermal-wax prints, should:	a.	be dry mounted at a temperature of 285 °F.
		b.	be cold mounted to prevent damage.
		c.	never be overmatted.

8.4 PRACTICAL TIPS

Spotting

Act quickly to remove an overly dark tone.

If you apply too much dye or use a mixture that is too dark for the surrounding area, you can try to rescue the print by quickly removing some of the dye. Keep an absorbent piece of paper, a soft cloth, or a cotton swab next to you when you work, and use it to blot away excess dye before it dries. By soaking up some of the tone, the area will appear lighter. You may also try to immediately add a tiny drop or water to the area and then blot it dry to remove more dye. Be careful about the amount of water and the blotting action: dye might bleed onto the surrounding area and make it darker. The best way to avoid spotting disasters is simply to build up the tone gradually.

Fiber-base

Flattening your fiber-base prints.

Fiber-base prints curl up quite significantly during drying. You place them on drying racks with the emulsion side down to prevent this, but they will always need flattening before mounting or display. To flatten your fiber-base prints after they have dried completely, you use a mounting press. Heat the press to 180ºF and insert your print *face down* between two cover sheets or boards for as long as it takes to flatten it (normally a couple of minutes). Avoid cover sheets with a strong texture because this might mark the surface of the print, and be sure to remove all dust particles from the cover sheets and the print before pressing. The pressure is quite strong in the press, and even the smallest particle may cause an indentation in your print. Dust is also prone to get permanently embedded in the surface of the print when it is hot and soft. After removing the print from the mounting press, keep it flat under moderate pressure until it has cooled down to prevent it from curling back up.

Print positioning

Use a soft weight to position your print in the overmat.

After an overmat has been cut, it is time to position the print and attach it to the backing board. This is rarely difficult if the overmat crops the image with some margin, but if you have decided to mount the photograph with a tiny border, it can be both time consuming and frustrating to get these borders to appear equal in the overmat window. The trick is to keep the print fixed between each lowering and raising of the overmat to check its position. To achieve this, you need to place a reasonably heavy weight in the center of the print. Make sure that you wrap the weight in a soft cloth or a photo glove to prevent scratches or other damage to the print surface. With the weight in place, you can make minor adjustments to the print position and be assured that the print stays in the same spot until you have attached it with photo corners or tacked it to the backing board.

Overmat corners

Finish the corners of an overmat with a razor blade.

When cutting a beveled overmat, it is best not to cut further than necessary at the corners. Cutting too far will leave a line beyond the window that is unsightly and certainly frowned upon by professional frame shops. However, if you cut too short, the window piece of the mat board will not be entirely free of the overmat borders, and the result can be even worse if the corners are torn. The trick is to cut as close as you can without letting the blade scar the border. If you find that you cut too short, do not attempt to insert the blade of the mat cutter again to finish the job. The result will not be good. Instead, pick up a razor blade and carefully cut the remainder while holding the blade at the same angle as the beveled edge.

8.5 JOURNAL

8.5.1 OVERMATTING GUIDE

Overmatting is not difficult, but it requires several measurements that need to be applied correctly. This guide contains worksheets that will help you get these measurements and the math right for your first overmatted prints. The borders on an overmat do not have to be equal. If the proportions of the print do not match the proportions of the mat board or the frame, it is customary to make three sides equal and leave more space at the bottom of the mounted print.

1 Measure the image area.

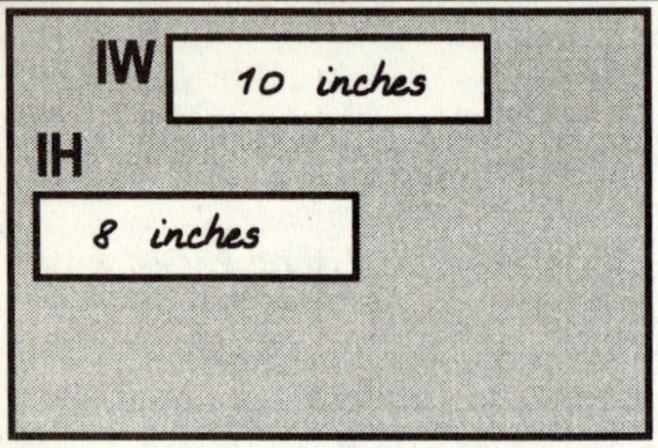

Measure the height and width of the image area. If you intend to crop the image with the overmat, measure only the area you would like to see through the window.

2 Plan the mount dimensions.

Measure the height and width of the mat board.

Subtract the width and height of the image area from the width and height of the mat board to determine the borders. Divide by two.

14 − 10 / 2 = 2
12 − 8 / 2 = 2

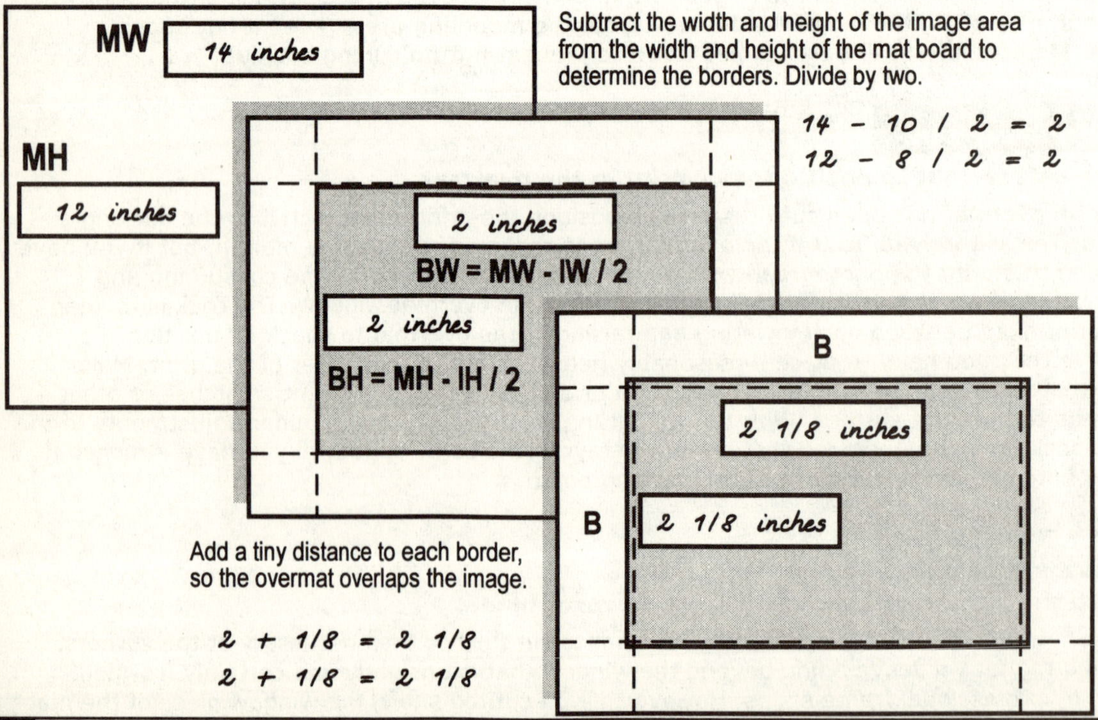

Add a tiny distance to each border, so the overmat overlaps the image.

2 + 1/8 = 2 1/8
2 + 1/8 = 2 1/8

3 Mark the cuts on the mat board – then follow steps 3 – 6 outlined below.

1 Measure the image area.

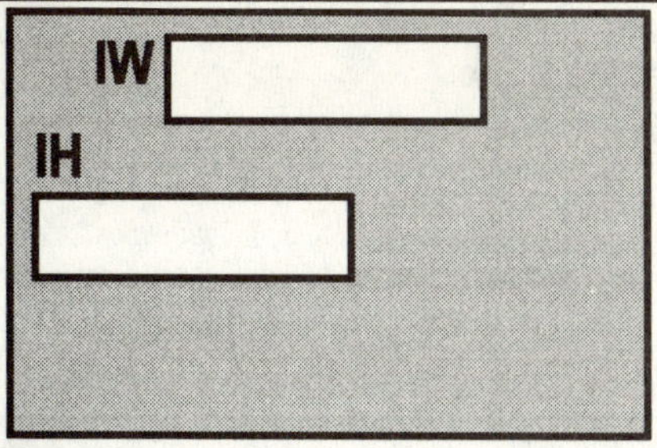

Measure the height and width of the image area. If you intend to crop the image with the overmat, measure only the area you would like to see through the window.

2 Plan the mount dimensions.

Measure the height and width of the mat board.

Subtract the width and height of the image area from the width and height of the mat board to determine the borders. Divide by two.

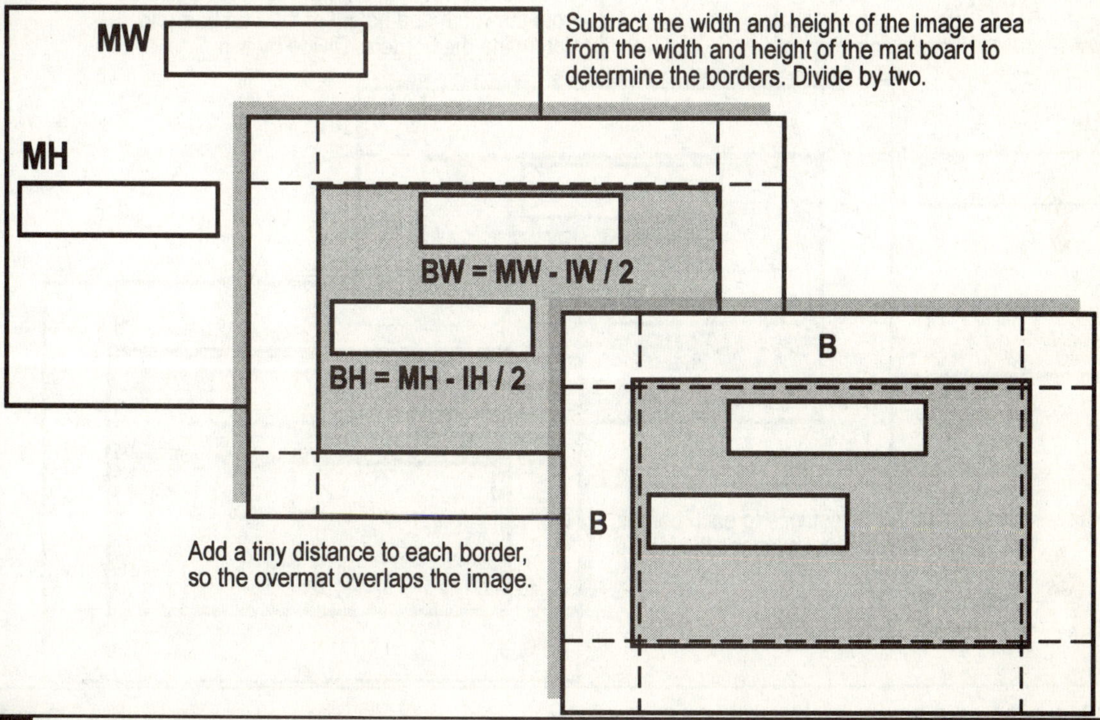

Add a tiny distance to each border, so the overmat overlaps the image.

3 Mark the cuts on the mat board.

Mark the inside of the board with a pencil according to the measurements above. A T-square aligned with the mat edge is useful to make sure that the lines are straight and square.

4 Cut the overmat.

Cut the overmat with a sharp knife. If you are using a mat cutter for a beveled cut, make sure that you are cutting each side from the right angle. Use a metal ruler as a guide and erase the remaining pencil marks when you are done.

5 Position and attach the print.

Position the print between the overmat and the backing board. Use a weight (must not scratch the surface) to hold the print in position until you have attached it with photo-corners or marked its position for dry mounting.

6 Attach the overmat to the backing board.

Use hinges at the top edge to attach the overmat to the backing board.

1 Measure the image area.

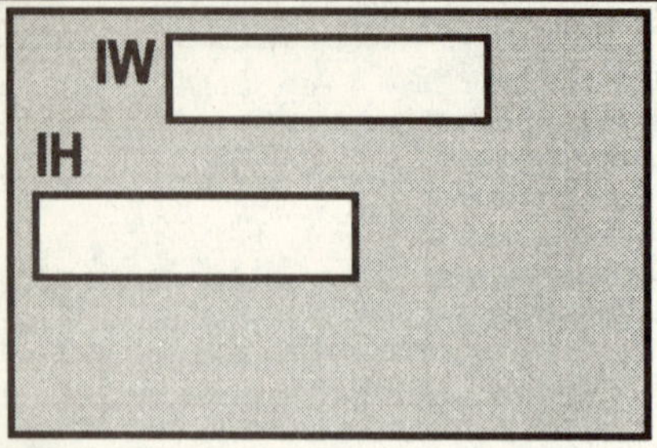

Measure the height and width of the image area. If you intend to crop the image with the overmat, measure only the area you would like to see through the window.

2 Plan the mount dimensions.

Measure the height and width of the mat board.

Subtract the width and height of the image area from the width and height of the mat board to determine the borders. Divide by two.

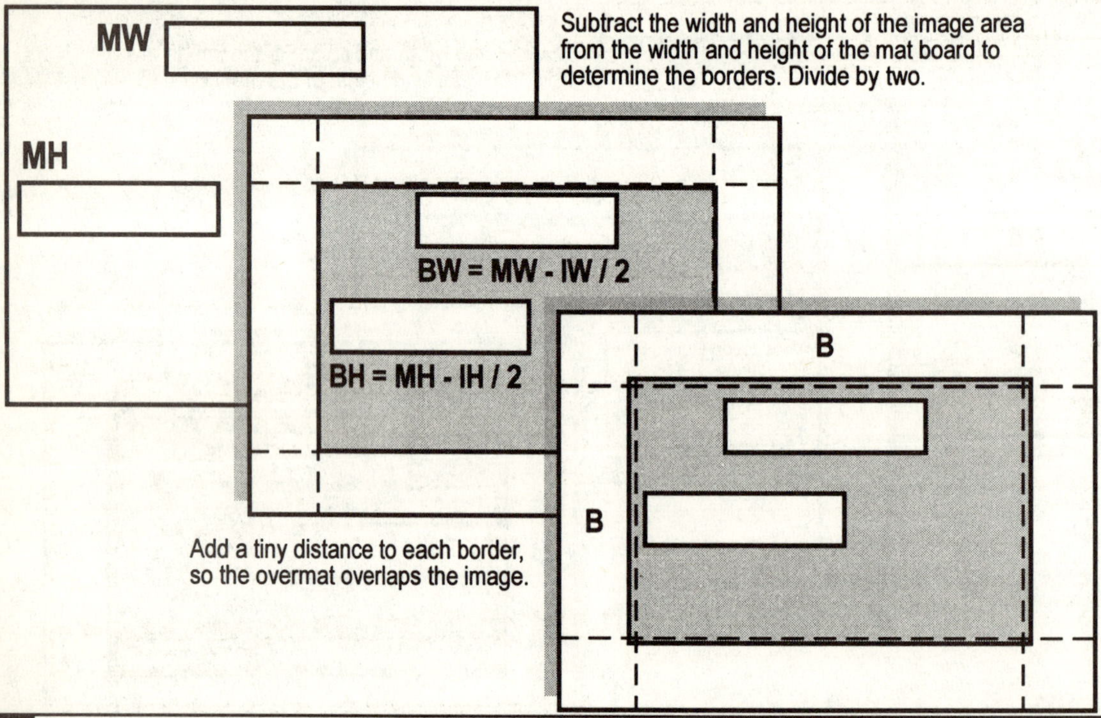

Add a tiny distance to each border, so the overmat overlaps the image.

3 Mark the cuts on the mat board.

Mark the inside of the board with a pencil according to the measurements above. A T-square aligned with the mat edge is useful to make sure that the lines are straight and square.

4 Cut the overmat.

Cut the overmat with a sharp knife. If you are using a mat cutter for a beveled cut, make sure that you are cutting each side from the right angle. Use a metal ruler as a guide and erase the remaining pencil marks when you are done.

5 Position and attach the print.

Position the print between the overmat and the backing board. Use a weight (must not scratch the surface) to hold the print in position until you have attached it with photo-corners or marked its position for dry mounting.

6 Attach the overmat to the backing board.

Use hinges at the top edge to attach the overmat to the backing board.

1	Measure the image area.

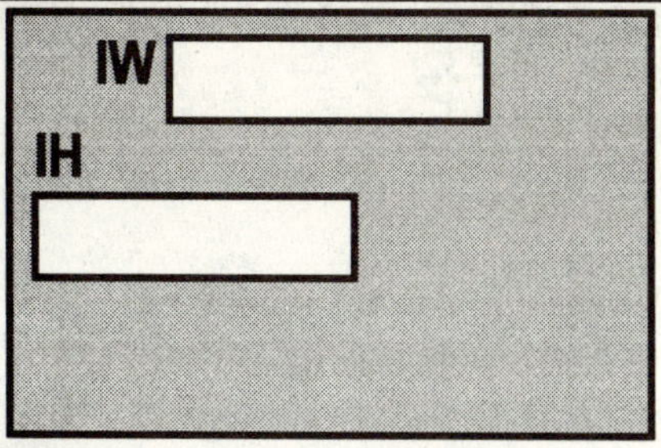

Measure the height and width of the image area. If you intend to crop the image with the overmat, measure only the area you would like to see through the window.

2	Plan the mount dimensions.

Measure the height and width of the mat board.

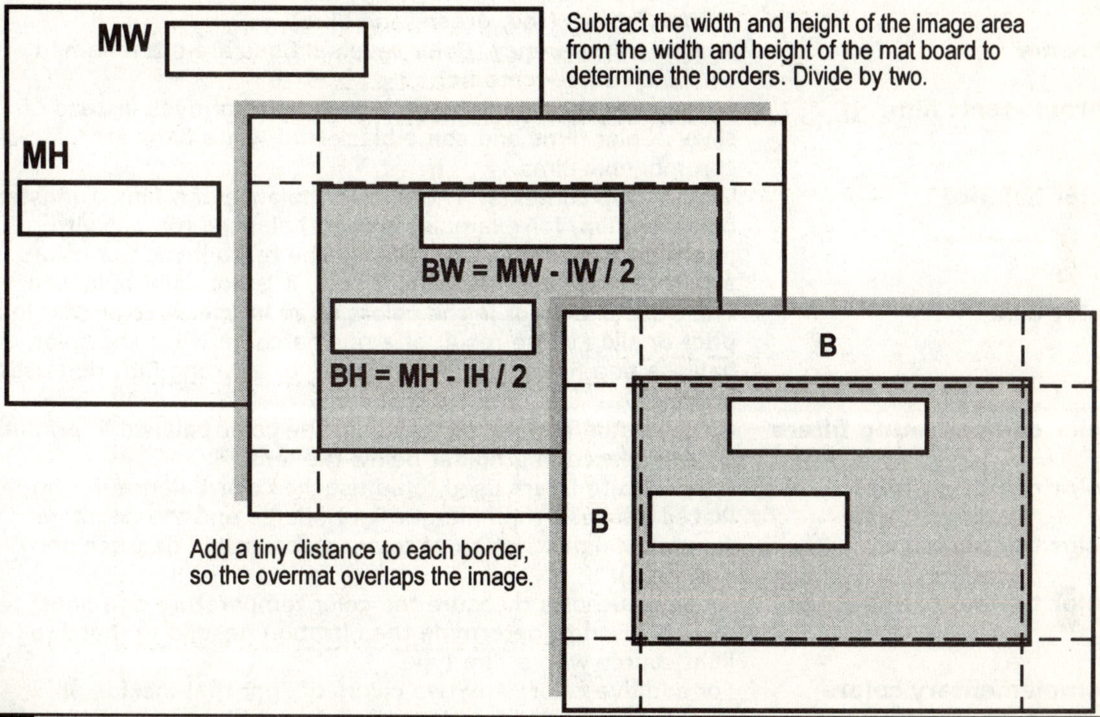

Subtract the width and height of the image area from the width and height of the mat board to determine the borders. Divide by two.

Add a tiny distance to each border, so the overmat overlaps the image.

3	Mark the cuts on the mat board.

Mark the inside of the board with a pencil according to the measurements above. A T-square aligned with the mat edge is useful to make sure that the lines are straight and square.

4	Cut the overmat.

Cut the overmat with a sharp knife. If you are using a mat cutter for a beveled cut, make sure that you are cutting each side from the right angle. Use a metal ruler as a guide and erase the remaining pencil marks when you are done.

5	Position and attach the print.

Position the print between the overmat and the backing board. Use a weight (must not scratch the surface) to hold the print in position until you have attached it with photo-corners or marked its position for dry mounting.

6	Attach the overmat to the backing board.

Use hinges at the top edge to attach the overmat to the backing board.

9 COLOR

9.1 GLOSSARY

Additive color	A way of producing colors of light by mixing the three additive primary colors (red, green, and blue).
Chrome	A color transparency. Color reversal films are often named with the suffix - chrome.
Chromogenic film	A film where the final image is composed of dyes instead of silver. Color films and some black-and-white films are chromogenic films.
Color balance	Used in two contexts: 1. The color balance of a film. Tungsten-balanced film, for example, is color balanced for use with incandescent lamps (3200°K). 2. The reproduction of colors in a print. If the print has a color cast, it is not color balanced.
Color cast	The trace of a color in the colors of an image. A color cast in a print or slide is the result of a mismatch between the color balance of a film and a light source, or a wrong filtration used in printing.
Color compensating filters	(CC) Gelatin filters used to adjust the color balance in printing. Usually placed in a holder below the lens.
Color printing filters	(CP) Acetate filters used to adjust the color balance in printing. Placed between the enlarger light source and the negative.
Color temperature	A numerical description of colors measured in degrees of Kelvin (K).
Color temperature meter	A device used to measure the color temperature of a light source. Used to determine the filtration needed to match a light source with a film type.
Complementary colors	For additive color: Any two colors of light that include all wavelengths of light and thus produce white when combined. For subtractive colors: Any two dye-colors that absorb all wavelengths and thus produce black when combined.
Daylight film	Color film balanced to produce white at 5500°K (midday sun and electronic flash).
Dichroic head	An enlarger head that contains adjustable color filters in the three subtractive primary colors (cyan, magenta, and yellow).
Filter	A piece of colored glass or gelatin placed in front of the lens to adjust the color balance of the light striking the film.
Hue	A technical term for color. The wavelength of light that gives a color its name, such as yellow, independent of its saturation or value.
Kelvin	The unit used to measure the color temperature of light.
Latitude	The amount of overexposure and underexposure possible without significant loss of quality in an image. Reversal films have very little latitude.
Photoflood	An incandescent lamp.
Primary colors	Basic colors from which all other colors can be mixed.
Reversal film	A film that produces a positive image.

Saturation	The purity of a color independent of its hue or value. The more gray a color contains, the lower its saturation.
Slide	Most accurately used to describe a 35mm transparency mounted for projection. Also used for reversal or transparency films - slide film.
Subtractive colors	A way of producing colors by mixing dyes that contain the three subtractive primary colors (cyan, magenta, and yellow).
Transparency	A positive image on film viewed by transmitted light.
Tungsten film	Color film balanced to produce white at 3200ºK (tungsten lights, regular light bulbs).
Tungsten light	A light source containing a thin tungsten filament that emits light when heated. Also called an incandescent light.
Type A film	Color film balanced to produce white at 3400ºK (photofloods).
Type B film	Tungsten balanced film - 3200ºK.
Value	The overall lightness or darkness of a color. Value and saturation are actually different. A color can be dark and still retain high saturation. In digital imaging, the term value is often replaced by brightness.

9.2 SUMMARY

171 **Color**

Color photography can sometimes produce unexpected results: We have quite strict expectations with regards to the accuracy of color in a photograph. This chapter will explain how color is controlled to render "natural" looking results.

172 **Color: Additive or subtractive**

All colors can be created either by adding or subtracting the primary colors: The additive method was used for early color films, while all modern films employ the subtractive method. **In additive mixing:** The red, green, and blue additive primaries can be mixed to produce any color. The sum of all three additive primaries is white. **In the subtractive method:** The cyan, magenta, and yellow subtractive primaries absorb red, green, and blue wavelengths and thereby subtract them from white light. Mixed in varying proportions they can produce any color. The sum of all three subtractive primaries is black.

173 **Color photographs: Three image layers**

A color photograph begins as three superimposed black-and-white negatives: Color film consists of three emulsion layers, each responding to a different part of the spectrum. In descending order from the top layer, they respond to blue, green, and red light. **Colors are created during development:** The developer converts the light-sensitive silver halide crystals to metallic silver. During development, a colored image of dye is also formed in each of the three emulsion layers. The blue-sensitive layer forms a yellow image, the green layer a magenta image, and the red layer a cyan image. The silver is finally bleached out to leave only the colored images. This basic process is used for color negatives, color transparencies, and color prints.

174 **Choosing a color film**

The look of color films is linked to film speed: Slower films have finer grain, better sharpness, more tones, higher contrast, and enhanced color saturation compared to faster films. **Even within the same film speed range, different films produce different color balances:** The overall appearance of the colors may range from warm (a yellowish tint) to cold (a bluish tint). Which film you choose is really a matter of personal preference.

174 **Color film characteristics**

Negative film: These produce a negative that can easily be printed. The names for these films are often adorned with the suffix - color. **Reversal film:** These films produce a positive image that is best suited for direct viewing or projection. Positives can also be printed, but the process is toxic and quite expensive. Reversal films often have the suffix – chrome in their name. **Professional films:** Films marked "Professional" are aged to reach the best color balance when they are sold. They should be used immediately and kept refrigerated. Amateur films have less exacting color standards, and they will reach their optimum color balance sometime during their life span. Refrigeration is not necessary unless they approach the expiration date. **Color balance:** Daylight films are color balanced for use in daylight and with electronic flash. Tungsten-balanced films are intended for use with incandescent lamps. **Type S/Type L films:** Some films are intended to produce the best results with certain light sources within a particular exposure range. S stands for "Short" – daylight-balanced films with exposures of 1/10 or shorter. L stands for "Long" – tungsten-balanced films with exposures of 1/50 to 60 seconds.

176 - 177 **Instant color films**

Instant color pictures are a favorite with photographers because the processing takes care of itself: It is simple for the user, but the technology involved is complex. **Polaroid makes a variety of instant color films:** Some films and formats are intended solely for Polaroid's cameras, but instant film for use with special backs in standard medium- and large-format cameras is also available.

178 - 179 **Exposure latitude: How much can exposures vary?**

Accurate exposure is particularly important with color reversal film because the film in the camera becomes the final transparency or slide: Reversal films only tolerate about 1/2 stop underexposure and about 1/3 stop overexposure before colors are seriously affected. **Color negative film has more exposure latitude, and a picture can be lightened or darkened when the negatives are printed:** It tolerates at least 1 stop underexposure and 1 or 2 stops of overexposure. Minor exposure mistakes can be corrected in printing. **In contrasty lighting, color film is not able to record color and details accurately in both very light highlights and very dark shadows:** The contrast range of the scene is greater than the exposure range of the film. Expose for the most important part and bracket other exposures. Use artificial lighting or reflectors to reduce the contrast in the scene. **It is easier to get good exposures with color if lighting is flat:** You will not experience contrast problems, but the colors are likely to be less vibrant in subdued light. Please see page 179 for some illustrations of exposure latitude.

180 - 181 **Color balance: Color temperature and the color balance of film**

Color films sometimes record colors that the photographer did not see when the shot was made: Different light sources actually have a distinct "color", which is not seen by the human eye. Film does not have this ability to adapt – it can only see one particular color as white, while other light sources will appear with a specific color. **The balance of colors in light is measured as color temperature on the Kelvin scale:** It is used as a measure of the wavelengths present in light, and runs from red at low temperatures towards blue at the higher end of the scale. **Different color films are made for different color temperatures:** Daylight film (also for use with electronic flash) is balanced for 5500°K. Tungsten-balanced color film for incandescent lamps (including ordinary light bulbs) is balanced for 3200°K. There is also a Type A tungsten film for use with photolamps balanced at 3400°K. **What happens if the color balance of light does not match the color balance of your film:** Light sources or conditions that do not match the three types of film will have an unusual color balance. **Color balance is more important with reversal films than with negative film:** Since the positive image is often the final product, it must be accurately color balanced when it is taken. Negative films can to some extent be corrected during printing. You can use colored filters to balance the color of the light. For tungsten film exposed in daylight, place an 85B filter on your lens. For daylight film exposed in tungsten light, place an 80A filter on your lens. **Some natural light conditions do not match the color balance of any film:** Sunsets or snow in shadows will produce a reddish or bluish color cast respectively. You can use a Skylight 1A filter to correct a slightly blue color cast. **Fluorescent lights create a similar problem: their light does not match the balance of any film:** With daylight film, photographs taken under fluorescent lights will turn greenish. Use a FL or magenta filter to correct the color balance.

182 - 183 **Filters to balance color**

Filters can correct the color balance a lot – or a little: Electronic flash matches daylight film, incandescent lamps match tungsten film, and photolamps match type-A film. You can use filters to match the color of your light source with the film more closely. Special color meters are available that measure the color of the light. **It is important to balance the light the way you want it when you make color slides:** The slide is often the final product. Color negatives are also easier to print when properly color balanced. **An exposure increase is needed with a filter:** A filter removes some wavelengths of light and this loss must be compensated for with an exposure increase. TTL metering compensates for this automatically. With a hand-held meter, increase the exposure according to the filter factor. Please see page 182 for a comprehensive listing of filters for color photography. **If you are mixing fluorescent light with flash:** Filter the flash to match the color temperature of fluorescent light and attach a FL correction filter to your lens.

184 - 185 **Color casts**

Reflected light can also reflect colors: A subject can take on the colors reflected from a nearby surface. While the eye adapts to see white colors, film does not have this ability. Colors are recorded according to their color temperature. **A color cast may or may not be a desirable addition:** We have very set expectations as to the color of things, and a color cast might give an unwanted impression. Sometimes, however, it might be used as a creative tool. **Colors can add the impression of heat or weight in a picture:** Take the psychological effect of color into consideration when composing or arranging your picture. **Color can affect the illusion of depth:** Warm colors protrude in the picture plane while colder colors recede.

186 - 187 **Color changes throughout the day**

Colors in your photographs will vary depending on the time of day that you made them: Early or late in the day, colors take on quite warm and golden properties. **In the earliest hours of the day, before sunrise, the world is essentially black and white:** There is very little color. **As soon as the sun rises, the light warms up:** Filtered by the atmosphere, the light takes on warm, reddish qualities. **The higher the sun climbs in the sky, the greater the contrast between colors:** The contrast between colors increases as they take on their true hue. Daylight film is balanced for the midday sun. **As the sun goes down, the light begins to warm up again:** The light gradually turns toward red as sunset approaches. **After sunset, there is a good deal of light left in the sky, often tinted by sunset colors:** Light often lingers in spectacular colors before it turns to darkness. **Finally, just before night, colors fade:** Colors disappear and the world once more turns black and white. **At dusk, at dawn, sometimes indoors, the light may be so dim that exposure times become very long:** The reciprocity effect must be accounted for with color films. For exposures of 1 second and longer, the exposure must be increased more than the customary stop. An exposure reading of 1 second should be exposed for one stop more, a reading of 10 seconds for two stops more, and a reading or 100 seconds for 3 stops more. Some color films are not intended for long exposures. Refer to the exposure information supplied by the manufacturer. **Very long exposures can change the color balance:** Long exposures affect the three emulsion layers of color films differently, creating a shift in the color balance of the film. Filters may be used to compensate for some of this change.

188 - 189 **Developing color film**

Process color materials carefully: Processing color films is similar to processing black-and-white films, but color materials are much more sensitive to changes in temperature and time. Even the slightest shifts in processing can invoke drastic changes in color balance and density. **Most photographers use a commercial lab for developing color films:** It is convenient and specialist machines carefully monitor the processing. **Some photographers prefer to do their own color film processing:** It could be marginally cheaper, but the results are usually less reliable. Few labs maintain their processing machines so badly that the results are unacceptable. **Color films can be pushed:** Color reversal films are processed in E-6 chemistry. Color negative films are processed in C-41 chemistry. Standard processing produces the best results. It is possible to give your lab instructions to push (you underexpose and the lab overdevelops) the film, usually at a slight increase in processing costs. **Cross processing:** Color films can be cross processed, reversal film in C-41 chemistry and vice versa, to get unexpected results in terms of contrast, color, and saturation.

190 - 191 **Making a color print from a negative: Equipment and materials**

Paper and chemicals for printing from a color negative - Color prints from color negatives can be made with negative/positive processes: You use paper intended for color negatives and process it in RA-4 chemicals. **Check the manufacturer's instructions:** Make sure that paper and chemicals are compatible. Keep color-paper refrigerated and warm it up gradually to room temperature before use. **Equipment for printing - Enlarger:** An enlarger with a tungsten or quartz-halogen bulb can be used. **Heat absorbing glass:** Some enlargers may require a heat absorbing glass to prevent damage to color negatives and filters. **Voltage control:** Changes in the voltage will affect the color balance. Color enlargers must have a voltage stabilizer.

Filtration: Placing filters of the subtractive primaries (cyan, magenta, and yellow) in the path of the enlarger light alters the color balance of the print. A filter is named after its density. **If the enlarger has built-in dichroic filters:** Knobs on the enlarger head control filtration. **If your enlarger has a drawer for holding filters between the lamp and negative:** Acetate color filters can be used. **If your enlarger is an older model that does not have a filter drawer:** Use better quality gelatin filters below the lens. **Color print viewing filter kit:** Colored filters used to determine the color cast of a test strip or print. **Equipment to process the print - For manual processing:** A plastic processing-drum is used to process films manually. **The next step up is mechanized agitation:** A motor drives the drum and keeps it at a set temperature. **A completely automated processor does everything for you:** Most color printing facilities have automatic processors. In addition, you need standard printing equipment. **Record keeping:** Keep track of filtration and enlarger aperture settings to make your results repeatable.

191 **Your personal standard filter pack**

The first step in color printing is to make test prints to establish a standard filter pack: Once you have found the best filtration for a normal negative, subsequent negatives will only have slight variations in filtration. **You will need a negative (or a transparency, if you are using reversal materials) that is of normal density and color balance:** It should contain a range of colors, including flesh tones, and neutral grays. **Make a note of the filtration that makes a good print from the negative:** Use this filtration to make your first test with all negatives.

192 - 193 **Exposing a test print**

The following pages show how to make prints from a color negative: Evaluation for color balance is the most important part of color printing. **Keep darkroom light to a minimum:** Since color paper is obviously sensitive to all colors, handling in total darkness is strongly recommended. **Consistency is vital every time you make a print:** Keep exposure and development procedures consistent. **Contamination will cause trouble:** If you are handling the developing chemistry, be extra careful to avoid contamination. **Color chemicals are more toxic than black-and-white chemistry:** Follow the instructions and handle all chemicals safely. **Making a test print step by step:**

1. Prepare the negative.
2. Set up the enlarger.
3. Compose and focus the image.
4. Set the lens aperture.
5. Make the first test exposure.
6. Continue making the test exposures.
7. Process the paper.
8. Evaluate the print.

194 **Judging density in a print made from a negative**

Color prints are judged – and adjusted – first for density (the darkness of the print), then for color balance: Evaluate the density in the mid-tones, but make sure that shadows are dark with detail and highlights are bright with tone and texture. Exposure affects the color balance, so once the correct density has been determined, you can start working on the filtration to adjust the color balance. Be aware that changes in the filtration may require adjustments in exposure. **The illumination for judging a color print is important:** Ideally it should be evaluated under the same lighting conditions as where it will finally be viewed. Prepare an area with controlled lighting to make your judgment consistent. Work with average viewing distances and an average intensity of the viewing light.

195 - 196 **Judging color balance in a print made from a negative**

The first print you make from a negative usually needs some change in the color balance: You alter the filtration to adjust the color balance of the print. Evaluate dry prints. **You can check your print against pictures whose colors are shifted in a known direction:** A ring-around chart, such as the one reproduced on page 196, can be a useful guide for determining color casts. **A better method for evaluating prints is to look at them through colored viewing filters:** By looking through a filter of a color opposite to the color cast, you get an idea of how much the filtration needs to be altered. **To correct the color balance of a print made from a negative:** Make the opposite color change in the enlarger filtration from the color change you want in the print. Work with the magenta and yellow filters, and remove a color cast from the print by adding that color to the filter pack. **The cure for a print with too much magenta is to add – not decrease – the magenta in the filter pack:** The added magenta will absorb more magenta and make the print more green. **Similarly, excess blue is corrected by lightening the filter that absorbs blue, the yellow filter:** Adding yellow, on the other hand, will make your print more blue.

195 **Using viewing filters to correct the color balance**

Viewing filter kits help you determine any changes needed in the color balance of a print: The white-side entries are for color negative filtration changes. **Hold the filter a few feet away from the print:** Look at the mid-tones in the print and flick the filter in and out of your vision to discern any changes. If you don't move the filter in and out, you will gradually adjust to the color cast of the print.

195 **Balancing a print made from a negative**

Use this table to adjust the color balance of a print from a negative:

Too magenta	Add M
Too red	Add M + Y
Too yellow	Add Y
Too green	Subtract M
Too cyan	Subtract M + Y
Too blue	Subtract Y

197 **More about color balance and print finishing**

After you change the filtration of a test strip, you may need to make a final exposure change: The altered density of the filter pack affects the amount of light reaching the paper. Yellow changes have very little effect, while magenta usually requires an exposure increase or reduction for every 3-5 units added or subtracted. **Do not end up with all three subtractive primaries (Y, M, C) in your filter pack:** This produces neutral density (gray) with no effect on the color balance. You only increase the exposure time needed. Subtract the lowest number from all three packs to remove neutral density. **Dodging and burning in a color print is feasible to some extent:** Local changes in exposure will affect both the density and the color balance of these areas. **You can also change color balance locally:** Dodge and burn through colored filters to control the color balance of these areas. **Color prints may need spotting:** There are retouching dyes available for color prints. These come in a variety of colors and must be mixed carefully before application. **Mount prints to protect them and to give a finished look:** Avoid heat mounting color prints if you can. Use either cold mount or vacuum mount. The backing board must be perfectly smooth, otherwise the print will pick up the texture of the board. **Protect color prints from excess light:** Color prints fade when exposed to light. Color materials are, however, getting more stable.

198 **Making a color print from a transparency**

You can make color prints from transparencies (slides) using reversal color print materials: The procedure is similar to color negative printing, except that most processes are reversed. **Clean the transparency carefully before you place it in the enlarger:** Specks of dust will become black spots in the print, which are hard to remove. **For best results, print from a fully exposed transparency with saturated colors and low to normal contrast:** Although low contrast paper is available, contrasty slides usually require complex dodging and burning in. **Be careful if you handle any color processing chemicals:** Chemicals used for processing reversal prints are very toxic. Please be extra careful when you handle them. Read the instructions carefully. **Materials and equipment needed for printing from a transparency:** The equipment is basically the same as for color negative printing, but the paper and processing chemicals are different. Be aware that the glossy surface of reversal papers is extremely glossy.

199 **Judging a print made from a transparency**

Unlike printing from a negative, reversal print materials respond the same way that slide film does when you expose it in the camera: Exposure and color balance adjustments are the opposite of those used for color negative materials. If the print is too dark, increase the exposure. If the print is too light, reduce the exposure. To remove a color cast from the print, subtract that color from the filter pack. **Evaluate and adjust density first:** Density affects the color balance. **Then evaluate color balance:** Use the same methods as those suggested for color negative materials. The black side of the viewing filters is for reversal materials. **When overall density and color balance are good, look for areas that need dodging or burning:** The actions are reversed. You darken an area by dodging it during the basic exposure time. You lighten an area by burning in after the basic exposure time. **Whatever you do, keep notes:** As for color negative materials, extensive notes will make printing much easier in the long run.

199 **Balancing a print made from a transparency**

Use this table to adjust the color balance of a print from a slide:

Too magenta	Subtract M
Too red	Subtract Y + M
Too yellow	Subtract Y
Too green	Add M
Too cyan	Add Y + M
Too blue	Add Y

Notes

9.3 TEST

FILL IN THE BLANKS

1 Color films are made of ____________________ emulsion layers.

2 ____________________ film has very little exposure latitude.

3 The three subtractive primary colors are ____________________, ____________________, and ____________________.

4 Type S films are intended for ____________________ exposures.

5 Color temperature is measure in degrees of ____________________.

6 Polaroid is a manufacturer of ____________________ color films.

7 Tungsten films are color balanced to produce white at ____________________ °K.

8 ____________________ films are color balanced to produce white at 5500°K.

9 When evaluating a color print, you consider ____________________ first and then color balance.

10 If your print from a color negative is too magenta, you add ____________________ to the filter pack.

MULTIPLE CHOICE – CIRCLE ONE OR MORE

1 When the three subtractive primary colors are mixed together in equal amounts, they produce:
   a. white.
   b. red, green, and blue.
   c. black.

2 When judging a color print, it is important that it is done:
   a. under the enlarger light with the correct filtration dialed.
   b. in lighting conditions that resemble those where the print will finally be displayed.
   c. under an 80A safelight.

3 When yellow, magenta, and cyan are all added to the filter pack, the result is:
   a. a red and cyan color cast.
   b. neutral density.
   c. reversal light.

4 If your print has a green color cast, you view it through a:
   a. green viewing filter.
   b. yellow viewing filter.
   c. magenta viewing filter.

5 To make a print from a transparency lighter, you must:
   a. increase the exposure.
   b. reduce the exposure.
   c. add neutral density to the filter pack.

6	Colored filters are usually used in color photography to:	a.	add an overall red cast to a scene.
		b.	match the color balance of a film with the color balance of the light source.
		c.	remove the silver glare from the emulsion of the film.
7	Color negative films are processed in:	a.	E-6 chemistry.
		b.	C-41 chemistry.
		c.	T-Max chemistry.
8	If your print from a color negative is too yellow, you:	a.	subtract yellow from the filter pack.
		b.	add yellow to the filter pack.
		c.	add cyan to the filter pack.
9	If you add magenta to the filter pack, the color of your print from a negative would shift towards:	a.	green.
		b.	magenta.
		c.	blue.
10	When your print from a negative is too blue, you can make it more yellow by:	a.	subtracting yellow from the filter pack.
		b.	adding yellow to the filter pack.
		c.	adding yellow and cyan to magenta in the filter pack.

9.4 PRACTICAL TIPS

Color printing

Keep track of your progress while printing.

When you are printing color, you usually make several tests before the print exposure and color balance is right. You always start with the standard filter pack and make adjustments until the print is exactly the way you want it. During this process, it is extremely helpful to track your changes in a sequence to make each adjustment more predictable. For example, if you can see how much an added density of 8 magenta altered the color balance of your print compared to the previous version, you are in a better position to judge exactly how many units more or less of magenta the print may need. The best way to keep track of your adjustments is to write on the back of the test prints themselves. Do this after the print has been fully processed. Number the sequence and write down the exposure time, the aperture, and the filtration. If you keep these records as you print, it will speed up the process, and you will most likely get a final print in fewer attempts and with less paper wasted.

Number: 1	*Number: 2*	*Number: 3*
Time: 8 seconds	*Time: 9 seconds*	*Time: 9 seconds*
Aperture: f8	*Aperture: f8*	*Aperture: f8*
Filtration: 75M 48Y	*Filtration: 83M 48Y*	*Filtration: 83M 53Y*
Next: +1 sec. +8M	*Next: +5Y*	*Next: +2Y (Final?)*

9.5 JOURNAL

9.5.1 FILTERS FOR COLOR PHOTOGRAPHY

Filters are mainly used in color photography to match the color balance of the light source with the color balance of the film. Find the filter factors for the filters you have and enter them in the table provided. Consult the reference below and include the actual exposure increase in stops. If you use your filters on a SLR camera with through-the-lens metering, you must perform a simple metering test to determine the actual exposure increase needed. See 4.4 Practical tips for a description of the procedure.

FILTER FACTOR ▾									
1	1.2	1.5	2	2.5	3	4	5	6	8
0	1/3	2/3	1	1 1/3	1 2/3	2	2 1/3	2 2/3	3
EXPOSURE INCREASE IN STOPS ▴									

FILTERS FOR COLOR PHOTOGRAPHY Table page 182 in the textbook describes use ▾	Filter factor ▾	Exposure Increase ▾	Manual exposure increase SLR metered exposure + ▾
81A Yellow	1.2	1/3	None
Linear Polarizer	2.5	1 1/3	+ 1 stop

9.5.2 STANDARD FILTER PACKS

The standard filter pack is the filtration required to make a print with correct color balance from a normal negative or transparency (the filtration will not be the same). Once you have established the standard filter pack for printing, you start with this filtration and make only minor adjustments for individual negatives. Paper manufacturers often list a standard filter pack on their packaging, but this will most likely be wrong. Film type, developing, the density of the enlarger filtration, and the paper processor all affect the color balance of the print, and you need to standardize these factors to establish your standard filter pack. Start by choosing a film, develop your rolls in the same commercial lab, print on the same enlarger, and use the same paper processor to ensure consistent and predictable results. The actual procedure is simple. After printing a few normal negatives with a good range of familiar colors to your satisfaction, you'll notice that the filtration for each of them is either identical or within a unit or two. Further printing will help you to narrow down or confirm the standard filter pack. Enter your standard filter pack(s) in the tables below. If you are printing in a school lab, you probably need a standard filter pack for each enlarger you are using.

STANDARD FILTER PACK ▸	Example		Filtration ▾		
Film ▾	Paper ▾	Enlarger ▾	C	M	Y
Fujicolor NPS 160	Fuji Crystal Archive	Room D Omega	00	57	49
Notes ▸	Keep the lever for white light / filter density in the middle position while printing.				

STANDARD FILTER PACK ▸			Filtration ▾		
Film ▾	Paper ▾	Enlarger ▾	C	M	Y
Notes ▸					

STANDARD FILTER PACK ▸			Filtration ▾		
Film ▾	Paper ▾	Enlarger ▾	C	M	Y
Notes ▸					

STANDARD FILTER PACK ▸			Filtration ▾		
Film ▾	Paper ▾	Enlarger ▾	C	M	Y
Notes ▸					

STANDARD FILTER PACK ▸			Filtration ▾		
Film ▾	Paper ▾	Enlarger ▾	C	M	Y
Notes ▸					

STANDARD FILTER PACK ▸			Filtration ▾		
Film ▾	Paper ▾	Enlarger ▾	C	M	Y
Notes ▸					

STANDARD FILTER PACK ▸			Filtration ▾		
Film ▾	Paper ▾	Enlarger ▾	C	M	Y
Notes ▸					

9.5.3 COLOR PRINTING RECORDS

While you are printing, it is preferable to keep your printing records on the back of the test prints (see 10.4 Practical tips). The tables below are devised for information about the final exposure and filtration for specific negatives. They will help you establish the standard filter packs above, and save you time and paper if you choose to print a particular negative again. Instructions for color balancing a print made from a negative or transparency have been included for your reference. Please see the example below for use of the records.

BALANCING A PRINT MADE FROM A COLOR NEGATIVE

PRINT IS	DO THIS	ALTERNATIVELY DO THIS
Too magenta	Add M	Subtract C+Y
Too red	Add M+Y	Subtract C
Too yellow	Add Y	Subtract C+M
Too green	Subtract M	Add C+Y
Too cyan	Subtract M+Y	Add C
Too blue	Subtract Y	Add C+M

BALANCING A PRINT MADE FROM A COLOR TRANSPARENCY

PRINT IS	DO THIS	ALTERNATIVELY DO THIS
Too magenta	Subtract M	Add C+Y
Too red	Subtract M+Y	Add C
Too yellow	Subtract Y	Add C+M
Too green	Add M	Subtract C+Y
Too cyan	Add M+Y	Subtract C
Too blue	Add Y	Subtract C+M

COLOR PRINTING RECORDS EXAMPLE

Film	Negative	Paper	Print size		Enlarger	Height	Exposure		Filtration		
			H	W			Sec.	f/	C	M	Y
23	Frame 2	Ilford	8	10	Omega D	47cm	7.5	5.6	00	57	49
23	Frame 8	Ilford	8	10	Omega D	47cm	8.0	5.6	00	59	49
23	Frame 16	Ilford	8	10	Omega D	47cm	7.5	5.6	00	57	46
23	Frame 19	Ilford	8	10	Omega D	47cm	7.5	5.6	00	57	49
4x5	#24	CA	20	24	Omega B	62cm	9.5	8	00	68	55
4x5	#28	CA	20	24	Omega B	62cm	10	8	00	70	55
4x5	#31	CA	20	24	Omega B	62cm	9.5	8	00	67	54

COLOR PRINTING RECORDS

Film	Negative	Paper	Print size		Enlarger	Height	Exposure		Filtration		
			H	W			Sec.	f/	C	M	Y

COLOR PRINTING RECORDS

Film	Negative	Paper	Print size		Enlarger	Height	Exposure		Filtration		
			H	W			Sec.	f/	C	M	Y

COLOR PRINTING RECORDS

Film	Negative	Paper	Print size		Enlarger	Height	Exposure		Filtration		
			H	W			Sec.	f/	C	M	Y

10 DIGITAL CAMERA

10.1 GLOSSARY

Bit (Binary digit) The smallest unit usable by a computer. There are 8 bits in a byte.

Bit depth The number of bits that are used to store a pixel's color information for display. The higher the bit depth, the more information can be stored, and the more colors can be displayed.

Bitmap The display of an image on the computer screen in a single layer of pixels mapped in a grid.

Byte A unit of digital data. There are 8 bits in a byte and 1024 bytes in a kilobyte.

CCD (Charge-Coupled Device) The sensor that has replaced film in digital cameras. It converts light into a string of binary digits and thereby records an image file.

Channel An image component that contains the pixel information for an individual color. Grayscale images have one channel. RGB images have three channels - red, green, and blue.

Color balance The color temperature of the light source is color balanced with a recording mode on the digital camera. Some cameras refer to this setting as white point or white balance.

Compression An algorithm that organizes and stores the image data in a way that reduces the file size compresses the image. Some formats, like JPEG, compress the file by permanently discarding image data.

Contrast The difference between the lightest and darkest areas of a scene or the pixels in an image file. Digital cameras have limited exposure latitude so many models offer contrast control.

Digital camera A camera that uses a CCD instead of film to capture and record an image in digital form.

Digital image file A digital image is converted into a string of data and stored as a digital image file. The computer reads and translates the data into an image again.

Digital imaging Image-editing method where an image is transformed into digital data to be read and altered by a computer.

Digital noise Colored pixels not part of the actual scene. Noise often shows up in dark areas when a digital camera is used with a high ISO rating.

Dpi (Dots per inch) A unit used to measure the resolution of a printer or an imagesetter. ppi is the term used to describe the input resolution of a scanner and a bitmapped image.

Grayscale An image that contains black, white, and up to 256 shades of gray.

Hardware The components of a computer system responsible for the physical processing and display of data.

Histogram A graph showing the number of pixels at each level of brightness in an image. The histogram is used as a guide to perform non-linear adjustments of contrast in an image.

JPEG (Joint Photographic Experts Group) A compression algorithm (file format) for photographic images. It reduces the file size by discarding image data.

Kilobyte A larger unit of digital data. There are 1024 bytes in a kilobyte and 1048576 bytes in a megabyte. The unit is often used to describe the size of a small computer file.

LCD (Liquid Crystal Display) The technology used on digital camera monitors.

Megabyte A unit of digital data frequently used to describe the file size of digital imaging files. A megabyte contains 1048576 bytes.

Pixel Short for picture element. The smallest unit in a digital image that can be displayed, changed, and stored. A digital image is made of tiny pixels arranged in a grid.

Ppi (Pixels per inch) The term used to describe the resolution of a bitmapped image.

Photoshop Short for Adobe Photoshop. The most common software application for digital imaging.

Printer A digital output option that transfers the digital image to paper or film.

RAM (Random Access Memory) The system memory of a computer used to run applications, to process information, and for temporary storage.

Rasterize The conversion of an object-oriented image (such as a Vector graphic) into a bitmapped image. All computer files are rasterized when they are printed.

Reaction time The time it takes for a digital camera to focus and set the exposure and then download the image to memory.

Resolution The amount of information in an image. It is measured in ppi (pixels per inch) for a digital image and a monitor display. The resolution of a printer is referred to as dpi (dots per inch), and the term lpi (lines per inch) is used for a halftone screen.

RGB The three additive primary colors (red, green, and blue) are used to project color on a computer monitor. Also an image mode in Adobe Photoshop.

Scanner A device that reads and converts a paper photograph, a negative, or a slide into a digital file.

Software Computer program used to manipulate data according to the user's directions. Adobe Photoshop is a common digital-imaging software package.

TIFF (Tagged Image File Format) A common file format for bitmapped images.

USB (Universal Serial Bus) The connector port frequently used to transfer images from a digital camera to a computer.

Notes

10.2 SUMMARY

203 **Digital imaging**

Digital imaging is changing photography by speeding up and simplifying many photographic processes: Where speed is of the essence or heavy manipulation of the photographic image is desired, digital imaging has become the standard way of processing photographs. **You don't necessarily need a digital camera to use digital imaging:** Negatives and slides can be scanned and converted to image files for input into a computer. **However, digital cameras now represent the fastest-growing segment of the camera market:** A digital camera is really a computer with a lens and as such it blends seamlessly into the booming market of electronic goods.

204 **A computer with a lens**

A digital camera produces an image by converting the tones of a scene into numbers: A CCD captures the light and translates it into data. **There are many advantages to using a digital camera:** Unlike film, the storage media is reusable. Corrections are easily made on the spot since results are viewable instantly. You can apply separate controls and settings to individual shots. Further changes can be made with image-editing software, and the file can be disseminated both by traditional means and electronically. **Some costs accompany the advantages:** The cost of equipment with a quality comparable to film is prohibitively high at the moment, but prices are constantly dropping. Consider also that just as a camera used with film demands a darkroom, a digital camera usually requires a computer and a printer. Please see page 204 for an introduction to digital camera features and functions.

205 **Pictures into pixels**

The image that comes through the lens on your camera is in analog form: It is on a continuous variable scale. **For computer use, the image is converted to digital form using a CCD:** Light-sensitive cells are arranged in a grid. Each cell records the intensity of the light and its color with the aid of a red, green, and blue filter. **Each position on the grid is recorded as a solid-tone pixel:** Along with its position, the data for each pixel contains brightness and color values. **Once the image is digitized, you can use image-editing software:** The software changes the value of one or more pixels to alter the image.

206 **Using a digital camera: Getting started**

Every digital camera is different: Read the manual to fully understand all the features and functions of your camera. **Make sure your camera has fresh batteries:** Unlike film-based cameras, there are seldom mechanical features on digital cameras. **Turn your camera off and insert a memory card:** The type of memory card or other storage media vary from camera to camera. Make sure you purchased the right kind. **Select the resolution and compression:** Lower resolution means a reduced image quality, but you will be able to store more images on your card. Choose according to the final use of the images. **Select the exposure mode:** The modes are familiar from conventional cameras – fully programmed, aperture priority, shutter priority, and manual. You might also be able to select manual or automatic focus. **Turn on the LCD monitor or view the data display panel:** Go to the menu for ISO settings. As with film, lower numbers give better results, but you might need a high rating in dim light. **If your camera allows it, select the color temperature for the dominant light source:** Sources may include tungsten, fluorescent, sunlight, cloudy, and outdoor shade.

Frame your picture by looking through the viewfinder or using the LCD monitor: Proceed as normal to focus and check the exposure, or let the camera perform some of these tasks for you. Leave the power of the camera on until the transfer is complete, and review your image on the monitor if desired. It can be discarded or stored. **You can review all your pictures on the LCD monitor in a "thumbnail" size:** This will give you an overview of what you have captured, but it does drain batteries so keep the review short.

207 **Memory and resolution**

A memory card in a digital camera is a removable device that stores your images until they are transferred to a computer: The size of the files and the capacity of the card determines how many photographs you can store. There are different kinds of memory cards and your camera will only accept one of them. Extra cards are useful when downloading is not an option and you wish to take more pictures. **The amount of memory you will need depends on the resolution:** Resolution is a measure for the number of pixels in an image. The more pixels, the better the image quality. **Unfortunately, you can get too much of a good thing:** High resolution means large files, which take up more space on your memory card and more space on your computer. Compression is a way of reducing the file size so the image is easier to store and handle. **When a memory card is filled, you need to transfer its contents to your computer:** Once the card is empty, it can be filled with new image files again.

208 - 209 **Choosing the quality you need**

Quality versus amount of memory: The larger an image is in terms of memory, the higher its quality. A memory card can consequently store only a few images of high quality and many more images of lower quality. The final use for the files and the amount of storage space you have available determines the resolution setting. **To achieve smaller digital files, your camera either uses fewer pixels to take pictures, compresses image files, or does both:** Low quality uses a lower resolution or compresses more compared to high quality. **Digital cameras let you choose:** You can set both resolution and compression modes on more advanced digital cameras. **How good is good enough:** For the Web and electronic display, a low quality is usually adequate. For prints and reproductions, use the maximum quality. Keep in mind that you can always throw away data during editing, but you can not fully recover what was never recorded. The box on page 208 explains the rudimentary principles of file compression.

210 **Monitors and viewfinders: Seeing what you've got**

Most digital cameras have a LCD (liquid crystal display) monitor on the back of the camera: The monitor displays the image focused on the image sensor. It may be hard to see in some situations, so an optical viewfinder is still found on most digital cameras. **One of the great advantages – and pleasures – of using a digital camera is the ability to see your picture almost as soon as you take it:** Cameras usually have several modes that allow you to view all the images recorded in a variety of formats, including a "contact sheet" of thumbnail-sized images. **If the picture was not what you wanted, you can delete it:** Deleting images will free up space on your memory card, allowing you to capture new versions of a scene. You can safeguard images against accidental deletion. **Digital cameras also provide an optical viewfinder, like those on conventional cameras:** The viewfinder image and the image recorded by the lens is not the same due to parallax. The LCD monitor allows you to view an image exactly the way the camera sees it, which is especially useful for close-ups. There are also SLR digital cameras.

211 **Delays and focal length**

You may discover a frustrating delay with some digital cameras between the moment you press the shutter release and the instant the camera exposes the image: The camera needs this time to determine focus, exposure, and color balance. Less of a problem with expensive cameras. You may press the shutter release button halfway with most models to perform these functions before exposing the image. **Once you press the shutter release, there is another delay as the camera downloads the image to the memory card:** While the transfer is taking place, the camera does not normally allow you to take another picture. Do not interrupt this transfer in any way – you may damage your camera or memory card. **A lens on a digital camera doesn't take longer to operate, but it does act as if it is longer focal length than you might expect:** Since the CCD is much smaller than 35mm film, lenses will comparatively be of a longer focal length on digital cameras. **You will have more depth of field than you might expect, too:** Depth of field is, in part, an effect dependent upon the focal length of the lens. Longer lenses produce less depth of field, and since digital-camera lenses hover around the 10-15mm bracket, they have very extensive depth of field. **Zoom options enlarge the effective focal length even more:** Digital zooming enlarges the individual pixels in an image without optically moving closer to the subject. Image quality deteriorates with digital zooming. **A macro feature on some digital cameras lets you get an enlarged image by focusing very close to the subject:** If this is done optically, it does not have the disadvantages of digital zooming.

212 **Per-frame ISO settings**

Traditional cameras let you change your film speed by roll: You select a film speed for the conditions you will be photographing under and the image quality you need. **Digital cameras let you change your camera's light sensitivity (the equivalent of film speed) frame by frame:** This will allow you to customize the film speed for each shot. **Digital noise may become evident at higher ratings:** Colored specks, normally in dark areas, and banding of the image may occur with high ISO settings. **You can minimize noise and other undesirable effects of high ISO settings by shooting at the lowest practical ISO rating:** Use the lowest value possible for the exposure you need. **Image-editing software can also help reduce noise:** Filters may help by discarding pixels that are too different from adjacent pixels, but this is really a poor option.

214 **Contrast and exposure control**

Some digital cameras let you adjust the contrast for each shot in order to get good tonality in both light and dark areas: Increase the contrast for low-contrast scenes and reduce the contrast for high-contrast scenes. It is preferable to make these adjustments with the camera instead of image-editing software. **The exposure latitude of digital cameras (their tolerance for under- or overexposure) is something like that of color slides – not much:** In contrasty scenes, the range of values might be too much for the camera to record. **Some cameras let you confirm that your picture has the tonal range you want:** A histogram will give you all the information you need. Less expensive models might only have plus and minus settings for contrast control. **Many digital cameras, especially less expensive ones, tend to overexpose highlights:** Meter and expose for the highlights as you would with a conventional camera and slide film. Use fill flash to remove noise in shadows and reduce the contrast.

215 **Color balance**

You can use your digital camera to adjust color balance while shooting: Different light sources have different color temperatures. Refer to chapter 9 for comprehensive coverage of this. **Sunlight, for instance, is bluer than the light emitted from a tungsten light bulb:** They have different color temperatures. With film, you use colored filters to achieve the desired color balance. **You do not need color-correcting filters with a digital camera:** Some cameras adjust automatically while others let you specify the light source. It is better to make these adjustments while shooting rather than with image-editing software. **Some models let you set the color balance even more exactly:** Activate the white balance control and point the camera at an object that is white to color balance the light.

216 **Choosing a digital camera**

Many types of digital cameras are available, from completely automatic to full-function professional models: Pick features according to your needs and budget. Keep in mind that the digital camera you buy today will be available for half the price tomorrow. Some say; buy the most expensive you can afford and the camera will be useful longer. **Creative control:** Manual features will give you creative control over the image. **Lens choice:** Again, the choices really depend on your budget. Existing camera systems with interchangeable lenses are expensive, and fixed zoom lenses on digital cameras provide a decent compromise. **Image quality:** The more pixels a digital camera can record, the higher its resolution, and the better the image quality. A 3-megapixel camera is required to make good 8x10 prints. **Flash:** Make sure that built-in flash can be manually turned off. Otherwise, flash functions very much as it does for conventional cameras. **Reaction time:** If you like to work quickly in a candid way, make sure that the time spent by the camera preparing for an exposure and downloading a picture is not excessive. **Types of memory:** More memory will allow you to store more pictures, but you may also purchase additional removable cards for cameras with a reduced maximum storage capacity. **Batteries:** Rechargeable NiMH or lithium batteries provide extra life for your camera. An AC adapter is useful for use inside or in the studio. External battery packs is another option. **The most common types of digital cameras are:** Point-and-shoot digital cameras, medium-priced digital compact cameras, professional digital SLR cameras with interchangeable lenses, digital backs that attach to medium-format cameras, and digital backs for 4x5-inch and 8x10-inch view cameras. Page 216 offers a more comprehensive description of each type.

Notes

10.3 TEST

FILL IN THE BLANKS

1 Digital imaging requires that you use either a digital camera or a ____________________ to convert your picture to a data file.

2 Digital cameras use a ____________________ instead of film to capture light emitted from a subject.

3 Digital images are usually stored on a ____________________ card.

4 A digital image is constructed of tiny ____________________ arranged in a grid.

5 An LCD ____________________ on digital cameras allow you to see images soon after they were captured.

6 A camera with a resolution of 1600X1200 pixels captures a total file size of 3.2 ____________________ for a color image.

7 ____________________ is a way of reducing the file size for storage.

8 You need ____________________ bits per pixel to display 256 colors in an image.

9 The quality of a digital image ____________________ with the number of pixels in the image.

10 The JPEG algorithm is considered a ____________________ compression method since it discards image data.

MULTIPLE CHOICE – CIRCLE ONE OR MORE

1 The LCD monitor on a digital camera usually allows you to:
- a. review all the pictures stored on the memory card.
- b. see exactly how the subject appears on the CCD.
- c. focus the image on the ground glass.

2 Due to the smaller size of the CCD compared to 35mm film,:
- a. lenses of the same focal length will appear longer on a digital camera.
- b. lenses of the same focal length will appear shorter on a digital camera.
- c. lenses of the same focal length will appear the same on a digital camera.

3 A digital exposure with a high ISO setting may:
- a. show increased grain in the highlights.
- b. display digital noise in the dark areas.
- c. produce banding.

4 Most advanced digital cameras have:
- a. a narrow exposure latitude.
- b. all the contrast grades, from 1-5.
- c. contrast controls.

5 With digital exposures, the most crucial part to expose for is the:

a. shadows.
b. midtones.
c. highlights.

6 The color balance for a particular light source is set on a digital camera by:

a. using color-correcting filters in front of the lens.
b. selecting the light source for your picture on a data panel menu.
c. manually changing the CCD to suit the color temperature of the light.

7 The term reaction time in digital photography may refer to:

a. the time elapsed between pressing the shutter and the actual exposure being made.
b. the time it takes for the camera to download the picture to the memory card.
c. the speed you use when physically pressing the shutter.

8 There are 1024 bytes in a:

a. bit.
b. kilobyte.
c. megabyte.

9 With a digital camera, you can:

a. review your picture immediately.
b. discard any pictures you don't like to free up space on the memory card.
c. set an ISO rating for each individual shot.

10 The number of pictures stored on a memory card can be controlled by:

a. setting a high or low image resolution.
b. choosing a file compression option.
c. storing only 1 bit per pixel for your color images.

Notes

10.4 PRACTICAL TIPS

Visualization

Visualize your technical decisions with a digital camera.

You will repeatedly hear the term visualization when you are dealing with photography. In the chapter on exposure, for instance, you are asked to compare the values in a scene to middle gray and make exposure compensations based on your visualization. Chapter 7 on printing suggests that you do a straight print and then visualize local changes in value that are later applied through dodging and burning. The concept of visualization comes to a culmination in the Zone System devised by Ansel Adams that is covered in chapter 15. According to this method, photography is not simply about mechanically securing a latent image that bears the direct imprint of a subject. Every step of the process (exposure, development, and printing) is used for an interpretive effect, so you could say that the image initially comes before the world it is intended to capture. Visualization in Zone System terms, then, means that the photographer sees the final image on the ground glass before embarking on a series of decisions that will translate this vision. With a digital camera, the idea of visualization to support technical choices is equally important, despite the immense flexibility of digital data. In addition to the usual options surrounding shutter speed and aperture settings used to shape the photograph, you also have to contend with image resolution and compression. To make informed choices about these settings, it is necessary to know the final use for the pictures. A resolution of 1600x1200, for instance, will capture a lot of useless data for an image intended to be sent as a tiny email attachment, and a resolution of 640x480 will only give you a detailed print that is about 2 inches tall. Contrast controls and color-balance settings add to this repertoire of choices. The LCD monitor found on many digital cameras is perhaps an extension of the persistent need for visualization in photography. What you visualize with your inner eye and what you finally see is now only an instant apart and subject to immediate revision.

Camera to digital darkroom

Dealing with the low resolution of affordable digital cameras.

Even advanced digital cameras that have a price tag of several thousand dollars currently only support resolutions of about 2400x1500 pixels. Some quick math will tell you that the biggest print of high quality (300dpi) such a camera can produce is only 8x5 inches. This is not exactly value for money, unless your images are destined for the Web or a publication printed on newspaper stock. The problem is that bicubic resampling of the data to increase the image size in an application like Photoshop is destructive to the file. Genuine Fractals, a Photoshop plug-in developed by the Altamira Group, offers a better solution to this problem. It employs a more intelligent algorithm when the computer calculates the new pixels (a process known as interpolation) that must be added to the image in order to make it larger. The dialog box on the right shows the resizing options offered by Genuine Fractals. More info can be found at www.altamira-group.com.

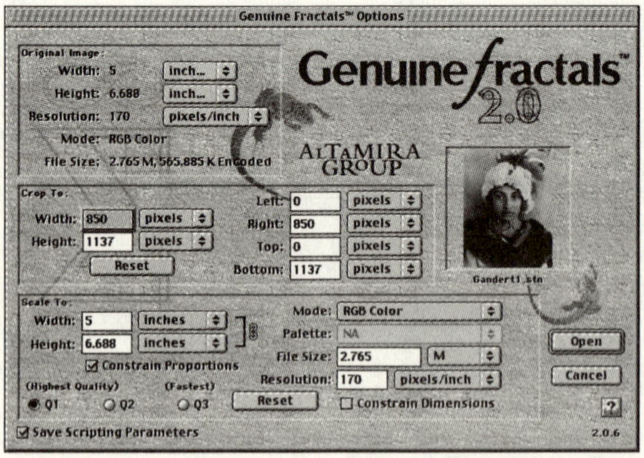

10.5 JOURNAL

10.5.1 DIGITAL CAMERA SETTINGS

The tables compiled below will allow you to work through the features of several digital cameras. If you do not own one, they may of course be used for equipment borrowed from school. An instruction manual might be a useful aid, but you can also find most of the information on the markings and menus of the camera itself. Expensive cameras will have many entries in each category, while cheaper models might not have all the features or only one or two settings.

CAMERA MAKE AND MODEL ▸	Olympus C-3030 Zoom									
Lens optical zoom range ▸	6.5mm to 19.5mm									
Lens digital zoom range ▸	1 - 2.5x									
Apertures ▸	2.8	4	5.6	8	11					
Shutter speeds ▸	800	500	250	125	60	30	15	8	>	16 s.
Exposure modes ▸	Program	S-Priority	A-priority	Manual	QT Movie					
ISO settings ▸	100	200	400							
Resolution settings ▸	2048x1546	1600x1200	1280x960	1024x768	640x480					
Compression settings ▸	JPEG -	settings	and	TIFF -	settings					
Color balance settings ▸	Daylight	Overcast	Tungsten	Fluorescent	(Auto)					
Memory card type ▸	SmartMedia up to 64 MB.									
Output ports ▸	Serial	USB	NTSC							

CAMERA MAKE AND MODEL ▸										
Lens optical zoom range ▸										
Lens digital zoom range ▸										
Apertures ▸										
Shutter speeds ▸										
Exposure modes ▸										
ISO settings ▸										
Resolution settings ▸										
Compression settings ▸										
Color balance settings ▸										
Memory card type ▸										
Output ports ▸										

CAMERA MAKE AND MODEL ▸

Lens optical zoom range ▸

Lens digital zoom range ▸

Apertures ▸

Shutter speeds ▸

Exposure modes ▸

ISO settings ▸

Resolution settings ▸

Compression settings ▸

Color balance settings ▸

Memory card type ▸

Output ports ▸

CAMERA MAKE AND MODEL ▸

Lens optical zoom range ▸

Lens digital zoom range ▸

Apertures ▸

Shutter speeds ▸

Exposure modes ▸

ISO settings ▸

Resolution settings ▸

Compression settings ▸

Color balance settings ▸

Memory card type ▸

Output ports ▸

Notes

11 DIGITAL DARKROOM

11.1 GLOSSARY

Bit (Binary digit) The smallest unit usable by a computer. There are 8 bits in a byte.

Bit depth The number of bits that are used to store a pixel's color information for display. The higher the bit depth, the more information can be stored, and the more colors can be displayed.

Bitmap The display of an image on the computer screen in a single layer of pixels mapped in a grid.

Byte A unit of digital data. There are 8 bits in a byte and 1024 bytes in a kilobyte.

CD - ROM (Compact Disc - Read Only Memory) A CD that stores digital files. Your computer needs a CD - ROM drive to read the disc.

Channel An image component that contains the pixel information for an individual color. Grayscale images have one channel. RGB images have three channels - red, green, and blue.

Color balance The software adjustment of color information in an image file so the colors in an image look either natural or enhanced.

Curves A Photoshop command for non-linear tonal adjustments in an image.

Digital camera A camera that uses a CCD instead of film to capture and record an image in digital form.

Digital image file A digital image is converted into a string of data and stored as a digital image file. The computer reads and translates the data into an image again.

Digital imaging Image-editing method where an image is transformed into digital data to be read and altered by a computer.

Dpi (Dots per inch) A unit used to measure the resolution of a printer or an imagesetter. ppi is the term used to describe the input resolution of a scanner and a bitmapped image.

File size The amount of data an image file contains. Usually expressed either in kilobytes (for small images) or megabytes (for large images).

EPS (Encapsulated PostScript) A file format used for images imported into a page-layout program such as Adobe InDesign or Quark Xpress.

GIF (Graphics Interchange Format) A file format used for displaying simple graphics or logos on the Internet.

Grayscale An image that contains black, white, and up to 256 shades of gray.

Hardware The components of a computer system responsible for the physical processing and display of data.

Histogram A graph showing the number of pixels at each level of brightness in an image. The histogram is used as a guide to perform non-linear adjustments of contrast in an image.

Indexed color A one-channel image mode that can contain up to 256 colors arranged in a table.

Interpolation	The recoloring of pixels to rebuild the image after its dimensions or resolution has been altered. Interpolation with a scanner uses software to add samples to the scan that were not present in the image.
JPEG	(Joint Photographic Experts Group) A compression algorithm (file format) for photographic images. It reduces the file size by discarding image data.
Kilobyte	A larger unit of digital data. There are 1024 bytes in a kilobyte and 1048576 bytes in a megabyte. The unit is often used to describe the size of a small computer file.
Layer	Essentially a division of image data into distinct and manageable portions. A layer in Photoshop allows you to work on a defined section of the image without disturbing data contained by the other layers.
Levels	A Photoshop command for tonal adjustments in an image with the graphical aid of a histogram. Non-linear.
Megabyte	A unit of digital data frequently used to describe the file size of digital imaging files. A megabyte contains 1048576 bytes.
Modem	A device that converts (modulates and demodulates) digital signals from your computer to analog signals that can be transmitted over the phone lines and vice versa.
Pixel	Short for picture element. The smallest unit in a digital image that can be displayed, changed, and stored. A digital image is made of tiny pixels arranged in a grid.
Ppi	(Pixels per inch) The term used to describe the resolution of a bitmapped image.
Photo CD	Usually refers to a commercial service where image files are scanned and put on a CD.
Photoshop	Short for Adobe Photoshop. The most common software application for digital imaging.
Printer	A digital output option that transfers the digital image to paper or film.
PSD	(Photoshop Document) The native Photoshop file format used to preserve the entire working space of this software package. Used while an image is still being worked on or if changes may be desirable at a later date.
RAM	(Random Access Memory) The system memory of a computer used to run applications, to process information, and for temporary storage.
Rasterize	The conversion of an object-oriented image (such as a Vector graphic) into a bitmapped image. All computer files are rasterized when they are printed.
Resolution	The amount of information in an image. It is measured in ppi (pixels per inch) for a digital image and a monitor display. The resolution of a printer is referred to as dpi (dots per inch), and the term lpi (lines per inch) is used for a halftone screen.
RGB	The three additive primary colors (red, green, and blue) are used to project color on a computer monitor. Also an image mode and working space in Adobe Photoshop.
Scanner	A device that reads and converts a paper photograph, a negative, or a slide into a digital file.
Selection	An area of an image in digital imaging that can be modified while the rest of the image remains unaffected. The boundary that defines a selection can be moved independently of its pixel content.
Software	Computer program used to manipulate data according to the user's directions. Adobe Photoshop is a common digital-imaging software package.
TIFF	(Tagged Image File Format) A common file format for bitmapped images.

11.2 SUMMARY

219 — **Digital darkroom**

Almost any result you can produce in a traditional darkroom – and some that you can't – can be achieved with the help of a personal computer: Image-editing software allows you to change an image in almost any way you like. **Digital imaging preserves quality from one generation of an image to another:** A digital image is a set of numbers. The image changes if the numbers change, but it remains the same if the numbers are not altered through software. **Regardless of how much you have manipulated a digital image, once finished you can print it now – or in six months, a year, or more and still get the same results from the original file:** The data will not change and the image is infinitely repeatable in the same configuration. **Digital imaging can simply enhance an image or radically change it:** Since you manipulate flexible data, there is really not limit to how you may tweak it and thereby the appearance of the image.

220 - 221 — **Digital imaging: An overview**

To understand digital imaging, compare it to conventional photography: Exposure can be compared to capture, and the translation of an image into a digitized form is the digital equivalent of recording the image on film. Software manipulations and output is comparable to the work traditionally done in the darkroom. **You won't need to purchase every part of the system yourself:** Most schools and universities have the necessary equipment, and you can also use professional service bureaus. **This chapter presumes that you are reasonably comfortable working with computers:** To perform digital imaging tasks, you first need a basic knowledge of the operating system of a computer and how to perform simple tasks such as opening and saving files. Please see page 220 for a breakdown of the components of a digital imaging system.

222 - 223 — **Scanning a photograph**

To capture an image, you have to get it into a digital form that a computer can use: You can either use a digital camera or a scanner to convert negatives, slides, or prints into a digital form. Film provides a better image quality than most digital cameras, so it is still widely used even by self-confirmed digital photographers. **Film scanners:** These work with transparencies and negatives; usually in the 35mm format but more expensive models accept large formats up to 4x5 inches. **Flatbed scanners:** Scan prints or other reproductions. Many have the option of a transparency adapter. **Drum scanner:** The best type of scanner, which comes at a hefty price. It scans negatives and slides for files with amazing image quality. **Scanning software controls the process:** It offers you control over how the image will be scanned. **If you don't have access to a scanner yourself:** You can scan your images at a service bureau. **Photo CDs:** Again, a commercial service. **If you are doing the scanning yourself:** You need to determine the scanner settings for resolution, size, and image values based on your final use for the image file. Page 223 shows a screen capture of Umax scanner software. Scanner software looks marginally different, but the controls are very similar.

222 — **Setting the quality of your scan**

First you need to determine how the image will be displayed: Always base your scan on the final image size and resolution. Once you have determined these, you can enter the right information into the scanner software. Some final display or print resolutions are:

Web	72 ppi.
Newspaper	150 ppi.
Photographic inkjet or dye-sublimation	300 ppi.
Glossy magazine, book	300 ppi.
Film recorder	600 ppi.

To avoid resampling the image, you need to capture a sufficient number of pixels in your original scan to support the final output. For example, if the final output is a 8x10-inch print at 300 ppi and your original negative is 4x5 inches, you need to scan at 600 ppi to get the desired number of pixels in the image. Once you have resized it, the file will fit the output requirements.

224 - 225 **The digital photograph: Image size, resolution, and file size**

Image size, resolution, and file size are important because these factors affect many aspects of digital imaging: The larger the file size, the more image data for the scanner or computer to process and store, and the slower the processing of the data. Resolution is a measure for how many pixels an image contains, and image size is a measure for how large the image will be at different resolutions. **What do you want to do with your print:** Always scan your image to the final output resolution and size. If this proves impossible, it is possible to resample the image. **The Image Size command in Photoshop lets you specify the final size of your photograph as well as its resolution and file size:** However, always save a copy of your raw scan in case you need to revert back to the beginning. Bending the image data repeatedly will eventually make it fall apart with disastrous results. **Resampling:** This allows you to reduce or increase the size and/or resolution of an image by discarding or adding pixels to the original file. For photographs, resampling is seldom desirable as it causes image deterioration. Try to scan your images with the correct number of pixels and resize them without resampling. Pages 224 - 225 shows the Photoshop dialog box for Image Size and its use.

226 - 227 **Working memory, storage, and transmission**

Working with digital photographs requires considerable computer memory: The random-access memory, or RAM, on your computer is used to manipulate and edit digital images. Aim for an amount of RAM that is at least three times the largest file sizes you will be working with. **Storing a digital image keeps it available for later use:** You can easily store your images on the hard drive of your computer, but it quickly fills up with large digital image files. **External storage devices:** The best options for large digital images include Zip disks (100 or 250 MB), Jaz cartridges (1 GB), CD-ROMs (650-700MB), or DVD-RAM (5.2 GB double sided). **You can create a database within which you can store, index, search for, and quickly retrieve images:** Cataloging software can help you with this. **When you save a file from a digital camera or scanner, you will get a choice of different formats:** The most common file formats for digital imaging are:

PSD (.psd)	Photoshop Document format retains all the information, channels, masks, and layers of an image. Used while you are working on an image in Photoshop or are likely to return to it later for more work.
JPEG (.jpg)	Compresses an image by discarding pixels that it deems unnecessary for viewing of the image. Used for photographs on the Web or for archiving of digital images.
GIF (.gif)	A web format used for graphics with simple blocks of color. Fading in favor of PNG.
TIFF (.tif)	A common format for page-layout programs.
EPS (.eps)	Frequently used for page-layout programs.

There are several ways to transfer an image from one device to another, such as from a computer to a printer: These include removable storage media, modems, and networks.

228 - 229 **Your work area and tools**

The tools and commands used to manipulate an image are part of image-editing software: Tools are displayed on the screen as small icons or as word commands in pull-down menus. **One of the most important commands is called Undo:** Found under Edit > Undo, it reverts back to the step before the last action. The History palette allows you to undo a number of steps specified in the preferences. **There are usually two or three ways of accomplishing almost anything with digital-imaging software:** Some achieve the same result, but there are often differences that make one method preferable to another for a certain operation. Keep in mind that it is possible to destroy the image data, so save a copy of the raw scan. Pages 228 - 229 introduces you the work area and tools of Adobe Photoshop 6.

230 - 231 **Selection tools**

Selection tools let you extend photographic techniques: They define an area so you can edit it locally without affecting the rest of the image. There is no limit to how small or large the area might be or what shape it can assume. **The first step is to learn how to use one or more of the tools that select an area:** The tools all serve the same function, but they select pixels in different ways. You choose the tool and method best suited to the area you wish to select. By choosing Select > Inverse you can reverse the selection, which is worth keeping in mind if it is easier to select parts of the image surrounding your intended selection area. The selection tools in Photoshop include the Marquee, Magic Wand, Lasso, and Pen tools. The Quick Mask mode is another method of masking off parts of an image for selection with one of the drawing and painting tools. Please see pages 230 – 231 for illustrations of these tools in action.

232 – 233 **Preparation: Repositioning and cropping**

You can crop any digital image, whether it was scanned or imported from a digital camera: Cropping simply means that you discard all the pixels outside the cropped area. If an image was scanned crooked, you can rotate it with the Image > Rotate Canvas command. **Slides, negatives, and images from digital cameras sometimes must be rotated:** This might be an aesthetic decision or a correction. **The cropping tool:** Select the area to be cropped and rotate the selection to straighten the image simultaneously if necessary. Page 232 shows the cropping tool in action.

234 – 235 **Adjusting the image overall: Adjusting color balance**

There are several ways to adjust color balance with image-editing software: Choosing Image > Adjust > Variations allows you to see several versions of potential changes simultaneously. Hue is the color of an object, saturation refers to the purity of the color, and brightness is the lightness or darkness of the color. You set these options when you adjust the color balance for shadows, midtones, and highlights (see page 235). **More exact changes:** Other options include the Color Balance and Hue/Saturation commands under Image > Adjust. It is preferable to make all these changes on an adjustment layer. Please see 11.4 Practical tips below.

236 - 237 **Making tonal adjustments**

How do you control the lightness, darkness, or contrast of an image in the digital darkroom: The most obvious command is Image > Adjust > Brightness/Contrast, but you must NEVER EVER use this for the reasons explained in 11.4 Practical tips below.

There are other more precise controls of brightness and contrast in the Image > Adjust menu: These include Levels and Curves. Levels offers a graphical representation, a histogram, of the distribution of tones in the image, which is a useful aid in making tonal adjustments. Levels also allow you to conveniently set the white and black point for highlights and shadows. See these pages in the textbook for detailed instructions.

238 - 241 **Using layers**

With layers you can combine one or more images: Using the Layers palette, you can also select one layer and work on this without affecting the other layers (parts of the image). Effects and adjustments can also be applied to individual layers. **Layers are the ultimate Undo command:** By adding an image or adjustments on a new layer, you can keep or discard it without affecting the rest of the image. **This page and the following two pages show how to make composites using layers:** The methods include simply moving one image onto another with the Move tool, merging images by selecting parts of an image and moving it to another on a new layer, and using a layer to mask parts of the layer underneath it when combining images. Pages 238-240 illustrate these techniques step by step. **Working in multiple layers creates large files:** When you are finally done with an image, flatten it to reduce the file size before saving.

242 – 243 **Special effects: Retouching and other adjustments**

Adjustments such as retouching can be tedious with conventional photographs: With digital imaging, you can retouch your image once and save the changes in an image file. There are other ways of enhancing the image explored on these two pages: **Repairs and spotting:** Easily performed with the Clone Stamp tool. Try to reduce the opacity to build up gradually. **Dodging and burning:** There are dedicated tools for this in Photoshop, but 11.4 Practical tips below gives you a much better method. **Sharpen with Unsharp Mask:** Found under Filter > Sharpen > Unsharp Mask, this filter increases the apparent sharpness of an image by increasing the contrast between adjacent pixels. Excessive sharpening creates artifacts. **Add blur:** You can use the Gaussian blur filter on parts of your image for an effect similar to extremely narrow depth of field.

244 – 245 **Converting color to black and white**

Among the many processes the computer has simplified is the conversion of color images to black and white: In the darkroom, you usually have to use a special black-and-white printing paper to produce decent prints from a color negative. With digital imaging, it is easy to convert a color image into a monochrome equivalent. **The simplest way to convert a color photograph to black and white is to select Image > Mode > Grayscale:** This conversion of image mode actually discards all the color information, which is not always desirable. The method offers no control over the translation of color into black and white. It is also possible to desaturate the colors of the image until it appears black and white. **Like a color film image, a digital color image is composed of three primary colors, red, green, and blue:** Please ignore the description in the textbook, and mix the three channels in Image > Adjust > Channel Mixer. Check the tiny monochrome box and adjust the three channels until you find a mix with the right contrast and amount of detail in shadows and highlights. After completing the mix, you can convert the RGB image to the grayscale mode if you wish. See 11.4 Practical tips below.

245 **Filters for special effects**

Filters are one approach to creating special effects in digital imaging: Instant effects like filters quickly wear off, though. Try to invent your own creative solutions, and generally shy away from package deals like the filter effects. Of course, there could be ways of using filters creatively, too.

246 – 247 **Printing and display: Printers**

There are many types of printers that will bring a digital image to life on paper: Most demand special papers and inks to achieve truly photographic prints. For best results, use the materials supplied by the manufacturer of your printer. **All color dyes fade:** The longevity of inkjet materials is rapidly improving and the market is currently swarming with archival inks. **Printers fall in two categories:** They either produce a series of small dots to convey a continuous tone or overlay varying amounts of ink to build a color. **Inkjet printers:** These spray a fine mist of inks in 4 or 6 colors onto the paper. Capable of producing photographic quality prints. **Black-and-white photographers:** Piezography is a specialized printing method for black-and-white prints with inkjet printers. It demands special ink cartridges and software. **Laser printers:** Cheaper to operate but not really suitable for fine photographic output. **Dye-sublimation printers:** These are expensive printers, which only support small paper sizes. The print quality, however, is outstanding. **High-performance film recorders:** Output image files onto continuous tone film that can be printed conventionally.

246 **Monitor calibration**

You may need to calibrate your monitor and check the settings on your printer or scanner: The goal is to calibrate your digital imaging system of scanner, monitor, and printer so you can work on the presumption that what you see is what you get. The way your computer system and software takes care of this is slightly different on PC and Mac platforms. Please consult specialist literature on this topic.

248 **The Internet: Resource and gallery**

Photographers are increasingly using the internet: It contains a wealth of information, mailing lists, and newsgroups concerned with photography. You can also display your own photographs on the Internet with your own Web page. **The World Wide Web is the part of the Internet that shows pictures:** The www, which comes to you through browser software, now has the capability to display text, graphics, photographs, sound, and video. **How do you get on the Internet:** Schools usually have a direct connection. They are connected to a computer, which is a part of the Internet. You can also use a modem and the telephone lines to access the Internet via a dial-up connection. Your computer dials another computer, which is part of the Internet, and transmits data over the phone line. The ISP (Internet Service Provider) or your school owns the computer you dial up and often charge a fee for usage. To view and navigate the Internet, you use a browser such as Microsoft Internet Explorer or Netscape Navigator. **You can create your own Web page:** You need space on a server (a computer permanently hooked up to the Internet) to store your page, and the ability to either write HTML code or use one of the many software packages intended for Web authoring. In addition, it is helpful to know how files can be transferred over the Internet using the FTP protocol. **You must change your photo files into a form usable on the Internet:** Photographs are displayed in the JPEG format. It allows you to weigh file size versus image quality to balance the download time with how your image will finally appear. The GIF format is intended for simpler forms with less than 256 colors.

Keep your file sizes small: Larger images take longer to download, and viewers of your Web page will not wait very long for your photographs to appear. It is better to use small images of high quality than large images of reduced quality.

249 **CD-ROMs**

What is a CD-ROM: Compact Disc – Read Only Memory. It is a CD than can display data written on it, but new data can not be added to the disc. **Advantages of a CD–ROM:** Its large storage capacity (650-700MB), low cost, protected environment, and relative permanence makes the CD a great way to distribute or store your images. **CD-ROMs are popular because they can be multimedia and interactive:** Multimedia implies a combination of more than one medium, for example photographs and text. Interactivity demands user input for a narrative to progress. **Make your own CD-ROM:** You must learn a software application such as Macromedia Director to program the CD. Another option is to write the presentation in HTML code, distribute it on a CD, and let users view your photographs in their Web browser. The box on page 249 describes the process and some of the software applications that can be used to make a CD-ROM.

250 - 251 **Ethics and digital imaging**

Are there times when an image should not be changed, even though it is possible to do so: When it is impossible to detect changes to a photograph, it raises questions about the veracity of all photographs. Digital imaging has thus come to be seen as a threat to photography, even as the death of the qualities associated with the analog photograph. **Advertisers often take considerable leeway with illustrations:** We have come to expect that advertising exaggerates and takes certain liberties with photographs. **Photojournalists usually follow fairly strict rules concerning photographic alterations:** By applying certain standards as to what constitutes a "real" photograph, this group hopes to continue presenting us with the reality it produces and conveys. Of course, the news industry relies heavily upon the analog relationship between subject and object established by photography, and it is consequently most threatened by the influx of digital imaging. **As the use of digital imaging increases, will photography lose its reputation for accurate representation of reality:** The question is rather if photography was not always a creation or manipulation rather than a simple "window on the world". **Working photographers are also concerned about financial matters:** Since there is no loss of quality in translation with digital files and because they are easily copied, copyright issues and ownership debates have reached a new level with the emergence of digital imaging. **Pedro Meyer, for many years a documentary photographer, found digital imaging gave him the freedom to tell stories, though not in the traditional documentary way:** Meyer pioneered the documentary versus digital debate with the publication of his book and CD-ROM "Truths and Fictions" in 1995. Look for it in your library.

252 - 253 **Enhancing reality**

With digital imaging, you can control your photograph in ways that may not be evident to anyone but yourself: They do not break the conventions of traditional camera images. It is this facility that has put the "truth to appearance" of photography into question.

254 - 255 **Going beyond reality**

Digital imaging can also step beyond reality: Heavy manipulation tends to leave the photography behind in favor of a more graphic and illustrative approach. See these last two pages for some colorful examples.

11.3 TEST

FILL IN THE BLANKS

1 When an image is scanned, it important to have decided on the final output ____________________ and print size.

2 An image displayed on the Internet should have a resolution of ____________________ ppi.

3 Resolution is a measure for how many ____________________ an image contains.

4 Resampling can reduce the image size and resolution by ____________________ pixels from the image.

5 It is not recommended to ____________________ the image size or resolution through resampling.

6 The ____________________, or Photoshop Document, format allows for the greatest flexibility when working on an image file.

7 The JPEG format is the best choice when significant ____________________ of the image is required.

8 Photoshop ____________________ all serve the same basic function of manipulating the value of pixels in an image, but they perform this task is different ways.

9 The ____________________ command allows you to return to the state before the last action.

10 The Lasso is considered a ____________________ tool.

MULTIPLE CHOICE – CIRCLE ONE OR MORE

1	The Magic Wand tool selects pixels of:	a.	contrasting colors.
		b.	similar color and value.
		c.	opposite colors and values.
2	Hue is the:	a.	purity of a color.
		b.	color of an object.
		c.	brightness of a color.
3	The histogram is a graph:	a.	for the digital noise level in an image.
		b.	for the distribution of tonal values in an image.
		c.	for the number of pixels in an image.
4	In a high-contrast image, the columns in a histogram are tallest:	a.	in the middle of the graph.
		b.	toward both ends of the graph.
		c.	only at the bottom edge of the graph.

5	The eyedropper tools found in the dialog box for image adjustments with Levels:	a. allow you to select and set the highlight and shadow values. b. remove digital noise from the image so you can see it clearer. c. add clarifying pixels to the image in areas where they are employed.
6	Layers in Photoshop allow you to:	a. organize and work efficiently with complex composite images. b. apply adjustments and changes to an image on a layer to leave the original intact. c. control the opacity of layered elements in an image.
7	To digitally remove dust and specks in an image, the best tool for the job is:	a. the Burn tool. b. the Clone Stamp tool. c. the Paintbrush tool.
8	The Unsharp Mask filter has the effect of:	a. blurring an image for a narrow depth of field effect. b. extending the depth of field in an image. c. altering the contrast between adjacent pixels in an image for a sharper appearance.
9	Converting a color image file to black and white is best done by:	a. tweaking the color settings on your monitor. b. mixing the red, green, and blue color channels before converting to Grayscale mode. c. dodge and burn with black as a foreground color and white as a background color.
10	Photographs on the Internet are displayed in the:	a. TIFF format. b. JPEG format. c. EPS format.

Notes

11.4 PRACTICAL TIPS

Scan tips

Some suggestions for the best possible scans.

- Use an original negative, transparency or print of good quality. Scanners can only record what is there from the outset.
- Scan at the appropriate resolution for your intended output size and resolution to avoid resampling the image. Use the scanner software or Photoshop to determine your correct scan resolution.
- Limit scans to the optical resolution of the scanner for photographs. Interpolation at higher resolutions simply means that the scanner software is adding pixels to your image to make it bigger.
- Adjust tones and color balance as best you can with the scanner software. Information lost in the scan can not be recovered later.
- Scan black and white images with a color setting to increase the bit-depth. The added information produces a better scan, and you can discard the extra bit-depth later.
- Align your scanning material perfectly on the flatbed or in the transparency carrier. It is best to avoid rotating the canvas in Photoshop for alignment. Try both, and you'll notice a difference.
- Sharpen the image in Photoshop after the scan by using Unsharp Mask, rather than using the sharpening tools in the scanner software. They usually offer less control and can be inferior.
- Be aware of Newton rings. If you use a glass carrier to hold your negative or transparency materials, you might notice small concentric circles in your scanned image. These are caused by light bouncing between two shiny surfaces. Try to separate the film a small distance from the glass.

Contrast control

Use non-linear adjustments to alter contrast in your image.

Adobe Photoshop offers several ways of altering the contrast in your image. Unlike traditional processing and printing techniques, digital imaging allows you to control image values locally with outstanding control, but to benefit from this ability you must avoid linear adjustments at all times. Linear contrast control moves all the values in your image either towards dark or light, and the danger is that you move the shadows or the highlights off the tonal scale so they print as pure black or pure white. This phenomenon is known as "clipping". The histograms below show the before (left) and after (right) effect of a 15 percent increase in contrast using the Image > Adjust > Brightness/Contrast command. Notice how many values have turned either black or white without texture and detail. Commands such as Brightness/Contrast or Auto Levels perform linear contrast adjustments and are likely to clip the tonal values in your image. Do not under any circumstances apply them to adjust contrast in your photographs. Use Levels or Curves instead to make non-linear corrections.

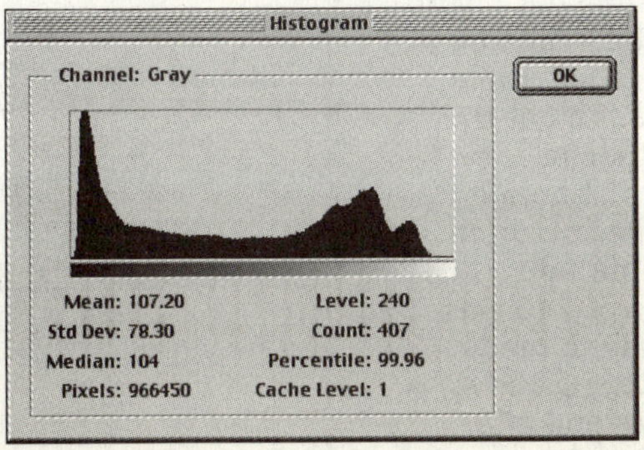

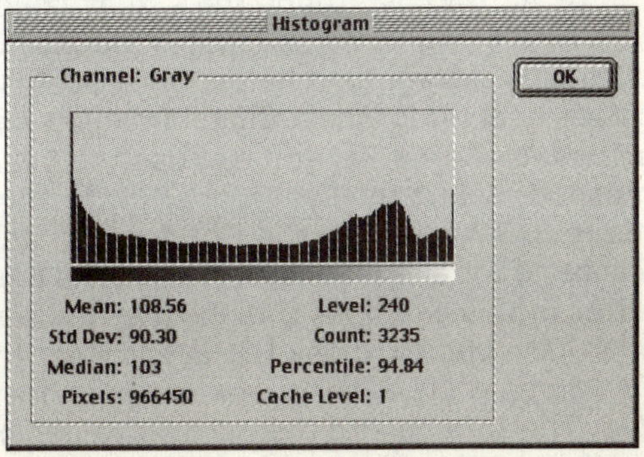

Adjustment layer

Use an adjustment layer to preserve the image data.

Your image will rapidly deteriorate if you keep changing the actual image data, so it is best to apply all changes on separate layers until you are completely satisfied. Even simple contrast controls are best done this way. To adjust the contrast in your image on a layer go to Layer > New Adjustment Layer > and then choose your adjustment method from the submenu.

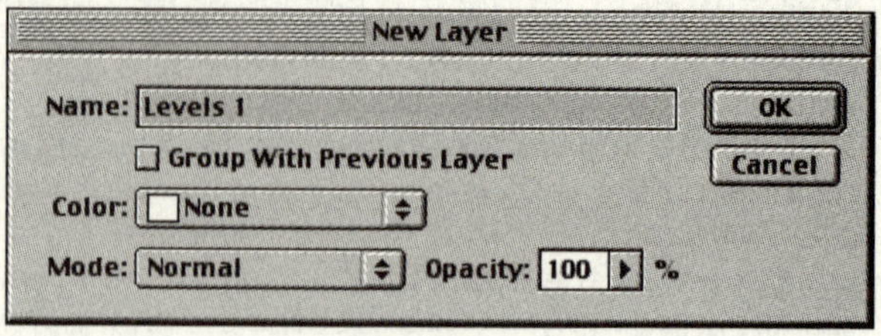

In this example, Levels was chosen as the adjustment option. A dialog box asking you to name the new layer and set its color, mode, and opacity will pop up. The settings in the illustration above are fine. Once you have clicked OK, the actual dialog box for the Levels will appear. You can now adjust the contrast exactly as you would if you had chosen this command through the Image > Adjust > Levels route explained in the textbook. Set your white and black points using the eyedropper tools, and finally apply the changes by clicking OK.

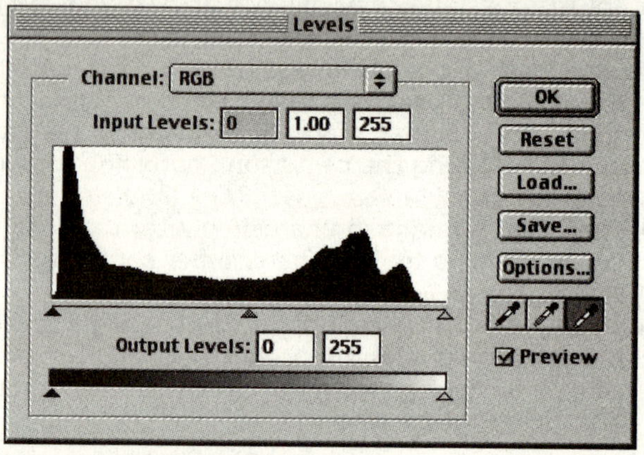

The beauty of using this method is that your contrast change will show up as a layer in the Layers palette. The name you gave it, Levels 1, and the histogram icon identifies it. By double-clicking on the layer, the Levels will reappear and you can adjust them again if necessary. Best of all, the layer can be discarded to leave the original image completely untouched by your adjustments.

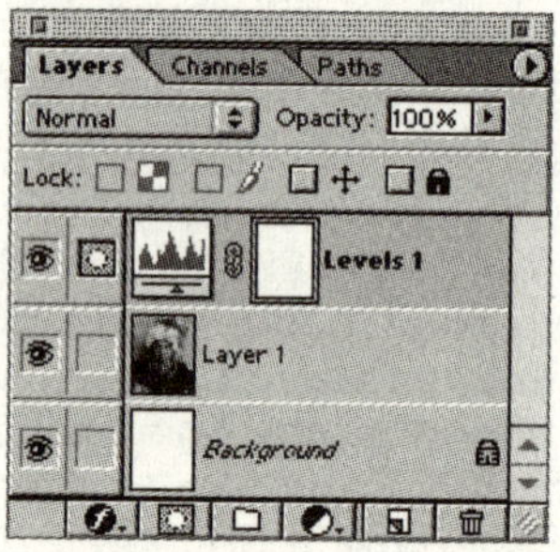

Digital light meter

Use the Eyedropper tool as a digital light meter.

It can be hard to determine the actual value of tones in your image simply by looking at the computer monitor. Placing the image on a neutral gray background helps, but visual inspection is not really accurate enough for most digital imaging applications. To get the exact value of an area, you can use the Eyedropper tool in Photoshop. Select the Eyedropper in the toolbox, set the area it reads to 3x3 Average in the Options bar, and place the cursor on your image to take readings. The results show up in the Info palette. In this example, a highlight area with a value of 240 was chosen. You can even use the Eyedropper tool this way to read tonal values while a dialog box, such as the one for Levels above, is active. The Info palette then shows values both before and after the adjustments you have currently set.

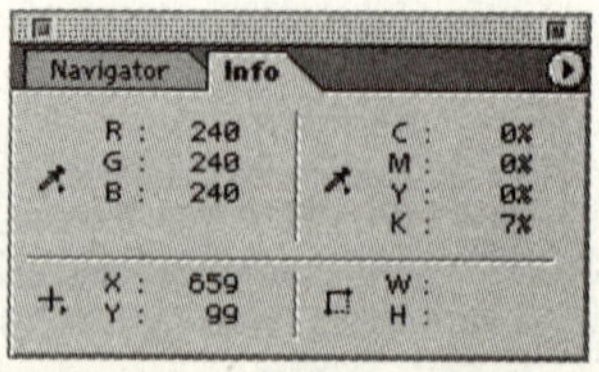

Color conversion

Use the Channel Mixer to convert your color images into black and white.

Every color image consists of three channels – red, green, and blue. These are mixed in varying proportions according to the data contained by each channel to display all colors on your monitor. You can take full advantage of this when you convert a color image to black and white. Choose Image > Adjust > Channel Mixer from the menu and a dialog box like the one on the right will appear. Check the Monochrome box to see how your image will appear in black and white, and slide the settings on the three channels until you have achieved exactly the tonal range and contrast you would like to see. The benefit of this method is that it offers complete control of the conversion without having to tweak and implicitly destroy the image data afterwards.

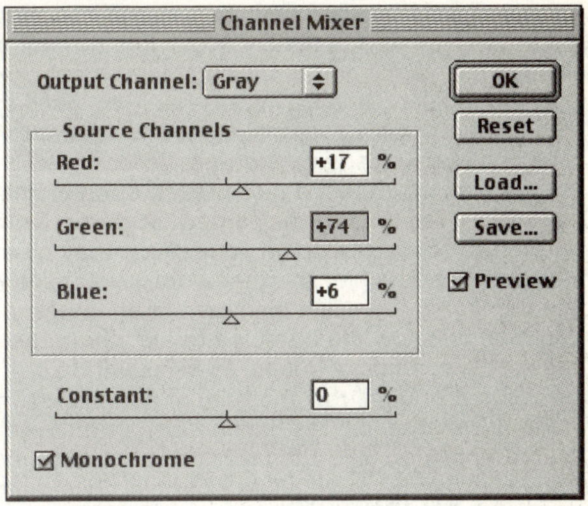

Burning and dodging

Perform burning and dodging on a separate layer.

There are special burning and dodging tools supplied in the Photoshop Toolbox, but they are frankly far inferior to the method outlined here. To avoid destroying the image data and allow for the correction of mistakes, you should perform local tonal adjustments on a separate layer. Select Layer > New > Layer from the menu and a dialog box like the one on the right will appear. The following options are crucial: Select Soft Light from the Mode menu and check the Fill with Soft-Light-neutral color (50% gray) box.

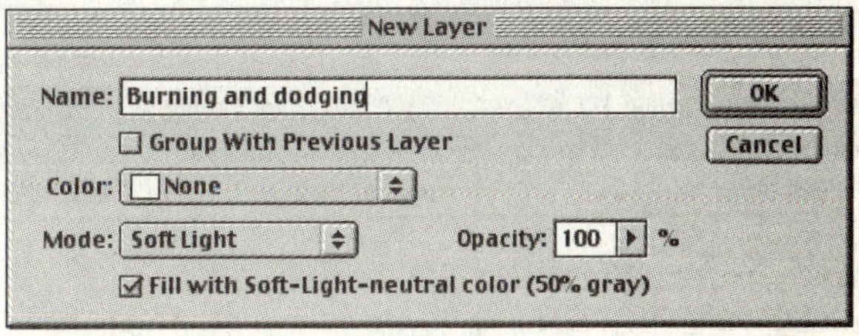

You will not notice a change to your image, but if you look at the Layers Palette, the new layer, named Burning and dodging in this case, has appeared and it is filled with 50% gray. Click on the layer to select it. To burn, you simply select a foreground color darker than 50% gray (RGB 128, 128, 128) and then paint or draw on the layer with any of the Photoshop tools designed for this. To dodge, you select a foreground color lighter than 50% gray and then use the tool of your choice to lighten an area. How much darker or lighter than 50% gray your foreground color is determines the amount of burning or dodging. Changes are visible on the image as you work. This method gives you outstanding control, and you can customize your tools for a specific job, from one pixel to the whole image. It also leaves the image data intact, and the new layer can be discarded or reworked at any time before you are completely satisfied and ready to finally flatten the image.

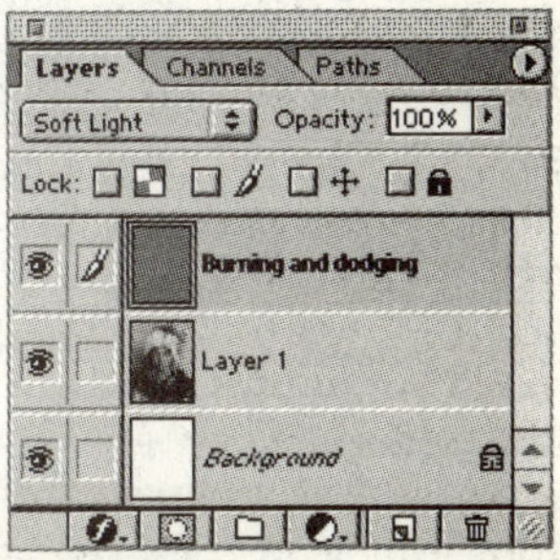

11.5 JOURNAL

11.5.1 SCAN DIARY

When you work on the computer, all the information you need with regards to your equipment and any image files is readily accessible through the machine itself. The files and folders it displays form such an organized environment that it perceptively keeps everything you need in an immaculate array. There is really no need to keep separate records of any kind. But anyone who owns a personal computer knows that the desktop is often littered with scattered icons and that underlying storage devices quickly fill up with junk data. The appearance of order is very often just a nice presentation of chaos. In the planning stages of a digital image, it is easy to fall prey to the somewhat deceptive neatness and flexibility of the computer system. As scans pile up on your disks, they must have a resolution that directly relates to the final output of the file. In other words, you have to plan ahead for every decision you make in digital imaging to import elements of an image with the highest quality possible. The brief scan diaries below are intended to aid you in the organization and execution of the initial stages of a composite image. Low-resolution scans are sometimes used when you have not yet secured original raw material or had access to the best equipment. Simply resample the image, insert the low-res file on a separate layer, and continue working on other aspects of your composition until the layer can be substituted for the final scan. The low-res files named *background* below serve as an example. Several versions were tried before a final background was selected and scanned at a high resolution. Images on the computer may seem infinitely moldable, but keep in mind that all resampling of image data is destructive if you are aiming for a high-quality photographic expression.

IMAGE/PROJECT TITLE ▸	*The usual suspect*	
Final output method ▾	Final output size ▾	Final output resolution ▾
Ink jet print	*8x10 inches*	*300 dpi*

HIGH-RES SCANS						
File name ▾	File format ▾	Pixel dimensions H/W ▾		Resolution ▾	Size H/W ▾	
large-dog	*.psd*	750	1200	300	2.5	4
small-dog	*.psd*	600	900	300	2	3
body	*.psd*	1200	2400	300	4	8
background	*.psd*	2400	3000	300	8	10

LOW-RES SCANS – Resampled before inserted on a layer in the final image.						
File name ▾	File format ▾	Pixel dimensions H/W ▾		Resolution ▾	Size H/W ▾	
Lsmall-dog	*.psd*	300	450	300	1	1.5
Lbackground	*.psd*	1200	1500	300	4	5
Lbackground2	*.psd*	1200	1500	300	4	5
Lbackground3	*.psd*	1200	1500	300	4	5

IMAGE/PROJECT TITLE ▸		
Final output method ▾	Final output size ▾	Final output resolution ▾

HIGH-RES SCANS

File name ▾	File format ▾	Pixel dimensions H/W ▾		Resolution ▾	Size H/W ▾	

LOW-RES SCANS - Resampled before inserted on a layer in the final image.

File name ▾	File format ▾	Pixel dimensions H/W ▾		Resolution ▾	Size H/W ▾	

IMAGE/PROJECT TITLE ▸		
Final output method ▾	Final output size ▾	Final output resolution ▾

HIGH-RES SCANS

File name ▾	File format ▾	Pixel dimensions H/W ▾		Resolution ▾	Size H/W ▾	

LOW-RES SCANS - Resampled before inserted on a layer in the final image.

File name ▾	File format ▾	Pixel dimensions H/W ▾		Resolution ▾	Size H/W ▾	

11.5.2 PHOTOGRAPHY SITES ON THE INTERNET

The Internet is a vast resource for photography. All these sites can be found as hyperlinks on the Companion Website developed for Barbara London and John Upton's Photography – 7th ed.

Archives / Collections

This list contains sites for archives and collections with substantial holdings of photographs. They usually offer some images online, but keep in mind that the screen seldom does a traditional photograph justice. Visit an archive or collection to fully appreciate the material qualities of their photographs.

Bibliotheque Nationale de France	http://www.bnf.fr/institution/anglais/estampgb.htm
Burns Archive	http://www.burnsarchive.com
California Heritage Collection	http://sunsite.berkeley.edu/CalHeritage
Denver Public Library	http://www.denver.lib.co.us/
George Eastman House	http://www.eastman.org
Harry Ransom Center	http://www.lib.utexas.edu/hrc/photography/
Library of Congress	http://www.lcweb.loc.gov/rr/print
New York Public Library	http://www.nypl.org/research/chss/spe/art/photo/photo.html
Polaroid Collection	http://www.polaroid.com/studio/exhibit/select3/index.html
Smithsonian	http://nmaa-ryder.si.edu/collections/
The Women in Photography	http://www.sla.purdue.edu/WAAW/Palmquist/Gallery.html
Zonezero	http://www.zonezero.com

Books

The list contains online photographic bookstores and publishers. Even if you can't physically handle the books, these sites are great for browsing. New titles are often listed well in advance of publication.

amazon.com	http://www.amazon.com
Arena Editions	http://www.arenaed.com
Barnes and Nobles	http://www.barnesandnoble.com
Bookfinder	http://www.bookfinder.com
Peachpit Press	http://www.peachpit.com
Photo Eye	http://www.photoeye.com
Prentice Hall	http://www.prenhall.com
Scalo Verlag	http://www.scalo.com
Twin Palms Press	http://www.twinpalms.com

Centers

These are centers for photography with an extensive agenda. They may exhibit work, offer artist's residencies, publish books and catalogs, collect photographs, offer degrees or workshops, and arrange events. Visit their sites to learn more about them.

Center for Creative Photography	http://www.creativephotography.org
Center for Photographic Art	http://www.photography.org
Center for Photography Woodstock	http://www.cpw.org
Friends of Photography	http://www.friendsofphotography.org
Houston Center for Photography	http://www.hcponline.org
International Center for Photography	http://www.icp.org
Light Factory	http://www.lightfactory.org
Light Work	http://www.lightwork.org
Photographic Resource Center	http://web.bu.edu/PRC/
Visual Studies Workshop	http://www.vsw.org

Education

The universities and schools on this list all have well established photography programs. The links lead to the homepage for each institution, and you can navigate to the photography department from there. Most sites give you an overview of degrees offered and some examples of faculty and student work.

Academy of Art College, San Francisco	http://www.academyart.edu
Arizona University	http://www.arizona.edu
Arizona State University	http://www.asu.edu
Art Center School of Design	http://www.artcenter.edu
Brooks Institute	http://www.brooks.edu
CalArts	http://www.calarts.edu
California State University, Fullerton	http://www.art.fullerton.edu
Cranbrook Academy of Art	http://www.cranbrook.edu
Indiana University	http://www.indiana.edu
International Center of Photography	http://www.icp.org
Maryland Institute	http://www.mica.edu
University of New Mexico	http://www.unm.edu/~finearts

Northern Arizona University	http://www.nau.edu
Ohio University	http://www.ohiou.edu
Parsons School of Design	http://www.parsons.edu
Pennsylvania State University	http://www.psu.edu
Pratt Institute	http://www.pratt.edu
Rhode Island School of Design	http://www.risd.edu
Rochester Institute of Technology	http://www.rit.edu
San Francisco Art Institute	http://www.sfai-art.com
Savannah College of Art and Design	http://www.scad.edu
School of Visual Arts	http://www.schoolofvisualarts.edu
School of the Art Institute, Chicago	http://www.artic.edu
Syracuse University	http://www.syr.edu
Temple University	http://www.temple.edu
Tisch School of the Arts / NYU	http://www.nyu.edu/tisch
University of California, Davis	http://www.ucdavis.edu
University of California, Irvine	http://www.cwis.uci.edu
University of California, Los Angeles	http://www.ucla.edu
University of California, San Diego	http://www.ucsd.edu
University of Illinois, Chicago	http://www.uic.edu
University of Illinois, Urbana-Champaign	http://www.art.uiuc.edu
University of Washington	http://net.art.washington.edu
Visual Studies Workshop	http://www.vsw.org
Washington University	http://www.artsci.wustl.edu
Yale University	http://www.yale.edu

Electronic media

Sites under this heading include the best or worst of Internet art. They do not address photography directly, but offer a crucial insight into the electronic environment of the digital image. Rhizome is a good place to start.

adaweb	http://adaweb.walkerart.org
Backspace	http://www.backspace.org
Easylife	http://www.easylife.org
Guggenheim Museum	http://www.guggenheim.org
Intelligent Agent	http://www.intelligentagent.com
Irational	http://www.irational.org
Jodi	http://www.jodi.org
Ljudmila	http://www.ljudmila.org
nettime	http://www.nettime.org
Potatoland	http://www.potatoland.org
Rhizome	http://www.rhizome.org
RTmark	http://www.rtmark.com
Superbad	http://www.superbad.com
Teleportacia	http://www.teleportacia.org
Turbulence	http://www.turbulence.org
Whitney Museum	http://www.whitney.org

Equipment

The list contains manufacturers of traditional photographic equipment, digital-imaging equipment, and some computer software companies with particular relevance to digital photography. You will find information about the products they offer on these sites.

Adobe	http://www.adobe.com
Agfa	http://www.agfaphoto.com
Beseler	http://www.beseler-photo.com
Bogen	http://www.bogenphoto.com
Bronica	http://www.tamron.com
Canon	http://www.usa.canon.com
Contax	http://www.contaxcameras.com
Epson	http://www.epson.com
Fuji	http://www.fujifilm.com
Genuine Fractals	http://www.altamira-group.com
Hasselblad	http://www.hasselblad.com
Ilford	http://www.ilford.com
Kodak	http://www.kodak.com
Konica	http://www.konica.com
Leaf	http://www.sinarbron.com
Leica	http://www.leica.com

LowePro	http://www.lowepro.com
Macromedia	http://www.macromedia.com
Mamiya	http://www.mamiya.com
Minolta	http://www.minolta.com
Nikon USA	http://www.nikonusa.com
Olympus	http://www.olympusamerica.com
Pentax	http://www.pentax.com
Phase one	http://www.phaseone.com
Photoflex	http://www.photoflex.com
Pinhole	http://www.pinhole.com
Polaroid	http://www.polaroid.com
PrintFile	http://www.printfile.com
Ricoh	http://www.ricoh.co.jp
Sekonic	http://www.sekonic.com
Sinar	http://www.sinarbron.com
Tamron	http://www.tamron.com
Tenba	http://www.tenba.com
Toyo	http://www.toyoview.com
Vivid Details	http://www.vividdetails.com
Vivitar	http://www.vivitar.co.uk/
Yashica	http://www.yashica.com

Equipment / Retail

These are equipment retailers with comprehensive sites. Browse their online stores to learn more about products you are interested in or to make price comparisons.

Abbey Camera	http://www.abbeycamera.com
B & H Photovideo	http://www.bhphotovideo.com
Bostick & Sullivan	http://www.bostick-sullivan.com
Calumet	http://www.calumetphoto.com
Focal Point	http://www.fpointinc.com
Freestyle	http://www.freestylesalesco.com
KEH	http://www.keh.com
Light Impressions	http://www.lightimpressionsdirect.com
Photographer's Formulary	http://www.photoformulary.com
Photoshopper	http://www.photoshopper.com

Galleries

This list of links offers a small selection of photography galleries. Their sites will usually offer examples of the work they exhibit and a list of the photographers they represent.

Alan Klotz/Photocollect, New York, NY	http://www.photocollect.com
Edward Carter, New York, NY	http://www.edwardcartergallery.com
Edwynn Houk, New York, NY	http://www.houkgallery.com
G.Gibson, Seattle, WA	http://www.halcyon.com/ggibson
Halsted Gallery, Birmingham, MI	http://www.halstedgallery.com
Howard Greenberg, New York, NY	http://www.howardgreenberg.com
Jane Corkin, Toronto, Canada	http://www.janecorkin.com
Janet Borden, New York, NY	http://www.janetbordeninc.com
John Stevenson, New York, NY	http://www.johnstevenson-gallery.com
Laurence Miller, New York, NY	http://www.laurencemillergallery.com
Partobject, Chapel Hill, NC	http://www.partobject.com
Paul Kopeikin, Los Angeles, CA	http://www.paulkopeikingallery.com
Peter Fetterman, Los Angeles, CA	http://www.peterfetterman.com
Photo Eye, Santa Fe, NM	http://www.photoeye.com/gallery/
Photographs Do Not Bend, Dallas, TX	http://www.flash.net/~pdnb
Photoportfolios, New York, NY	http://www.photoportfolios.com
Ricco/Maresca, New York, NY	http://www.riccomaresca.com
Robert Klein, Boston, MA	http://www.robertkleingallery.com
Robert Mann, New York, NY	http://www.robertmann.com
Robin Rice, New York, NY	http://www.nystyle.com/rrice/
Sepia International, New York, NY	http://www.sepia.org
Soho Triad Fine Arts, New York, NY	http://www.sohotriad.com
Stephen Cohen, Los Angeles, CA	http://www.stephencohengallery.com
Talli's Fine Art, New York, NY	http://www.photal.com
Wessel O'Connor, New York, NY	http://www.wesseloconnor.com
Weston Gallery, Carmel, CA	http://www.westongallery.com

Magazines / Journals

Some of these sites host the online version of regular photography magazines, while other offerings are exclusively Internet based. The sites are a tremendous resource for researching all aspects of photography. Bookmark your favorites.

Afterimage	http://www.vsw.org/afterimage/
American Photo	http://www.americanphoto.com
Aperture	http://www.aperture.org
Apogee Photo	http://www.apogeephoto.com
ArtByte	http://www.artbyteonline.com
Artforum	http://www.artforum.com
Atlas	http://www.atlasmagazine.com
Bit Weaver's Loom	http://www.bitweaver.com
Black and White World	http://www.photogs.com/bwworld/index.html
Blind Spot	http://www.blindspot.com
British Journal of Photography	http://www.bjphoto.co.uk
C: The Speed of Light	http://www.nearbycafe.com/adc/adc.html
Camera Arts	http://www.cameraarts.com
The Chronicle of Higher Education	http://www.chronicle.com
Communication Arts	http://www.commarts.com
Creative Camera	http://www.ccamera.demon.co.uk
The Critical Eye	http://www.thecriticaleye.com
CTheory	http://www.ctheory.com/ctheory.html
Dazed and Confused	http://www.confused.co.uk
Design and Publishing Center	http://www.graphic-design.com
The Digital Journalist	http://dirckhalstead.org
Esprit (RIT)	http://www.espritdomain.com
European Photography	http://www.equivalence.com
Eye Caramba	http://www.eyecaramba.com
f32	http://www.f32.com
Fotophile	http://www.fotophile.com
Fotoshow	http://www.fotoshow.com
Hyperzine	http://www.hyperzine.com
Journal E	http://www.journale.com
Lens Work	http://www.lenswork.com
Life	http://www.lifemag.com
Mythopoeia	http://www.myth.com
National Geographic	http://www.nationalgeographic.com/photography
New York Institute of Photography	http://www.nyip.com
Online Photography	http://www.onlinephotography.com
Outdoor Photographer	http://www.outdoorphotographer.com
Photo Arts	http://www.photoarts.com
Photo District News	http://www.pdn-pix.com
Photo Electronic Imaging Magazine	http://www.peimag.com
Photo Life	http://www.photolife.com
Photo Link	http://www.photolink.com
PHOTO Magazine	http://www.photo-magazine.com
Photo Metro	http://www.photometro.com
Photo Techniques	http://www.phototechniques.com
photographie.com	http://www.photographie.com
Photography in New York	http://www.photography-guide.com
The Pixel Foundry	http://www.pixelfoundry.com
Professional Photographer	http://www.ppmag.com
Publish	http://www.publish.com
ReVue	http://www.revue.com
Shutterbug	http://www.shutterbug.net
Sight	http://www.sightphoto.com
Urban Desires	http://www.desires.com
View Camera	http://www.viewcamera.com
Women in Photography	http://www.womeninphotography.com
Worldphoto	http://www.worldphoto.com
Zonezero	http://www.zonezero.com

Mailing lists

The Internet has many discussion groups devoted to photography. These are some popular forums listed by topic. To subscribe to lists without a portal site, enter the words included in the parentheses in the body, not the subject heading, of an email message. You will get directions on how to unsubscribe once you have joined.

Alternative Processes (SUBSCRIBE ALT-PHOTO-PROCESS-L)	alt-photo-process-request@usask.ca
Digicam (SUBSCRIBE DIGICAM)	majordomo@leben.com
egroups - Photography	http://www.egroups.com/dir/Arts/Photography
Epson Inkjet (SUBSCRIBE EPSON-INKJET)	majordomo@leben.com
Large Format	http://www.onelist.com
nettime	http://www.nettime.org/info.html
Panorama (SUBSCRIBE PANORAMA-L)	mailserv@cc.monash.edu.au
Photo News Network	http://www.photonews.net
PhotoBuzz	http://www.photobuzz.com
PhotoForum	http://www.rit.edu/~andpph/photoforum.html
Photojournalism (SUBSCRIBE PHOTOTUJ your name)	mailserv@vm.temple.edu
Photonet	http://www.photo.net/bboard/
Photoshopper	http://www.photoshopper.com/chat.html
Pinhole	http://www.pinhole.com/discussion
Pure Silver (SUBSCRIBE PURE-SILVER)	majordomo@tundraware.com
Rhizome	http://www.rhizome.org/subscribe
Stockphoto	http://www.stockphoto.net
Streetphoto	http://www.topica.com/lists/streetphoto

Museums

A list of museums devoted to the exhibition and collection of photographs. Visit their sites to view current exhibits and review schedules of upcoming events.

American Museum of Photography	http://www.photographymuseum.com
California Museum of Photography	http://www.cmp.ucr.edu
Canadian Museum of Contemporary Photography	http://cmcp.gallery.ca
Fox Talbot Museum of Photography	http://www.r-cube.co.uk/fox-talbot/
George Eastman House	http://www.eastman.org
Guggenheim Museum	http://www.guggenheim.org
J. Paul Getty Museum	http://www.getty.edu
Los Angeles County Museum of Art	http://www.lacma.org
Metropolitan Museum of Art	http://www.metmuseum.org
Museum of Contemporary Photography	http://www.mocp.org
Museum of Modern Art	http://www.moma.org
The Museum of Photographic Arts	http://www.mopa.org
National Gallery of Art	http://www.nga.gov
National Museum of Photography, Film, and TV (UK)	http://www.nmpft.org.uk
San Francisco Museum of Modern Art	http://www.sfmoma.org
Victoria and Albert Museum (UK)	http://www.vam.ac.uk/
The Whitney Museum of American Art	http://www.whitney.org

Organizations

The majority of the sites listed are professional organizations with a particular area of interest. Try their sites, if you seek information about the photographic practice they support. Other societies are more invested in the historical and aesthetic sides of photography.

Advertising Photographers of America	http://www.apanational.com
American Historical Photographic Society	http://www.aphs.org
American Society of Media Photographers	http://www.asmp.org
AIPAD	http://www.artline.com/associations/ipa/ipa.html
Association of Panoramic Photographers	http://www.panphoto.com
Camera Club of New York	http://www.interport.net/~ccny/
College Art Association (CAA)	http://www.collegeart.com
Copyright Clearance Center	http://www.copyright.com
The Copyright Society of America	http://www.csusa.org
The Daguerreian Society	http://www.daguerre.org
Electronic Frontier Foundation	http://www.eff.org

Media Photographers' Copyright Agency	http://www.mpca.com
National Press Photographer's Association	http://www.sunsite.unc.edu/nppa/
National Stereoscopic Association	http://www.nsa-3d.org
Photo Marketing Association International	http://www.pmai.org
Photographic Society of America	http://www.psa-photo.org
Photographic Society of France	http://www.sfp.photographie.com
Professional Photographers of America	http://www.ppa.com
The Royal Photographic Society (UK)	http://www.rps.org
Society for Imaging Science and Technology	http://www.imaging.org
Society for Photographic Education	http://www.spenational.org
University Photographers' Association	http://www.upaa.org
U.S Copyright Office	http://www.lcweb.loc.gov/copyright
U.S Patent and Trademark Office	http://www.uspto.gov
Women in Photography	http://www.womeninphotography.org

Photo History

A list of sites preoccupied with the historical analysis of photographs. They offer insightful texts, historical resources, and many extraordinary photographs from 1839 to the present.

Alternative Processes - Mike Ware	http://www.mikeware.demon.co.uk
American Museum of Photography	http://www.photographymuseum.com
Amercian Photographs - The First Century	http://nmaa-ryder.si.edu/collections/exhibits/ ➡ helios/amerphotos.html
Burns Archive	http://www.burnsarchive.com
City Gallery	http://www.city-gallery.com
Civil War Photography	http://www.civilwarphotography.com
The Daguerreian Society	http://www.daguerre.org
Daguerreotypes	http://lcweb2.loc.gov/ammem/daghtml/ ➡ daghome.html
Farm Security Administration	http://memory.loc.gov/ammem/fsahtml/ ➡ fsainfo.html
George Eastman House	http://www.eastman.org
History of Photography – Robert Leggat	http://www.kbnet.co.uk/rleggat/photo
Photography in Latin America (Spanish)	http://www.fotohistoria.org
Media History	http://www.mediahistory.com/photo.html
Photography in Japan	http://www.photojpn.org/HIST/hist1.html
Processes and Conservation - Luis Nadeau	http://www.photoconservation.com
Secrets of the Dark Chamber - Daguerreotypes	http://nmaa-ryder.si.edu/collections/exhibits/ ➡ secrets/index.html
Stereoviews	http://www.geocities.com/heartland/5873/
W. H. Jackson	http://www.fit.edu/InfoTechSys/resources/ ➡ cogsei/whjte.html
W. H. Fox Talbot	http://www.foxtalbot.arts.gla.ac.uk/
Women in Photography	http://www.sla.purdue.edu/WAAW/Palmquist/ ➡ gallery.html

Picture Agencies

A brief listing of commercial picture agencies and stock photography archives. Collectives like Magnum Photos employ some of the most renowned photojournalists working today.

Associated Press	http://www.ap.org
Black Star	http://www.blackstar.com/stock/index.html
Corbis	http://www.corbis.com
Magnum	http://www.magnumphotos.com
Reuters	http://www.reuters.com

Workshops

Sites for some of the most popular workshops offered. Courses at these places often feature distinguished instructors with special skills. A great opportunity to perfect a technique or expand on other aspects of your photography. Scholarships and internships are frequently available to students.

Anderson Ranch Workshops	http://www.andersonranch.org
John Sexton Workshops	http://www.johnsexton.com
Macacademy	http://www.macacademy.com
Maine Photographic Workshops	http://www.theworkshops.com
Palm Beach Photography Center Workshops	http://www.workshop.org
Photographer's Formulary's Workshops	http://www.workshopsinmontana.com
Santa Fe Workshops	http://www.sfworkshop.com

11.5.3 FILE FORMATS AND FILE EXTENSIONS

A file extension tells the computer what kind of file it is dealing with. It usually consists of three letters separated from the file name by a period – name.extension. This brief outline of file extensions is a useful guide to digital imaging and more elaborate multimedia work. You will no doubt come across many of these file formats while surfing the Internet. It may seem very extensive, but it is by no means exhaustive.

AU, AIF, AIFF, AIFC, SND	A sound file extension used on Macintosh and Unix systems.
AVI	A video file for Windows computers.
BMP, PCX	A bitmap image.
DCS 1.0, or DCS 2.0	(Desktop Color Separation) DCS files pre-separates the Photoshop image into five related files. One for each of the CMYK channels and one for these four channels combined. The newer 2.0 format has single and multiple file options, and it also preserves alpha and spot color channels. DCS files can only be printed on a PostScript printer.
DOC	A Microsoft Word document.
EPS	(Encapsulated PostScript) A PostScript image. The EPS format has many uses, and it is a good choice for output to an imagesetter or import into an illustration or a page layout program.
EXE	A self-extracting archive for DOS or Windows.
GIF	(Graphical Interchange Format). One of the most common graphics file formats on the Web. The GIF format is suitable for graphics with less than 256 colors and offers lossless compression. Patented by Compuserve, hence the Compuserve GIF credit in the Photoshop dialog box.
HLP	A HELP file for Windows.
HTM, HTML	An HTML (HyperText Markup Language) file. The files displayed in your Web browser window are HTML files.
HQX	A file with Macintosh BinHex compression. Opened by StuffIt Expander. You may encounter this extension when you download files on the Internet.
JPG, JPEG, JPE	(Joint Photographer's Expert Group) A graphics file. The most common file format for photographic images on the Web. JPEG files compressed with maximum quality are sometimes used to archive digital images that will not require further work.
MID, RMI	MIDI sound files.
MMM	Microsoft Multimedia Movie Player file format.
MOV, QT	Quicktime video files.
MP 2	The MPEG audio format.
MP 3	A CD quality sound format you will hear and read more and more about.
MPEG, MPG, MPE, MIV	(Moving Pictures Experts Group) A video format.
PDF	(Portable Document Format) Often used to transfer manuals or other documents electronically. Adobe Acrobat Reader is used to display these files independently of computer platform and software application.
PICT	A Macintosh file format used to save and display images. Not suitable for color separation, but an option if the image is intended for import into a video or animation program.
PIT	Macintosh Packit archive format.
PNG	(Portable Network Graphics) An emerging graphics file format primarily for the Web. New browsers support PNG images.
PS	A Postscript document.
PSD	A Photoshop Document format. The only format that can retain multiple layers and layer transparency, along with all the other adjustments you may have applied to the image. A PSD file basically preserves the entire working space of an image. It is the best choice if you want to rework it at any time, but few applications can read it.
RAM	A RealAudio sound file. A common format for streaming audio on the web.
RTF	(Rich Text Format) A text file that can be opened by many word processors.
SEA	A self-extracting archive for Macintosh. Expect to encounter this extension when you download files.
SIT	The StuffIt archive format for Macintosh. You will encounter this extension when you download files from the Web.
TIF, TIFF	(Tagged Image File Format) A common graphics format used for bitmapped images (photographs). A TIFF image can contain color management profiles and it can also be color separated. TIFFs can be saved with or without compression.
TXT, TEXT	A plain text file.
WAV	A standard sound format for Windows.
WRL	A VRML 3D object file.
XLS	A spreadsheet by Microsoft Excel.
ZIP	A common PKZIP archive file used for both Windows and Macintosh file compression. Expect to encounter this when you download from the Web.

12 LIGHTING

12.1 GLOSSARY

Artificial light	Light sources such as tungsten lights or electronic flash used by the photographer to light a scene.
Automatic flash	A programmed mode on an electronic flash unit where a light-sensitive cell cuts off the light when the film has been exposed correctly.
Ambient light	Refers to the light already present in a scene without the addition of artificial light. Also called available or existing light.
Available light	See ambient light above.
Axis lighting	Light pointed at the subject from a position close to the camera's lens.
Back lighting	Light that comes from behind the subject towards the camera.
Bounce light	Light that is reflected off another surface before it reaches the subject.
Broad lighting	Portrait lighting in which the main source of light illuminates the side of the face turned toward the camera.
Butterfly lighting	Portrait lighting in which the main source of light is placed high and directly in front of the face.
Catchlight	The reflection of a light source in a subject's eyes.
Contrast	The difference between the darkest and lightest areas in a subject.
Electronic flash	A tube containing gas that produces a brilliant flash of light when electrified. Also called a strobe.
Existing light	Also called ambient light or available light. See ambient light above.
Fill light	A source of illumination that lightens shadows cast by the main light and thereby reduces contrast in the photograph.
Filter factor	A number that indicates how many times the exposure must be increased to compensate for a loss of light.
Flash	A light source that emits a brief and bright burst of light. See electronic flash above.
Flashbulb	A forerunner to the electronic flash. Flashbulbs are used once and then discarded.
Flash meter	An exposure meter that measures the intensity of flash light.
Floodlight	An electric light designed to produce a broad and diffused beam of light.
Guide number	A number indicating the maximum intensity of a flash unit. The guide number is used to calculate manual flash settings. Divide the guide number with the flash-to-subject distance to find the correct aperture for an exposure.
Hot shoe	A bracket on top of the camera used to mount a flash unit and synchronize it with the shutter.
Illuminance	The strength of light falling on a given area of a surface. Measured by an incident-light meter.
Incandescent light	Light emitted when a substance is heated by electricity. For example, tungsten lights.
Inverse square law	A law of physics. At twice a given distance, a subject receives only one fourth of the light. The principle is used to calculate manual flash exposures.
Key light	The main light in a lighting arrangement.

Luminance The light reflected or produced by a given area of a subject in a specific direction measurable by a reflected-light meter.

Main light The principal source of light in a lighting set up. The main light defines the darkest shadows in a subject. Also called a key light.

Manual flash A mode of flash operation where the photographer manually adjusts the aperture opening to control the intensity of light required for a flash exposure.

Modeling light A small tungsten light built into some larger flash units. Used to predict the effect of lighting placements.

Narrow lighting A portrait set up in which the main source of light illuminates the side of the face partially turned away from the camera. Also called short lighting.

Photoflood An incandescent lamp that produces a very bright light but has a relatively short life.

Reflector A reflective surface used to bounce light from a source towards the subject. Most frequently used to lighten shadow areas and thereby reduce the contrast in a subject.

Short lighting A portrait lighting set up. See narrow lighting above.

Silhouette A scene or a photograph where the background is much more brightly lit than the subject.

Slave An electronic flash unit that fires when it detects light from another flash unit. Used to synchronize several flash units in a set up.

Spotlight An electric light that contains a small bright lamp, a reflector, and often a lens to concentrate the light in a small spot.

Strobe Abbreviation for stroboscopic. A light source that produces a series of brief pulses of light in rapid succession. Electronic flash is sometimes referred to as strobe.

Sync cord An electrical cord connecting a flash unit with a camera so that the two can be synchronized.

Synchronize To cause the flash unit to fire at the same time as the camera shutter is open.

Tenting A way to light a highly reflective object. Enclosing the object in a "tent" of translucent materials removes unwanted highlights and reflections.

Tungsten light Incandescent light from a tungsten filament heated by an electric current.

Notes

12.2 SUMMARY

259 **Lighting**

Changes in lighting will change your picture: Both indoors and outdoors, pay attention to how the light defines your subject. **Light can affect the feeling of a photograph:** Harsh or soft, light has a psychological effect on how a subject is perceived.

260 - 261 **Direction of light**

The direction of light is important because of shadows: The shadows, rather than the highlights, define your subject. Consider how the light is positioned in relation to your subject and how the shadows fall. Change the camera position to control the direction of the light if you are photographing with available light. **Before you shoot, take a moment to consider your alternatives:** You may also choose to make several exposures with different lighting conditions. If so, you will have several options to select from at the printing stage.

262 - 263 **Degree of diffusion: From hard to soft light**

Another important characteristic of lighting is its degree of diffusion: This ranges from contrasty and hard-edged to soft and evenly diffused. **Direct light creates hard-edged, dark shadows:** Light travels in direct lines from source to subject. The smaller the light in relation to the subject and the further away it is, the sharper and darker the shadows will be. **Diffused light scatters onto the subject from many directions:** Very obscure signs of directionality. Shadows are light with indistinct edges. Sources of diffused light are large in relation to their subject. **Directional-diffused light is partially direct with some diffused or scattered rays:** A mix of directional and diffused light, showing characteristics of both.

264 **Available light – outdoors**

What kind of light will you find when you photograph in available light, the light that already exists in a scene: You will encounter all types of light. Consider how it affects your subject and change this effect any way you can (your position, the subject's position, by introducing artificial light). **A clear, sunny day creates bright highlights and dark, hard-edged shadows:** Position the subject or yourself to control the direction of the shadows or move the subject into the shade where the light is diffused. You may want to use a reflector or a flash to lighten the shadows and thereby reduce the contrast in the scene. **On an overcast day, at dusk, or in the shade, the light will be diffused and soft:** It illuminates all parts of the scene evenly. **The light changes as the time of day changes:** Shadows are longer in the morning or just before sunset, enhancing the sense of texture and volume in a scene.

265 **Available light – indoors**

Available light indoors can be contrasty or flat, depending on the source of light: When there is only one source of light, the scene often has an extreme contrast. **When shooting indoors, expose for the most important parts of the picture:** Since the contrast may be too excessive for the film to record all areas of the scene, concentrate on the most important part and expose for that. **Light indoors is often relatively dim:** Select a very fast film for moving subjects. Use a tripod for still subjects.

266 **Artificial light: Lights and other lighting equipment**

Types of light – Photofloods: Lights with a tungsten filament. 3200 – 3400°K. Used with tungsten-balanced color film. **Quartz-halogen bulbs:** These contain a gas that prolongs the life of the tungsten filament. 3200°K. Used with tungsten-balanced color film. **Flash equipment:** Comes in many sizes and strengths. Attachments allow you to control the quality of the light. Used with daylight-balanced color film. **Reflectors and light-control devices - Bowl-shaped reflectors:** Used with photofloods to concentrate the light and direct it towards the subject. **Snoot:** A tube placed in front of the lamp housing to narrow the beam. **Umbrella reflector:** The light source is pointed away from the subject and into the umbrella, which bounces diffused light back towards the subject. **Reflector flat:** A flat piece of cardboard or other material used to bounce light toward the subject. **Flag or gobo:** A panel mounted on a stand and placed so it shields part of the subject or the camera from light. **Barn doors:** Panels mounted on the lamp housing to block part of the light. **Diffusers and filters – diffusion screen:** A translucent material placed in front of a light to diffuse it. **Tent:** Translucent material that wraps around the subject to remove unwanted highlights and reflections. **Softbox:** Completely encloses the light to produce a soft and even light. **Filter holder:** Accepts filters, gels, and screens to alter the light. **Supports for lights and other devices – light stands:** Holds lights or any other piece of lighting equipment in place. **Cross arm or boom:** A horizontal addition to a vertical stand. **Umbrella mount:** Used to mount an umbrella to a light stand. **Background paper or seamless:** Paper on large rolls used to isolate a subject in the studio.

267 **Qualities of artificial light**

The same properties are available in artificial light as in available light: You still work with direct and diffused light, but you are in a position to control the properties of the light by using lighting equipment. **The bigger the light source relative to the subject, the softer the quality of the light:** By varying the distance from your lights to the subject, you control the appearance of the shadows. **The more diffused the source, the softer the light:** Your selection of light sources and use of diffusing attachments such as umbrellas determines the amount of diffusion. **Use the type of light and its distance to control the light on your subject:** Add filters and diffusers to your lighting vocabulary, and you have complete control over the lighting.

268 - 269 **The main light: The dominant source**

Where do you start when making a photograph with artificial light: You normally work with available light already present outside, while artificial lights require that you start from scratch. **The most natural looking light imitates that from the sun - one main light casting one dominant set of shadows:** A multitude of shadows cast across the subject from a range of light sources can often be confusing, and certainly not flattering for portraits. By varying the position of the main light, you can get very different effects. See page 268 for a series of illustrations. **Some types of lighting have been traditionally associated with certain subjects:** The ability of lighting to emphasize or hide aspects of your subject has made these techniques desirable. **Lighting can influence the emotional character of an image:** Changing the light can have a strange effect on the personality depicted. **Most photographs made with artificial light employ more than one light source:** A fill light or a reflector is often used to lighten shadows and reduce the contrast in an image. Lights can also be used to control the value of the background.

270 **The fill light: To lighten shadows**

Fill light makes shadows less dark by adding light to them: Your eye automatically adjusts for differences in contrast as it travels between shadows and highlights. Film does not have this ability. You have to measure and control the contrast so it corresponds with the contrast range tolerated by the film. **Fill light is most useful with color transparencies:** They have a limited contrast range, and must be exposed correctly to secure a good result. Color negative materials are more forgiving, and some corrections can be made in printing. **Fill light can also be useful with black-and-white materials:** If the contrast range in the subject is more than 3-4 stops, fill lighting is usually desirable. It is of course possible to control the contrast during printing with black-and-white materials, but the results will invariably be better if corrections are made with lighting and/or development. **Artificial lighting often requires fill lighting:** One main light usually produces shadows that are too dark for most subjects. **Some daylight scenes benefit from fill light:** In strong sunlight, shadows are very dark and will often benefit from fill light. Close-up work outdoors is plagued by large shadows, which can be reduced through the use of fill light. **A reflector is a simple, effective, and inexpensive way to add fill light:** It is placed on the opposite side of the subject from the main light. A simple, white piece of card works well as a reflector. Keep in mind that it must be neutral in color to avoid creating a color cast. **A floodlight or flash can also be used for lighting:** It must be of a lower intensity than the main light to cancel out the shadows without adding its own. This can achieved simply by using a light of lower intensity, moving it further away from the subject, or diffusing it. **A black "reflector" is useful at times:** Black materials placed opposite the main light will absorb light and darken a part of the subject.

271 **To measure the difference between highlights and shadows**

With an incident-light meter: From the subject position, point the light meter first towards the main light and then towards the fill light. The difference between the readings amounts to the contrast range in the subject. **With a reflected-light meter:** Place a gray card on the side of the subject facing the main light and take a reflected-light reading. Move the card to the side of the subject facing the fill light and take another reading. The difference between the readings amounts to the contrast range in the subject.

272 **Lighting with flash**

Flash units provide a convenient means of increasing the light, indoors or out: Flash units come in several sizes, from camera mounted mobile units to large studio outfits. They are powered either by batteries or a separate power pack. **Professional photographers find flash particularly useful:** It is portable and predictable, which makes it useful in a range of situations, from fast moving subjects to dim light. **A camera-mounted flash unit is convenient to carry and use:** But the axis-lighting it provides may not be suitable for all subjects. A unit that can also be used from an off-camera position is more versatile. **The burst of light from electronic flash is very brief:** Flash light illuminates a scene for 1/1000 of a second or less. A drawback is that it is impossible to see how the light will affect the subject during this brief moment. Larger flash units use tungsten modeling-lights for this purpose, but experience will eventually allow you to predict the effect of various flash positions quite accurately. **Flash must be synchronized with the camera's shutter:** The hot shoe or a sync cord is used for this purpose. Cameras with focal plane shutters must be set to the flash sync speed or slower to ensure that the shutter is all the way open at one point during the exposure. The sync speed is usually marked in red, with an X, or a lightning symbol. Leaf shutters can be synchronized with flash at all speeds.

273

Flash equipment

Types of flash units: Built-in flash, hot-shoe flash, handle-mount flash, studio flash units, self-contained flash heads. Please see page 265 for a comprehensive description of each type. **Flash metering - Automatic flash:** These units have a sensor, which measures the light reflected from the subject and cuts off the flash when the exposure is correct. Most also have a manual mode. **Dedicated (or designated) flash:** Automatic flash units designed to be used with a particular camera. Flash and camera work together to expose the film automatically. **Through-the-lens metering:** TTL metering has a sensor inside the camera that reads the amount of light striking the film. A camera with TTL metering used with a dedicated flash unit is the ultimate set up for automatic flash exposures. **Flash meter:** A light meter capable of measuring the brief burst of light from flash. **Flash accessories – sync cord:** Synchronizes flash and camera so the flash fires when the shutter opens. **Flash slave unit:** Attached to a flash unit, it triggers this unit when exposed to the brief burst of light from another flash unit. **Modeling light:** A small tungsten light built into the flash head to better predict the effect of the flash. **Light modifiers:** Flash units can be used with a variety of focusing or diffusing attachments. **Describing flash power – A guide number in one way of describing a flash unit's power:** The guide number is an expression of a flash unit's power. The higher the number, the stronger the flash unit.

274 - 275

Basic flash techniques

The easiest way to light a scene with flash is with direct flash on camera: The lighting this placement provides, however, is both harsh and very two-dimensional. **You can get more varied and interesting lighting with the flash in other positions:** Light from above provides the most natural light, but side lighting also adds more volume and texture to your subject. The illustrations on page 266 show the effect of some placements. **Natural lighting, whether indoors or outdoors, rarely strikes a subject exclusively from one direction:** Bouncing the flash off other surfaces or placing reflectors near your subject will simulate this effect. **Aim the flash carefully so that the light doesn't create odd shadows or distracting reflections:** The shadow from flash lighting is very harsh. Pay close attention to where it falls in relation to your subject.

276

Manual flash exposures

Manually controlled flash units emit a fixed amount of light: The aperture is used to control the intensity of the light reaching the film and thereby the exposure. The light gets weaker the further it travels (the inverse square law), so the aperture must be opened up more and more as subjects move progressively further away from flash and camera. **Studio photographers and other professionals often use a flash meter:** This is the most accurate way of determining a flash exposure. When more than one flash unit is used, with bounced light, or with multiple firings of the same unit, a flash meter makes exposure calculation quite easy. It can measure both incident and reflected light. Most advanced light meters read both continuous light and flash.

Using a flash unit's calculator dial:
Your flash can help you calculate a manual flash exposure:
Most flash units have a calculator dial. Follow these steps:

1. Set the flash to manual.
2. Set the correct film speed on the calculator dial.
3. Set the shutter speed to the flash synchronization speed or slower.
4. Focus on your subject, and find the focusing distance on your lens.
5. Use the calculator dial to determine the correct aperture for this distance.

Manual exposures for bounce flash:

Bounce flash travels an extra distance: Calculate the complete distance the light has to travel for a manual flash exposure. Compensate for light absorbed by the reflecting surface by increasing the exposure. Follow these steps:

1. Follow steps 1-3 above.
4. Estimate the distance from the flash to the reflecting surface to the subject.
5. Find the aperture for this distance on the calculator dial.
6. Increase the exposure to compensate for light absorbed by the reflecting surface. Bracket.

Using a flash meter:

A flash meter the is the most accurate way to work with manual flash, including bounce flash: Follow these steps to use a flash meter:

1. Set the film speed on the meter and a flash synchronization speed on your camera.
2. Set up the meter as you would for a normal incident-light reading and activate it. Fire the flash manually and read off an aperture on the flash meter.
3. You can also synchronize the flash with the meter via a sync cord. When the meter is activated, the flash is fired. Read off an aperture on the flash meter.

277 **Automatic flash exposures**

Automatic flash units and automatic through-the-lens (TTL) camera systems react to the amount of light reflected back from the subject during the exposure: A sensor on the flash unit or in the camera cuts off the flash when enough light for the exposure is reflected back from the subject. **Dedicated flash units are designed to be used with a particular camera:** They offer additional features, such as the ability to balance the amount of flash with the existing light in a scene. **When doesn't automatic or TTL flash work well:** If areas surrounding the subject are either very bright or dark, these areas will reflect or absorb a disproportionate amount of the light. The result is underexposure (white surroundings) or overexposure (dark surroundings) of the main subject. **Bounce flash presents a special situation:** When the flash head can swivel to bounce the light while the sensor remains pointed in the same direction as your lens, the flash unit will calculate the exposure automatically as usual. Cameras with TTL metering also calculate bounced flash accurately. In all other cases, you must switch to manual exposure and determine the flash exposure yourself.

Sensor on flash meters light reflected from the subject:

An automatic flash that controls exposure with a sensor on the flash unit: The sensor cuts off the light when the exposure is correct. The calculator dial will allow you to determine which setting to use with automatic exposure. Follow the steps below:

1. Set the calculator dial to the film speed you are using.
2. Select the distance range within which you will shoot.
3. Set the camera to manual operation and the aperture for the distance range chosen in point 2 above.
4. Set the camera to a flash synchronization speed.
5. If desired, use the flash unit's test button to ensure that the subject will receive adequate light.
6. Compose the picture and make the exposure.

Sensor in camera meters light reflected from the subject:
A camera that automatically controls flash exposure through the lens: Sensors in the camera cuts off the light when the exposure is correct. Follow the steps below:
1. Set your flash to TTL operation.
2. Set the camera's exposure mode.
3. Select any f-stop on your lens.
4. Set the shutter speed to synchronize with the flash.
5. Use the test button on the flash unit to test the exposure.
6. Compose the picture and make the exposure.

278

Fill flash: To lighten shadows

Flash can be used as a fill light: In high-contrast situations, dark shadows can be lightened with an additional flash exposure. Use less flash than existing light to reduce the contrast and maintain some of the shadows from the main light. **Flash can increase the light on a fully shaded subject that is against a brighter background:** Again, flash is used to balance the contrast. **Color slide film and digital photographs particularly benefit from using flash for fill light:** Due to a limited exposure range, all contrast corrections are best done at the time of exposure. **There are other uses for flash plus daylight:** Experiment with the amount of flash used and try using flash in dim light with slow shutter speeds.

279

Flash plus available light

You can use flash outdoors during the day to lighten shaded areas: You balance the existing light with fill light from flash to achieve this. **Automatic operation:** Cameras with TTL metering can automatically balance fill light with available light. **Manual operation:** Follow the steps below:

First find the settings for a flash exposure:
1. Set camera and flash to manual operation.
2. Set the film speed on camera and flash.
3. Focus on your subject and find the lens-to-subject distance on the lens.
4. Find the correct aperture on the calculator dial.

Now, find the settings for an available-light exposure:
5. Meter the existing light. Find the equivalent exposure combination that allows you to use the aperture from point 4 above.
6. The above combination will make the flash exposure and the existing-light exposure equal.

How to balance flash and existing light if your flash has adjustable power settings:
7. Alter the power settings on your flash to 1/2, 1/4, 1/8, or 1/16 to make the shadows filled with flash darker.

How to balance flash and existing light if your flash does NOT have adjustable power settings:
7a. Drape a handkerchief or tissue over the flash to reduce the light output.
8. Move further away from your subject.

280 - 281

Controlling background brightness

You can use flash plus existing light to make the background lighter or darker: By altering the shutter speed in relation to the aperture for a correct flash exposure, the background will be lighter or darker. The technique is most suitable when the existing light is relatively dim. Please see page 280 for some examples of the effect and a step-by-step description of the procedure.

282 - 283 **Simple portrait lighting**

You don't need a complicated lighting arrangement for portraits – or many other subjects: Simple lighting is often the most natural and best. Too much of a production might also make your subject more conscious of being photographed. **Outdoors, open shade or an overcast sky provides a soft, even light:** Placing your subject in the open shade avoids the harsh shadows of direct light and prevents squinting. With color film, use a Skylight 1A or 81A (light yellow) filter to remove excess blue from the light. **Indoors, window light is a convenient source of light during the day:** Just watch for excessive contrast and place your subject away from the direct light, or use fill light to lighten the shadows. **A main light plus reflector fill is the simplest setup if you want to arrange the lighting yourself:** By using soft light with light shadows, you might not need complicated fill-light arrangements.

284 - 285 **Multiple-light portrait setups**

Conventional portrait lighting is realistic but flattering: In fact, most techniques are used to alter features so they fit ideas about ideal proportions. **A typical studio portrait setup uses a moderately long camera lens:** A long lens reduces the distortion experienced by shorter lenses. The subject's head is often turned to one side. **Your choice of main light affects the quality of the light:** Remember that it is the shadows that define your subject, so your choice of a direct or soft main light is crucial. **Another common portrait lighting setup is virtually shadowless:** Diffusing the light and adding a reflector/fill light will remove distinct shadows from your subject. Please see pages 284 - 285 for illustrated examples of short lighting, broad lighting, and butterfly lighting. **Flash units, direct or diffused, can be used:** The brief duration of flash makes it ideal for portraits. The drawback is that the effect of flash lighting is hard to observe before test exposures are made.

286 **Lighting textured objects**

Lighting for a textured object depends on whether you want to emphasize texture: Side lighting emphasizes texture. **Shadows must be seen if the texture is to be prominent:** Front lighting minimizes texture.

287 **Lighting reflective objects**

Photographing objects with glossy surfaces can be like photographing a mirror: Highlights and reflections (of camera and photographer) can be distracting and are usually unwanted. **Reflections can be controlled in various ways:** Move your lights around, hang strips of paper just outside the picture area, spray your subject with a dulling spray, place polarizing filters on lights and lens, or surround your subject with a tent made of a translucent material. **Using a camera that views through-the-lens is the best way to keep track of reflections:** Changes in lighting etc. will be immediately noticeable on the ground glass.

288 **Lighting translucent objects**

Try lighting translucent or partially transparent objects from behind: This technique will give the objects depth and luminosity and prevent distracting reflections caused by front lighting.

12.3 TEST

FILL IN THE BLANKS

1 ____________________ light has high contrast.

2 ____________________ light has low contrast.

3 Shadows are light and without distinct edges in ____________________ light.

4 Shadows are dark with sharp edges in ____________________ light.

5 According to the ____________________ law: at twice a given distance, a subject only receives a quarter of the light.

6 The ____________________ light defines the shadows in a subject.

7 Flash and camera are ____________________ when the flash fires as the shutter opens.

8 A continuously burning light is called an ____________________ light.

9 To diffuse the light from electronic flash, you can ____________________ the light off a nearby surface.

10 A flash exposure can be calculated manually by dividing the flash to subject distance into the ____________________ for the flash unit.

MULTIPLE CHOICE – CIRCLE ONE OR MORE

1	An electronic flash is also referred to as:	a.	lightning.
		b.	a strobe.
		c.	an incandescent light.
2	A flash exposure is generally given by:	a.	any shutter speed and f/16.
		b.	the flash sync speed or slower and an aperture determined by the lens-to-subject distance.
		c.	a shutter speed of 1/1000 and the minimum aperture.
3	The guide number of a flash unit is:	a.	a number given by the manufacturer to indicate the power of a flash unit.
		b.	a rating for use in adverse conditions with low visibility.
		c.	a reference to the instruction manual.
4	A fill light is normally used with a main light to:	a.	lighten the shadows.
		b.	reduce the contrast in a subject.
		c.	match the contrast of the subject with the contrast tolerated by the film.

5	The best way to ensure even illumination with flash is to:	a.	use one stop less exposure.
		b.	arrange most of the subject at the same distance from the flash.
		c.	reposition yourself so most of the subject is at the same distance from the flash.
6	Incandescent lights allow you to:	a.	directly observe how lighting decisions affect the subject.
		b.	meter the scene normally with an incident or reflected light meter.
		c.	freeze motion in moving subjects.
7	Automatic flash exposure is controlled by:	a.	a sensor in the flash unit.
		b.	the camera's standard light meter.
		c.	automatic shutter speed changes.
8	If flash is bounced off a surface before hitting the subject, the flash-to-subject distance used to calculate exposure is:	a.	the direct distance from flash to subject.
		b.	the distance from the flash to the reflecting surface.
		c.	the distance from the flash to the surface to the subject.
9	Light from a flash unit illuminates the scene for approximately:	a.	1 sec.
		b.	1/60 sec.
		c.	1/1000 sec.
10	Reflections in an object with a glossy surface can be removed or reduced by:	a.	using polarizing filters on both the lights and the lens.
		b.	changing the position of the lights.
		c.	placing the object in a tent made of translucent materials.

Notes

12.4 PRACTICAL TIPS

Flash

Diffuse your flash for softer light.

Flashlight is notoriously harsh, and it is not uncommon for a flashed subject to look like a deer in headlights. There are several solutions to this problem. If there are surfaces nearby, you can use them to bounce the light (as described in the textbook). Otherwise you can use these tricks to get a diffused quality of light.

Place a piece of translucent material such as white cloth or tracing paper over the flash to soften the light source. The beams are no longer travelling in direct lines from flash to subject, but are diffused by the added layer.

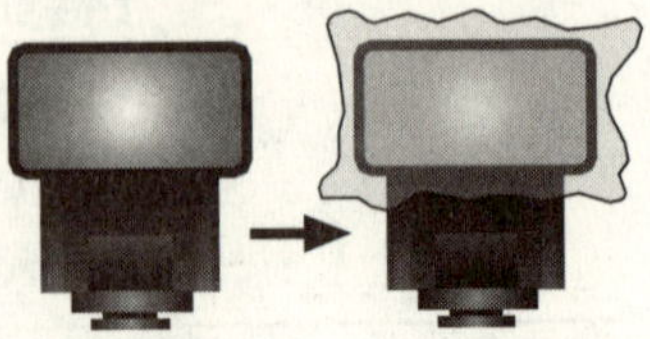

Another option is to add a small reflector to the flash and bounce the light off this and onto the subject. The flash must be pointed away from the subject and into the attached reflector. There are several models available for purchase, but you can also construct one yourself.

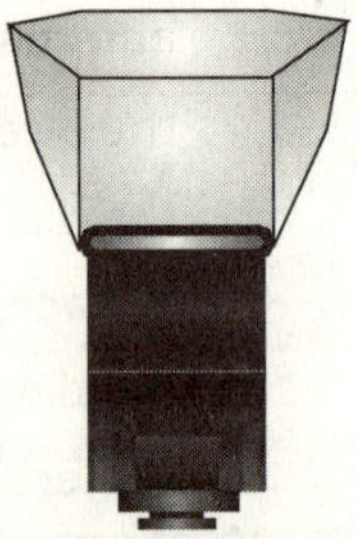

Exposure calculations are a little more complex with the above attachments. If you are using the automatic mode on the flash, use the test button as normal to make sure that you actually get enough light. With manual exposure, you need to test how much weaker the new and diffused light is compared to direct flash. Both techniques effectively change the guide number of the flash, and the best way to test is simply to shoot a roll with different exposures. Expect to increase the exposure by about two stops with the diffusing attachments.

Studio lighting

Mask off your lights with paper or card to control spill.

Artificial lights come with a multitude of attachments that are used to either focus the light into a point or to diffuse it over a wider area. But even with all this added equipment, it is not always easy to make the light fall exactly where you want with the intensity you had in mind. It is also fair to say that the more complicated a lighting set up becomes, the harder it is to control, and the more likely you are to end up with multiple shadows and other undesirable lighting effects. Instead of adding more lights to accentuate parts of your subject, you may consider removing light from select areas by masking off the lights you have already placed. Many studio photographers work in this way. Suspend a piece of black card or heavy paper from a couple of light stands in front of the light and proceed to cut holes in it to highlight areas of your subject. Inexpensive clamps from a hardware store are ideal for attaching the card to the stands. If you find that the light spreads more than you intended it to, simply cover part of the hole with some black masking tape or scraps of card. By using this method, one or two lights is usually enough, and you do not necessarily need all the extra equipment used to control the light. When it comes to lighting, simple approaches are often best.

12.5 JOURNAL

12.5.1 LIGHTING DIAGRAMS

This section of the journal will help you establish a record of lighting solutions and effects. When you are working on a lighting setup, note the positions of lights and reflectors in these diagrams. Use the symbols to indicate the direct or diffused quality of the light sources. By comparing the negative and print with these records, you will quickly learn how the placement of lights and reflectors model the subject. Since you are working in three dimensions (rather than the two dimensions of these pages), the diagrams are somewhat awkward to use. You have three viewpoints to work with - a frontal view, a view from above, and a side view. Combined with the distance markings, these perspectives should be adequate to enter the information you need. Use the view from above to estimate the angle your lights are positioned at. Please see the first diagram below for an example. Remember that there is no substitute for looking carefully at your subject in lighting.

KEY TO LIGHTING SYMBOLS ▾		
●	Subject	Your main subject
□	Background	A background used to isolate the subject
⬉	Main light positioned below the subject	Flash or incandescent lamp
➔	Main light positioned level with the subject	Flash or incandescent lamp
⬊	Main light positioned above the subject	Flash or incandescent lamp
⇖	Fill light positioned below the subject	Flash or incandescent lamp
⇨	Fill light positioned level with the subject	Flash or incandescent lamp
⇘	Fill light positioned above the subject	Flash or incandescent lamp
■	Reflector	White or silver surface
≋	Diffused light	Soft shadows, low contrast
\ι/	Direct light	Harsh shadows, high contrast
○	Spot light	Light falling on a select part of the subject

Notes

LIGHTING DIAGRAM EXAMPLE

View from the camera position

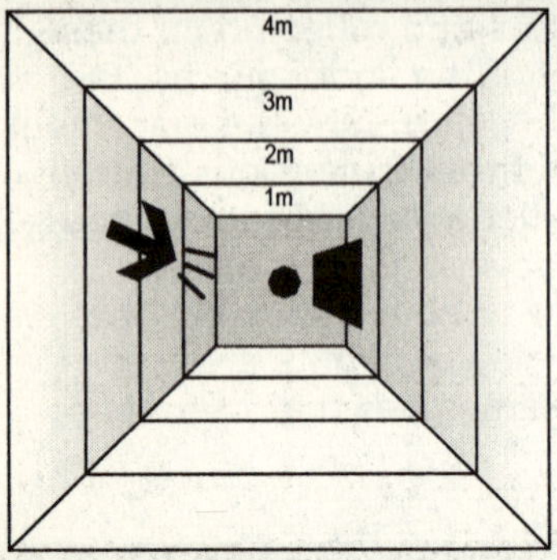

View from above

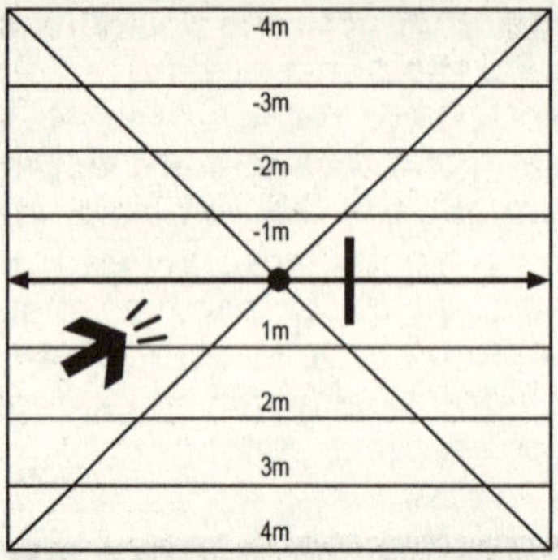

View from the side

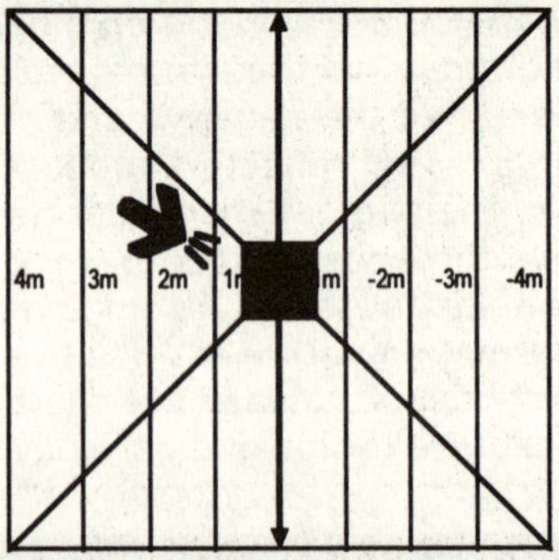

COMMENTS

This setup explored the use of a reflector. I used one Photoflood and a 20x24-inch piece of white card attached to a lighting stand. The main light was 2 meters away from and slightly above the subject. It was placed at an angle of about 60 degrees.

LIGHTING Ratio	EXPOSURE Information	NEGATIVES Rolls	Frames
3 : 1	I metered both sides of the subject and found a difference in exposure of 1.5 stops. The exposures were bracketed.	# 12	#16 - 36

CONTACT PRINTS

A small print of the subject.

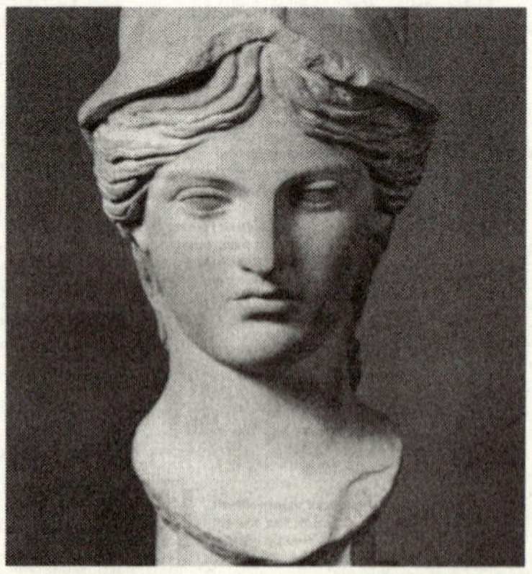

LIGHTING DIAGRAM 1

View from the camera position

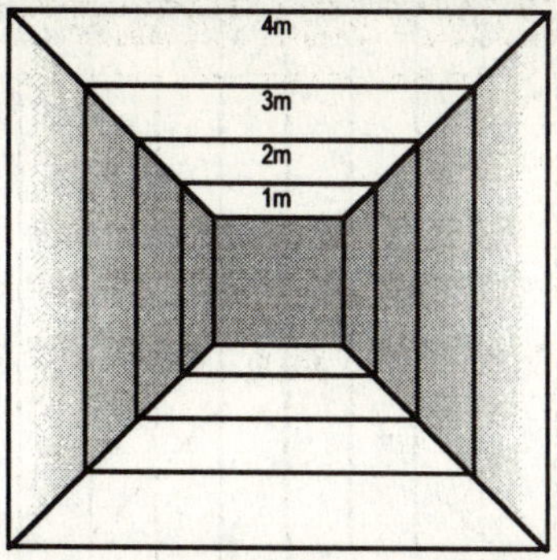

View from above

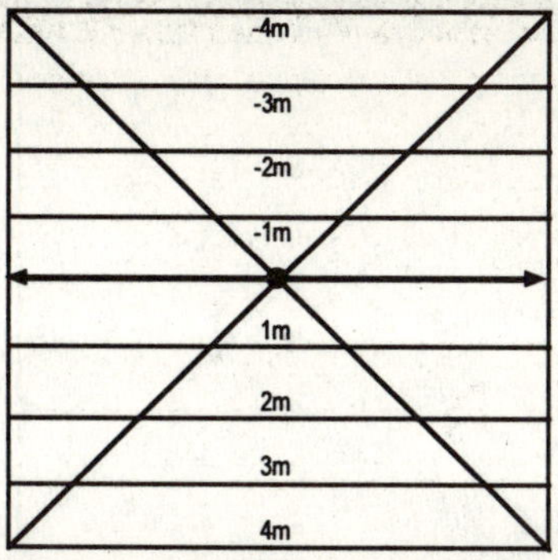

View from the side

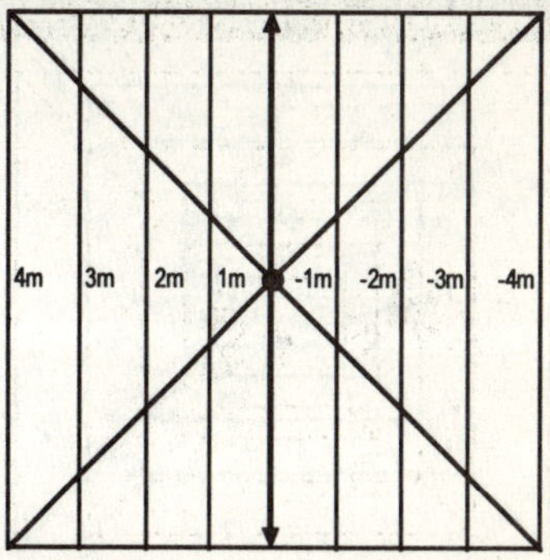

COMMENTS

LIGHTING Ratio	EXPOSURE Information	NEGATIVES Rolls	Frames

CONTACT PRINTS

LIGHTING DIAGRAM 2

View from the camera position

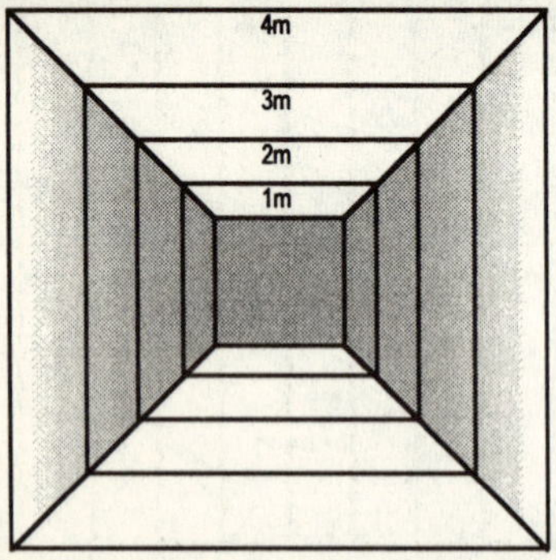

View from above

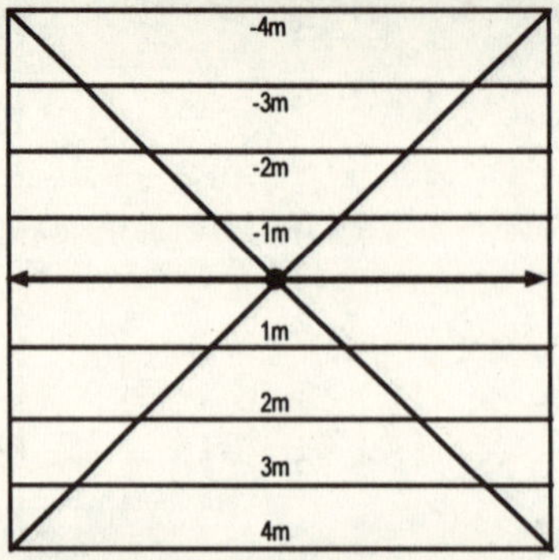

View from the side

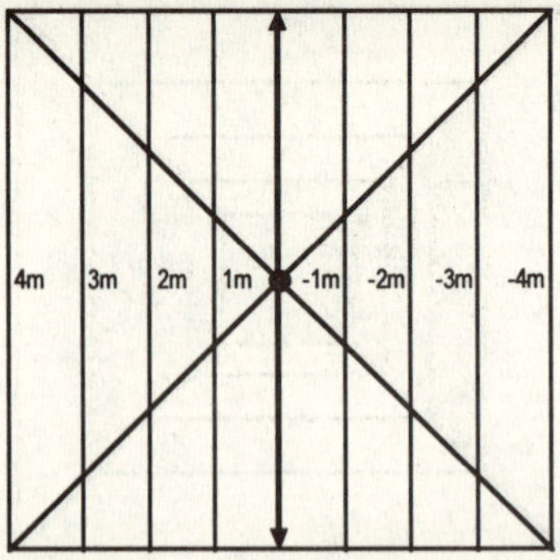

COMMENTS

LIGHTING Ratio	EXPOSURE Information	NEGATIVES Rolls	Frames

CONTACT PRINTS

LIGHTING DIAGRAM 3

View from the camera position	View from above	View from the side
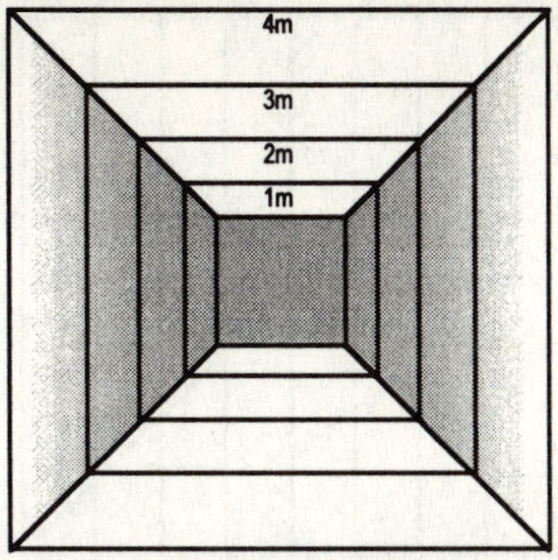	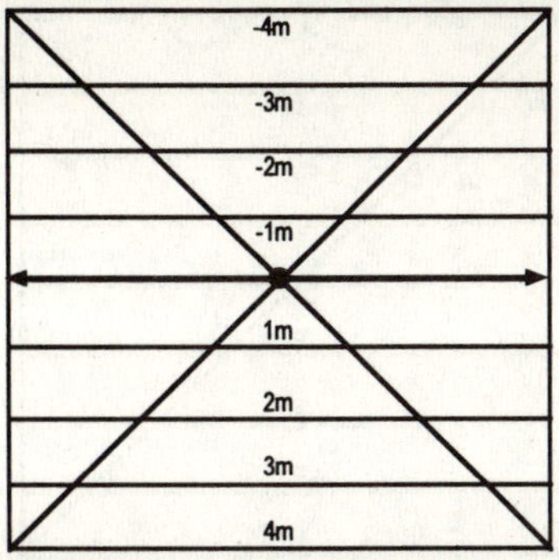	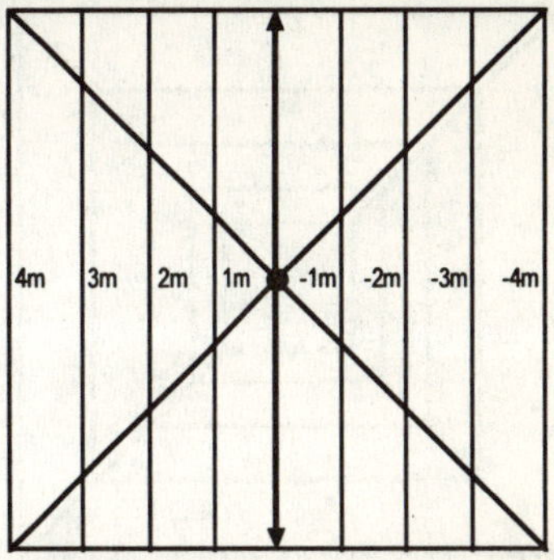

COMMENTS

LIGHTING / EXPOSURE / NEGATIVES

LIGHTING Ratio	EXPOSURE Information	NEGATIVES Rolls	Frames

CONTACT PRINTS

LIGHTING DIAGRAM 4

View from the camera position ▾ View from above ▾ View from the side ▾

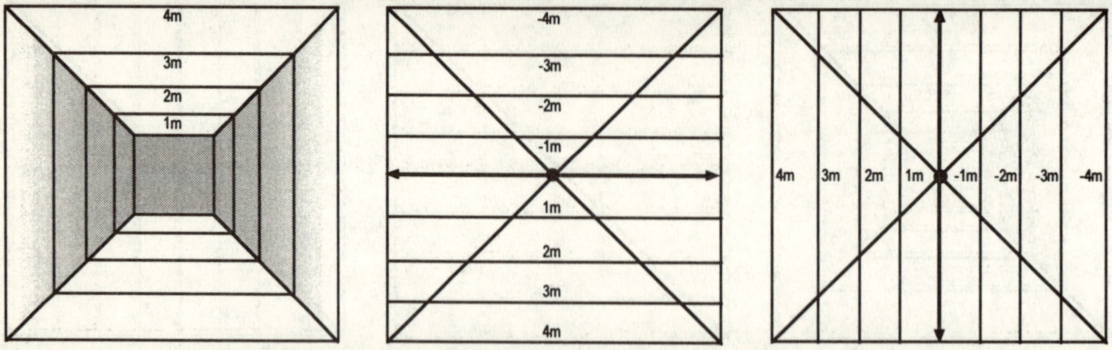

COMMENTS ▾

LIGHTING ▾ Ratio	EXPOSURE ▾ Information	NEGATIVES ▾ Rolls	Frames

CONTACT PRINTS ▾

LIGHTING DIAGRAM 5

View from the camera position	View from above	View from the side
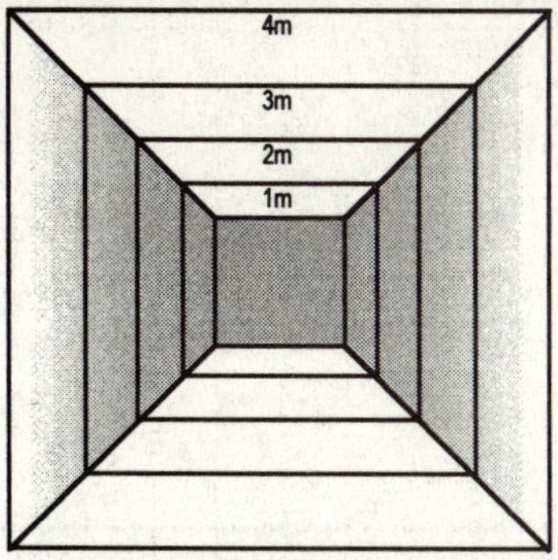	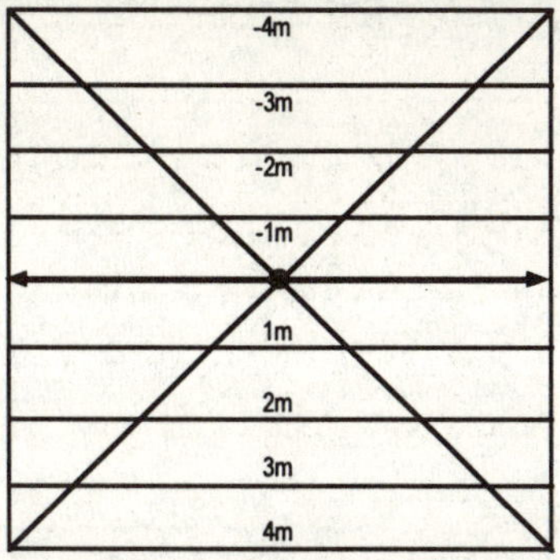	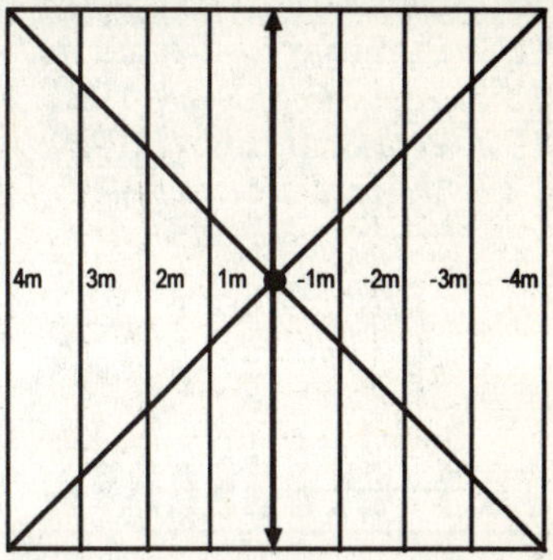

COMMENTS

LIGHTING Ratio	EXPOSURE Information	NEGATIVES Rolls	Frames

CONTACT PRINTS

13 SPECIAL TECHNIQUES

13.1 GLOSSARY

Bellows	An expandable piece of equipment mounted between lens and camera to adjust the distance between lens and camera. Bellows are used in close-up photography to alter the degree of magnification and the focusing distance.
Bracketing	The common practice of making several exposures on either side of what is perceived to be the correct exposure. Bracketing leaves room for slight error and gives more choice at the printing stage.
Circle of confusion	The tiny circle formed by a lens as it projects the image of one point in a subject onto the film.
Close-up	A photograph where the subject is magnified to the extent that it appears larger than normal.
Close-up lens	An attachment used in front of the lens to allow for close focusing.
Contact print	A print of exactly the same size as the negative it was made from.
Cross processing	The common name for the processing of color negative film in E-6 chemistry or color reversal film in C-41 chemistry.
Depth of field	The area from near to far in a photograph that appears sharp.
Diopter	A term used in photography to describe the magnifying power of a lens.
Enlargement	An image (usually a print) that is larger than the negative.
Exposure factor	The exposure factor indicates how many times the exposure time should be multiplied for an exposure increase. An exposure factor of 2 requires a doubling of the exposure time. The exposure factor can be converted to stops. A factor of 2 requires a 1-stop exposure increase.
Extension tube	A metal ring or tube mounted between lens and camera to allow for larger magnification and closer focusing.
Lith film	A film primarily used in the graphics industry. It produces a very high-contrast image.
Macro lens	A lens especially designed for close-up photography.
Non-silver process	A printing process that does not depend on the sensitivity of silver to form an image. The cyanotype and platinum prints are examples of non-silver processes.
Photogram	An image formed by placing objects directly on the printing paper and exposing them to light.
Polarizing filter	This filter removes reflections from reflective surfaces such as glass and water. It blocks light undulating at certain angles to a linear or circular screen created by the filter.
Sabattier effect	A partial reversal of the image tones in film or paper when it is exposed to light again during the initial development process.
Solarization	A reversal of image tones that occurs when film is massively overexposed.

13.2 SUMMARY

293 **Special techniques**

This chapter shows some of the alternative ways of taking photographs or making prints: There are many variations on the camera and print theme. **The main pitfall in manipulating a print is changing it merely for the sake of change:** Use special techniques as a means of communication.

294 - 295 **Copying techniques**

Copying a flat object: This might seem simple, but it actually demands close attention to detail and technique. All the principles of close-up photography apply if the subject is small, and in addition you must align the camera properly in relation to the subject and light it evenly. **The film to use depends on the copy:** Use fine-grain (slow) panchromatic film for subjects with an extended tonal range. For black-and-white line copy, use a high-contrast film like Kodalith Ortho or underexpose and overdevelop normal black-and-white film. **If you want a color reproduction:** Use a color film balanced for your light source. **A camera with through-the-lens viewing is best:** It allows for accurate positioning of the copy in the frame (crucial for slides) and makes it easier to notice bad lighting, glare, or reflections. **A steady support for the camera is vital:** Use a tripod and cable release. **The copy and the camera must be parallel to each other:** If the film plane is not exactly parallel to the surface of the copy and the lens is not pointing directly at the center of the copy, it will get distorted. Use the edges of the viewfinder or any grid lines on the ground glass to check alignment. **Oversize objects can be hung on the wall:** Center the tripod height and camera position close to the object and then move it further back to the same central point. **Your goal for lighting should be even, shadowless light over the entire surface of the copy:** By far the best option is to use incandescent lights positioned at an angle of 45° to the copy. **Check the evenness of the illumination:** With a hand-held meter (preferably incident), you can measure the corners and the center of the copy to make sure that the light is even. Place a gray card in these positions if you measure with a reflected-light meter. **Reflections can be a problem:** Polarizing filters on both the lights and the lens will remove most reflections. You can also try positioning the lights at a sharper angle. If the camera is reflected in the print, hide it behind a black board with a hole cut for the lens. **Meter the copy:** Use an incident-light meter or take a reflected-light reading off a gray card. Select an aperture in the middle of the range to get the best from your lens and some depth of field. **You may need to increase your basic exposure:** With extension tubes, bellows, a (polarizing) filter, or long exposures, you need to adjust the exposure manually. If you use a TTL meter, the meter will generally do this for you, unless you are dealing with the reciprocity effect. **Bracketing your exposures will insure your work pays off:** Bracket in smaller increments (1/3 stop) with color reversal film.

296 - 297 **Pinhole photography: Pinhole exposures**

Please see page 296 in the textbook for instructions on how to make a pinhole camera. **Exposing a paper negative - Select a paper:** Single-weight papers with low contrast (1 or 2) are ideal if a positive print is desired. **Load the paper into the camera in complete darkness:** Make sure that the pinhole itself is covered up before you leave the room. **Start by working outdoors in midday sun:** Paper has a very slow speed, so bright conditions are necessary to avoid extremely long exposures. **Keep the camera stationary during the exposure:** "Depth of field" extends from 3 inches to infinity with a pinhole camera. **Start with a trial exposure of 1 minute:**

Remove the tape over the pinhole and replace it after 1 minute to control the exposure time. Double or halve the time if your results are too light or too dark. **Exposing a film negative - Calculating an exposure with film:** Find your f-stop by dividing the diameter of the pinhole into the focal length of the camera (the distance from film to pinhole). Keep the units in either mm or inches, not both. Meter as usual and use this f-stop to determine the exposure time. **Or, simply make a trial exposure:** With ISO 100 film, a pinhole 0.57mm wide, and a "focal length" of 8 inches, try an exposure of 4 seconds in bright conditions. **Dealing with light leaks:** Place an unexposed piece of paper or a negative in the camera and leave it in the sun for a few minutes. Develop as usual. If there are any signs of light striking the paper or negative, tape or glue your box until they disappear.

298 - 299 **A Photogram: A cameraless picture**

A photogram is a kind of contact print: Placing objects, rather than negatives, directly on the printing paper and exposing it to light creates a photogram. **Any object that comes between the light source and the sensitized material can be used:** Experiment with opaque and translucent objects to get different effects. **A photogram can be made on printing paper, film, or a digital scanner:** A film negative can be printed after development. Color photograms are also a possibility. Placing an object directly on the scanner bed will create a photogram of sorts. There is a lens involved, so the result is more like a camera image.

300 - 301 **A Sabattier print: Part positive, part negative**

A Sabattier print is made by reexposing paper to light during processing: The result is an image that seems to contain both positive and negative qualities. Mackie lines separate adjacent highlights and shadows. Solarization is a frequently used but inaccurate term for this effect. **The unusual appearance results from a combination of effects:** The dark areas of the print remain largely unaffected, since they are almost fully developed. The light areas have plenty of unexposed silver-halide crystals, so they turn gray during the second exposure. Chemicals left from the first development retard further development in the border areas between light and dark, creating the Mackie lines. **There are several ways to produce a Sabattier print:** All you need is an exposure to light during the development process. Please see the box on page 301 for a basic procedure. Make a test print that covers the basic exposure times in one direction and the second exposure times in the other direction. Pick the square with the desired effect.

302 - 303 **Alternative processes: Cyanotyping**

Alternative processes offer many different choices when you want more than a straight black-and-white or color print: Older photographic printing methods are now frequently referred to as alternative processes. The cyanotype is one of the simplest, while platinum printing is both more demanding and more expensive. Please see page 302 for a technical description of the Cyanotype process.

304 **Cross processing**

Cross processing of color film produces unpredictable, but often interesting color shifts: Color negative film is ordinarily developed in C-41 chemistry and color reversal films in E-6 chemistry. It is possible to develop negative film in reversal chemistry and vice versa for a negative with increased contrast and highly saturated colors or a transparency with reduced contrast and muted colors. **Cross processing transparency film inherently increases contrast:** Shoot in low contrast, or overexpose your film by one stop to secure shadow detail. **If you use a lab to process the film:** Explain that you are not making a mistake by asking for cross processing. To avoid contamination, most labs only cross process films at the end of a day or at the end of a batch just before the chemistry is due for replacement. **When printing:** Your colors will be twisted, so don't even think about aiming for realism. Experiment.

305

Polaroid image transfer

With certain Polaroid materials, it is possible to transfer the image onto another surface (normally watercolor paper) during the development process. Please see page 305 for a description of the procedure. A related technique, Polaroid emulsion lifts, is described in 13.4 Practical tips for this chapter.

306

Handcoloring

With the aid of Marshall's Photo Oils or similar products, a black-and-white photograph can be hand colored for a muted effect. For a more expressive look that is less concerned with the transparency of the colors and how they blend into the emulsion, standard watercolors, acrylic paints, colored pencils, or pastels can be used. Page 306 shows some examples of hand coloring. The rest of the chapter describes other techniques, such as painting with light, and contextual practices like mixed media and installations.

13.3 TEST

FILL IN THE BLANKS

1. With ____________________ processing, color reversal film is developed in C-41 chemistry.
2. Solarization is a term inaccurately used for the ____________________ effect.
3. Light-sensitive iron salts form an image in the ____________________ process.
4. When copying a flat object, the lights should be positioned at an angle of ____________________ degrees to the copy.
5. A ____________________ filter may reduce glare and reflections in a copy.
6. In a pinhole photograph, ____________________ extends from about 3 inches to infinity.
7. When objects are placed directly on the printing paper and exposed to light, the result is a ____________________.
8. Alternative processes require ____________________ printing.
9. An ____________________ makes use of the site where the photographs are exhibited.
10. The copy and the camera must be ____________________ to each other to ensure reproductions without distortions.

MULTIPLE CHOICE – CIRCLE ONE OR MORE

1	By elevating objects from the paper in a photogram, you:	a.	increase the depth of field.
		b.	make the elevated objects less sharp than objects close to the paper.
		c.	alter the focusing distance of the paper.
2	If you use extension tubes or bellows in close-up copy work, you may need to:	a.	increase the exposure.
		b.	reduce the exposure.
		c.	use a neutral density filter.
3	Exposures of 1 second or longer are subject to the:	a.	reciprocity effect.
		b.	inverse square law.
		c.	Scheimpflug rule.
4	A Sabattier print is created by:	a.	printing on grade 5 paper and developing in acetic acid.
		b.	exposing the print to light during development.
		c.	printing a positive image on negative paper twice.
5	The lighting of a flat copy must be:	a.	contrasty to exaggerate shadows.
		b.	even and soft to ensure a uniform exposure of the entire copy surface.
		c.	done with a single light only.
6	Pinhole cameras can be used with:	a.	film, but not paper.
		b.	paper, but not film.
		c.	both film and paper, but not at the same time.
7	Cross processing:	a.	increases the color saturation and contrast in slide film processed in C-41.
		b.	makes negative film processed in E-6 muted in color.
		c.	turns black-and-white film processed in E-6 into infrared film.
8	The cyanotype image is:	a.	blue.
		b.	made of platinum metal.
		c.	usually contact printed.
9	To get a reasonably sharp pinhole image, the pinhole itself must:	a.	be at least 1 inch in diameter.
		b.	be very small to reduce the circles of confusion.
		c.	have clean edges.
10	Hand coloring photographs can be done with:	a.	specialist photo oils.
		b.	watercolors.
		c.	colored pencils.

13.4 PRACTICAL TIPS

Copy work

Make sure that the light is even and keep the same exposure.

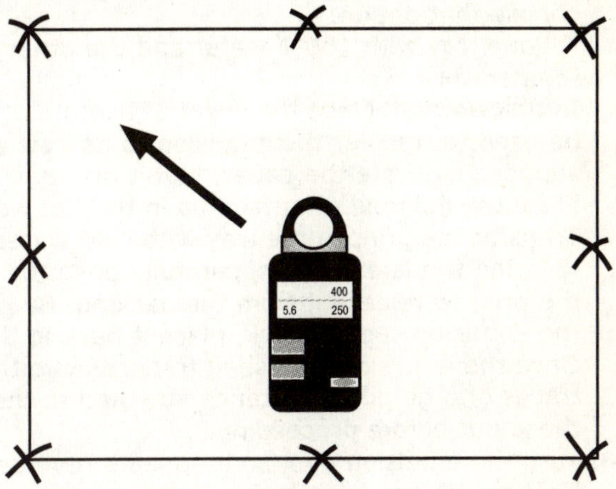

This is more a useful reminder than a tip. When you have set up your lights for copy work, you meter the entire surface of the copy with an incident-light meter to make sure that the light is even. Alternatively you can use a gray card to take reflected readings with the same procedure. Move the light meter around to get readings from the center and all the corners of the print. The readings should ideally be identical to assure that the print gets an even exposure. If there are hotspots, move your lights further away or diffuse them with umbrellas or softboxes to broaden the source. A difference of 1/3 stop does not seem like much, but it will be very noticeable in the final copy.

Once you are satisfied that the light is even, you can proceed to copy objects (of the same size) without altering the exposure. The intensity of the light will remain the same. Simply mark the location of your print on the wall, or on the baseboard of the copy stand, and place each new print in the same location. By keeping this in mind, you can work very quickly and efficiently. But the penalty for getting the initial exposure wrong is of course greater when your mistake is repeated with every reproduction.

Polaroid emulsion lifts

A starting guide to Polaroid emulsion lifts.

In the emulsion lift process, you remove the print emulsion from its original backing and transfer it to another support. This might be a traditional watercolor paper or basically anything you like. One option is to transfer the image to paper that is already marked in some way, like sheets of music or a page torn from an old book. Other materials such as glass and metal are also suitable. Keep in mind, though, that the support will get wet, so paper needs to be reasonably thick and sturdy to facilitate the process. Experiment with thinner and more fragile supports once you are comfortable with how the materials behave. The equipment needed is outlined below, and the step-by-step procedure is easy to follow.

Equipment checklist:

- ❑ Polaroid color film – one of the following types 108, 669, 59, 559, 809, or 64 Tungsten.
- ❑ Watercolor paper or other support for the emulsion.
- ❑ Thermometer capable of recording temperatures as high as 160ºF.
- ❑ Two darkroom trays.
- ❑ Thin latex gloves.
- ❑ A clock or timer.
- ❑ Either vinyl contact paper or silver spray paint.
- ❑ Sheet of clear acetate or mylar.
- ❑ Soft, flat brush (some prefer a rubber roller).

Polaroid emulsion-lift procedure

1. Expose and process your Polaroid print as normal.
2. The Polaroid print must be completely dry before you can start the emulsion lift. Leave it overnight or blast it with a hairdryer.
3. To prevent the print backing from dissolving in the hot water, cover the back of the print with vinyl contact paper or spray it with silver spray paint. Allow the paint to dry if you choose that option.
4. Fill one tray with 160°F water and the other with water slightly colder than room temperature.
5. In preparation, place the sheet of acetate at the bottom of the tray with cold water. It will be used to transfer the emulsion to its new support. If you are using paper as a final print support, saturate the paper, blot it dry, and place it on a clean and level surface.
6. Place the Polaroid print face up in the hot water and agitate it for about four minutes.
7. Transfer the print to the tray with cold water.
8. Wearing the latex gloves, carefully push the edges of the emulsion toward the center of the print to release it from the backing. Be patient, and do not apply excessive pressure. If the emulsion seems stuck, place it back in the hot water for a longer period.
9. Once the emulsion is pushed free, remove the backing from the water. There may be traces of a gel-like substance attached to the emulsion or floating in the water. Try to fish these out before proceeding.
10. Turn the emulsion over so it appears reversed with the front of the print facing down.
11. Holding the emulsion by two corners and supported by the sheet of acetate, lift it in and out of the water to smoothen any wrinkles.
12. Using the sheet of acetate, transfer the emulsion to its new support. Place it with the emulsion side down and the acetate on top. Apply light pressure to squeeze out water and firmly attach the emulsion. Remove the acetate.
13. Using the flat brush or your fingers, manipulate the emulsion until it is either free of wrinkles or has taken on the appearance you desire. A brush softened in warm water will be more precise and less likely to damage the emulsion. Push any air bubbles or large water drops towards the edges until they disappear. You may use a rubber roller to finally press the emulsion into its paper support. Do not touch after it has started to dry.
14. Hang the finished masterpiece to dry. You can flatten the new print in a dry mount press at 180°F. A glossy UV-protective spray can be used to add a uniform surface finish.

Notes

13.5 JOURNAL

13.5.1 SPECIAL-TECHNIQUE WORKSHEETS

Special techniques usually require some experiments before they are mastered. The instructive procedures described in the textbook and elsewhere are usually general guidelines that will produce acceptable results, but there are many variables that affect the outcome. Only after trying a process and adjusting it to suit your particular working conditions will these technique seem truly special in the sense that they enhance your images in exactly the way you want. The worksheets below will allow you to develop a reference library for special techniques with your own comments and modifications added to the standard procedures. Please see the completed example for detailed instructions on how to use them.
Some of the techniques you may want to experiment with include:

- Extreme close-up work.
- Pinhole photography.
- Photograms.
- Sabattier prints.
- Negative prints.
- Hand coated emulsions - liquid light.
- Alternative processes, including cyanotype, platinum, Van Dyke, and gum prints.
- Digital negatives for contact printing.
- Polaroid image transfers.
- Polaroid emulsion lifts.
- Hand coloring of photographs.
- Sandwiched negatives.
- Cross processing of color film.
- Mixed media applications.

Special-techniques bibliography

Albumen and Salted Paper Book: The History and Practice of Photographic Printing
James Reilly
Light Impressions, 1980
Alternative and Non-Silver Photographic Processes: Working Notes
Christopher James
Delmar Publishing, 2000
Breaking the Rules: A Photo Media Cookbook
Bea Nettles
Prairie Book Arts Center, 1992
Darkroom Dynamics
Jim Stone
Focal Press, 1979
Making Digital Negatives for Contact Printing
Dan Burkholder
Bladed Iris Press, 1999
New Dimensions in Photo Imaging
Laura Blacklow
Focal Press, 2000
Palladium Printing, Made Easy
Ted Rice
Eagle Eye, 1984
Pinhole Photography: Rediscovering a Historic Technique
Eric Renner
Focal Press, 1994
Silver Gelatin: A User's Guide to Liquid Photographic Emulsion
Martin Reed and Sarah Jones
Amphoto, 1996
The Darkroom Cookbook
Stephen G. Anchell
Focal Press, 1994
The Gum Bichromate Book: Non-Silver Methods for Photographic Printing
David Scopick
Focal Press, 1991
The Keepers of Light: A History and Working Guide to Early Photographic Processes
William Crawford
Morgan and Morgan, 1980

SPECIAL-TECHNIQUE WORKSHEET ▸	Polaroid emulsion lift.
Reference ▸	Student Lab Manual - see 13.4 Practical tips above.
Description ▸	The process works very much like outlined in the procedure. A Polaroid print is immersed in hot water to release the emulsion from its backing paper. The emulsion is then transferred to another support.

Adjustments to the standard procedure ▾

1	Point 3 - Tape the print to a piece of paper when spray painting to protect the image.
2	Point 4 - The water MUST be 160 degrees, otherwise the emulsion will not lift.
3	Point 9 - The sticky residue bonds the emulsion to the backing. REMOVE ALL!!!
4	Point 13 - Once the emulsion starts to dry, it will tear if pulled. Apply some water.
5	Point 13 - Using a soft, flat brush works best for this step. Soften in warm water.
6	Larger formats work better due to the loss of image area from wrinkles.
7	Used Polaroid type 59 color film - 20 4x5-inch sheets for the standard holder.
8	OPAQUE backing works best. On glass, it is hard to see the image properly.
9	
10	

Process sample ▾

A corner of my first 4x5-inch emulsion transfer. If air or water is left under the emulsion, as it was here, it will stretch and form a bubble when dry. Push out with brush and roll flat with a rubber roller while wet. The sample below (although a disaster) gives a good impression of the wrinkles formed.

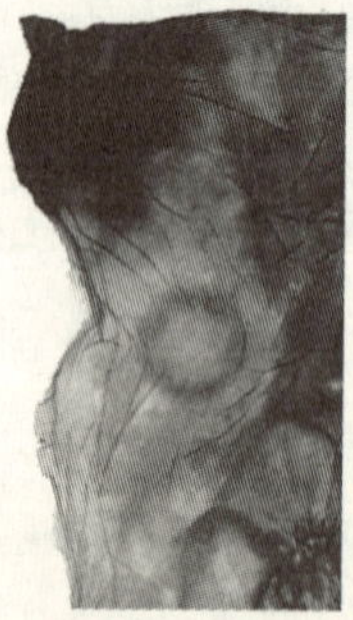

SPECIAL-TECHNIQUE WORKSHEET ▸

Reference ▸

Description ▸

Adjustments to the standard procedure ▾

1

2

3

4

5

6

7

8

9

10

Process sample ▾

SPECIAL-TECHNIQUE WORKSHEET ▸
Reference ▸
Description ▸
Adjustments to the standard procedure ▾
1
2
3
4
5
6
7
8
9
10
Process sample ▾

SPECIAL-TECHNIQUE WORKSHEET ▸
Reference ▸
Description ▸
Adjustments to the standard procedure ▾
1
2
3
4
5
6
7
8
9
10
Process sample ▾

SPECIAL-TECHNIQUE WORKSHEET ▸	
Reference ▸	
Description ▸	
Adjustments to the standard procedure ▾	
1	
2	
3	
4	
5	
6	
7	
8	
9	
10	
Process sample ▾	

SPECIAL-TECHNIQUE WORKSHEET ▸

Reference ▸

Description ▸

Adjustments to the standard procedure ▾

1

2

3

4

5

6

7

8

9

10

Process sample ▾

14 VIEW CAMERA

14.1 GLOSSARY

Bellows A flexible, light proof, and usually accordion folded part of the view camera located between the lens board in the front and the viewing screen in the back. Bag bellows are used with short-focal-length lenses to facilitate camera movements.

Changing bag A light proof bag where the photographer can insert her or his hands to load film when a darkroom is unavailable. Dust on the negative is often a problem when loading sheet film in a changing bag.

Covering power The area of the focal plane over which a lens projects an image that is acceptably sharp and evenly illuminated.

Cut film Another term for sheet film.

Dark slide The protective cover removed in the sheet-film holder when the film is loaded or exposed.

Fall The action of lowering the front or back of the view camera to position the image on the ground glass. Moving the front also affects the point of view.

Film holder Also referred to as a sheet-film holder. The light proof container that holds sheets of film when used in a view camera.

Focusing cloth A dark cloth used to shade the ground glass on a view camera for viewing and focusing.

Ground glass A piece of glass roughened on one side so that an image focused on it can be seen on the other side. The viewing screen in both reflex and view cameras are made of this type of glass.

Hanger A metal frame used to hold sheet film during processing in a tank.

Leaf shutter A shutter made of a circle of overlapping metal leaves. View camera lenses have a leaf shutter.

Notching code Notches cut in the margin of sheet film so that the type of film and its emulsion side can be identified in the dark.

Press camera A old type of sheet-film camera with a viewfinder and handgrip for hand-held photography.

Rise The action of raising the front or back of the view camera to position the image on the ground glass. Moving the front also affects the point of view.

Sheet film Film cut into individual flat pieces.

Shift The action of shifting the front or back of the view camera sideways to position the image on the ground glass. Moving the front also affects the point of view.

Swing The action of swinging the front or back of the view camera horizontally to change the plane of focus (front) or the shape of objects (back, and to a lesser degree front) in the image.

Tilt The action of tilting the front or back of the view camera vertically to change the plane of focus (front) or the shape of objects (back, and to a lesser degree front) in the image.

View camera A camera in which the taking lens forms an image directly on a ground-glass viewing screen. A film holder is inserted in front of the viewing screen before exposure. The front and back of the camera can be set at various angles to change focus and perspective.

14.2 SUMMARY

309 **View camera**

Why should a photographer use a bulky, heavy, slow-working view camera: Because what the view camera sacrifices in ease of use, it gains in possibilities no other camera offers. **A view camera's movements give you an extraordinary amount of control over the image:** The film and lens planes can be moved independently to control the appearance of the image. **The view camera's large film format is also an advantage:** The sharpest detail and the finest grain is found in enlargements from large negatives.

310 - 311 **Inside a view camera**

A view camera's movements give it the ability to change and control an image: The film and lens planes are parallel in most cameras. A view camera allows you to bring these planes out of alignment to change the image. **To make full use of a view camera's movements, you must use it with a lens of adequate covering power:** The image projected by a lens is circular. With a view camera, this circle must be large enough to accommodate movements of the rectangular negative format within the circle. When the rectangle gets too close to the edge of the circle, the image will be out of focus and darkened by the reduced brightness. The size of the image circle increases as the lens is stopped down. **View camera movements:** Rise and fall, shift, tilt, and swing. Please see page 311 for a breakdown of the view camera parts.

312 - 313 **View camera movements: Rise and fall**

Rise, an upward movement, and fall, a downward movement, change the placement of the image on the film: Moving the back places the film within various parts of the image circle. Moving the front places the image circle so it falls on various parts of the film. **Rise or fall of the back does not affect the shape of the subject:** Only the position of the object on the film changes. **Rise or fall of the front changes the point of view and to some extent the shape:** By moving the lens, you are effectively altering the camera's position in relation to the subject and thereby the shape of the subject. **Why not just raise and lower the camera:** You can do that, but small adjustments are easier to make with rise and fall. Besides, rise and fall of the back allows you to change the composition of the image without altering the point of view. The movements are illustrated on page 313.

314 - 315 **Shift**

Shift, a sideways movement, is the same as rise and fall except the movement takes place from side to side: The angles between the subject, lens, and film planes remain the same, only the placement of the image on the film is changed. **Since shift is simply a sideways version of rise and fall, the results are similar:** Shifting the camera back moves subjects in the same direction on the film. Moving the lens has the opposite effect. **Spatial relationships change with front shift but not with back shift:** The point of view changes with lens shifts. The movement is illustrated on page 315.

316 - 317 **Tilt**

Tilt, a forward or backward movement, can change both the shape and the focus of the image on the film: With tilt, you bring the planes of film, lens, and object out of alignment. Tilting the back of the camera changes the shape of objects significantly and the focus somewhat. Tilting the front of the camera changes the focus significantly without changing the shape of the object.

Tilting the back changes the shape: You alter the distance light has to travel to the film plane and thereby the shape of the object. **The rule is: The farther the image travels inside the camera, the larger it gets:** The degree of tilt will determine the amount of distortion/correction to an object. **Tilting the front changes the focus:** You alter the plane of focus, which will remain parallel to the lens plane. The effect of tilt is demonstrated on page 317.

318 - 319 **Swing**

Swing, an angled left or right movement, can change the shape or focus of the image: The effect depends upon whether the front or the back is moved. **Swinging the back of the camera changes the shape:** Moving the film plane alters the distance light has to travel inside the camera and thereby the shape of objects. **Swinging the front of the camera changes the focus:** Again, the plane of focus remains parallel to the lens plane as you move the lens. Swing is illustrated on page 319.

320 **Using a view camera to control the image**

The practical application of the view camera's ability to rise, fall, shift, tilt, and swing are virtually endless: These movements give you complete control over the placement of your image and the perspective and focus in your image. **Controlling the plane of focus and depth of field:** Tilt the lens plane so it is more parallel to the subject plane. See the Sheimpflug rule below. **Controlling horizontal perspective when shooting at a side angle to the subject:** Swing the camera back so it is parallel to the face of the subject and then swing the lens plane until it is parallel to the film plane. **Controlling vertical perspective when shooting from a low camera angle:** Tilt the camera back forward until it is parallel to the face of the subject and then tilt the lens plane until it is parallel to the film plane. **Controlling vertical perspective when shooting from a high camera angle:** Tilt the camera back backward until it is parallel to the face of the subject and then tilt the lens plane until it is parallel to the film plane. **Controlling the vertical placement of a subject in the image frame:** Use rise or fall of the camera back or front to position the subject. **Controlling the horizontal placement of a subject in the image frame:** Shift the front or back to position the subject.

321 **Controlling the plane of focus**

A view camera's movements let you control sharpness in an image: When you are photographing a plane that is not parallel to the lens plane, you might have difficulty rendering it all sharp even with the smallest aperture. **With a view camera you can adjust the plane of focus:** By bringing the lens plane and the subject plane into closer alignment (swinging or tilting the lens), the plane of focus will be aligned more closely with the subject plane. Stop down the lens if you want depth of field to extend even further. **Scheimpflug makes it even better:** When the planes of film, lens, and subject meet, the subject plane will be completely sharp. In other words, the lens and subject planes should not be parallel to render the subject plane sharp. Observe the effect of your movements on the ground glass of the camera to determine the point where the film, lens, and subject planes intersect. **If you want only part of the picture to be sharp:** Swing and/or tilt of the camera front allows you to position the focus plane anywhere you want in an image.

322 - 323 **Controlling perspective**

A view camera is often used in architectural photography for controlling perspective: It allows you to correct any distortion. **Photographing a building head on isn't always as easy as it seems:** Your position in relation to the building will inevitable create a distortion that can be corrected through camera movements.

Another problem arises if you want to photograph a building with two sides showing: First, tilt to correct converging vertical lines, then swing the camera parallel to one side of the building, usually the widest side. The correct procedure and its effect is illustrated on pages 322 - 323.

324 **Equipment you'll need**

Camera equipment: 4x5 view camera, lens, sheet-film holders, 4x5 film, sturdy tripod, focusing cloth, focusing magnifier or loupe, hand-held light meter, cable release, carrying case, Polaroid back, bag bellows, bellows extensions, rail extensions, and changing bag. **Equipment and chemicals for processing film:** Sheet film hangers, processing tanks, developing trays, film processing chemicals. Please see page 324 for a full description of each item.

325 **What to do first – and next**

A suggested procedure for view camera work:

1. Set up the camera and zero the controls. Level the camera.
2. Roughly frame and focus.
3. Make more precise adjustments. Apply camera movements.
4. Make final adjustments and lock down the controls.
5. Make an exposure. Remember to close the shutter before inserting the film and withdrawing the dark slide.

326 **Loading and processing sheet film**

Load film in total darkness into sheet-film holders that accept two sheets of film, one on each side: After exposure, turn the dark slide so the black side faces out. This is the best way to avoid double exposures. **The film must be loaded with the emulsion side out:** When the notches on sheet film are in the upper right-hand corner, the emulsion side is facing you. Check this with every sheet before inserting it in the holder. **Developing sheet film follows the same basic procedure as developing roll film:** Instead of one processing drum, you use three tanks or trays for developer, stop bath, and fixer. However, there are drums for sheet-film processing in daylight that produce very good results. Tank and tray development is done in complete darkness. Presoak your film in water to ensure even development. See 6.4 Practical tips. The development time for sheet film is different from roll film, and it is also dependent on the agitation pattern you use.

326 **Loading sheet film**

Dusting holders: Remove all dust from your film holders with a blower or a brush. Dust on the negative will cause dark specks in your print that are very difficult to remove. **Finding the notches:** The notches on sheet film are used to identify the film type. The packaging has an illustration of the pattern. When loading film, the notches should be in the upper right-hand corner so the emulsion is facing you when you insert the sheet into the holder. **Checking film insertion:** It happens that the sheet slips into the groove for the dark slide on one or both sides. If there is resistance when you insert the slide, remove the sheet and load it again. You can also carefully feel for the film guides in the holder to ascertain that the sheet is correctly loaded. Do not touch the film. **Unexposed/exposed film:** The top of the dark slide has a light and a dark side. Unexposed film should have the light side out. Exposed film should have the dark side out.

327 **Processing sheet film**

Loading hangers: Place the loaded hangers in a clean and dry tank to avoid damaging the film in the dark. **Tank processing:** Do not crowd the tank with hangers – keep 1/2-inch between them.

Tap the hangers on the edge of the tank after insertion to dislodge air bubbles from the surface of the film. **Tank agitation:** Agitate for 6-8 seconds every minute of the development time. Lift all the hangers completely out of the solution and drain to one side. Immerse the hangers and lift them up once more. Drain to the other side before immersing them again. **Tray processing:** Wear protective gloves for tray processing. Immerse each sheet of film in the tray with the emulsion side up. **Tray agitation:** Keep the film emulsion-side-up in a corner of the tray and shuffle the order bottom to top throughout the developing time. If you have one or two sheets, agitate by rocking the tray. See 15.4 Practical tips also. Complete the process (tank or tray) with stop bath and fixer. **Washing and drying:** A film washer for sheet film works best, but you can also wash a few sheets at the time in a tray with running water. Hang the film to dry from a corner.

14.3 TEST

FILL IN THE BLANKS

1 View camera ____________________ give you complete control over the shape of your subject and the plane of focus in your image.

2 The front and rear standards on a view camera are separated by a ____________________.

3 ____________________ describes a downward movement of either the front or rear standard on the view camera.

4 A normal lens for a 4x5-inch view camera is a ____________________mm lens.

5 The ____________________ the image travels inside the camera, the larger it gets.

6 Tilting the back of the camera changes the ____________________ of the image.

7 The image ____________________ formed by the lens must have adequate covering power to allow for camera movements.

8 The Scheimpflug rule states that the subject plane will be sharpest when the planes of film, lens, and subject ____________________.

9 The first step when setting up the view camera for a photograph should be to ____________________ it and zero the controls.

10 When the notches on sheet film are in the upper right-hand corner, the ____________________ side of the film is facing you.

MULTIPLE CHOICE – CIRCLE ONE OR MORE

1 To increase the depth of field in a scene, the lens:

a. can be tilted backward.

b. can be tilted forward.

c. must be parallel to the camera back.

2	Swing:	a.	moves the camera front or back up or down.
		b.	moves the camera front or back sideways.
		c.	twists the camera front or back around a vertical axis.
3	Shifting the lens alters the:	a.	depth of field.
		b.	focusing distance.
		c.	point of view.
4	To correct vertical perspective, you must:	a.	shift both front and back to the left.
		b.	make the back and front parallel to the face of the subject.
		c.	swing front and back around a vertical axis.
5	To control the horizontal placement of a subject in the image frame, you can:	a.	swing the lens.
		b.	tilt the back.
		c.	shift the front or back.
6	To ensure even development of sheet film, it is beneficial to:	a.	avoid agitation.
		b.	presoak the film in water.
		c.	add a little stop bath to the developer to retain the developing process slightly.
7	Dust in the film holder causes:	a.	white specks in the print.
		b.	clear areas where the dust was on your negative.
		c.	black specks that are hard to remove in your print.
8	Rise and fall controls the:	a.	horizontal perspective when shooting at an angle to the subject.
		b.	the vertical placement of a subject in the image frame.
		c.	vertical perspective when shooting from a high camera angle.
9	Before withdrawing the dark slide from the film holder, make sure that you:	a.	cover the ground glass with the focusing cloth.
		b.	close the shutter.
		c.	use a magnifying loupe to set the right aperture.
10	Swinging the front allows you to:	a.	increase the covering power of the lens.
		b.	adjust the plane of focus to make only a part of the scene sharp.
		c.	control the vertical perspective in a scene.

14.4 PRACTICAL TIPS

Focusing

The Scheimpflug rule in practice.

The Scheimpflug principle states that when the planes of film, lens, and subject meet, the subject plane will be completely sharp. Once you have set up your camera and decided on a plane of focus in the scene, you can use the Scheimpflug rule to make sure that it will be as sharp as possible. The procedure is quite simple. Envision that your plane of desired focus intersects one point in the foreground and one point in the background. Without tilting the lens, focus first on the nearest point you mentally selected, and then refocus on the furthest point. Use the rear standard to focus. The closest point will be at the top of your ground glass and the furthest point will be at the bottom of your ground glass.

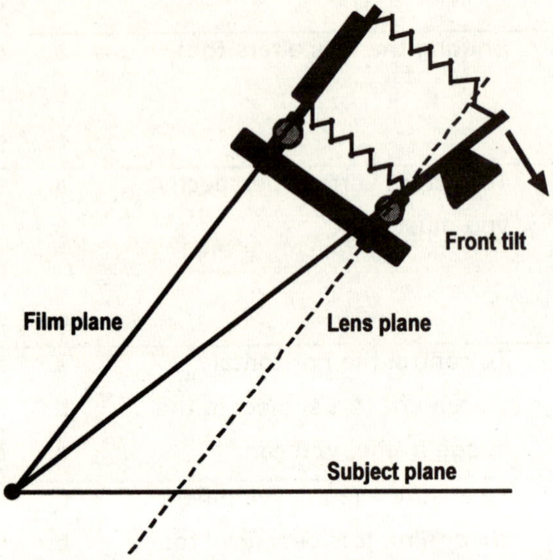

You have to move the rear standard a considerable distance between the two points of focus. Now tilt the lens in the direction indicated by the Scheimpflug principle. Focus on the point in the foreground and then refocus on the point in the background. The distance you moved the rear standard between the two focus points should have been reduced. Continue tilting the lens and focusing on both points until they coincide. The subject plane, the lens plane, and the film plane now intersect. If you find that the distance you move the rear standard between the two focus points starts to increase again, you have tilted the lens too far.

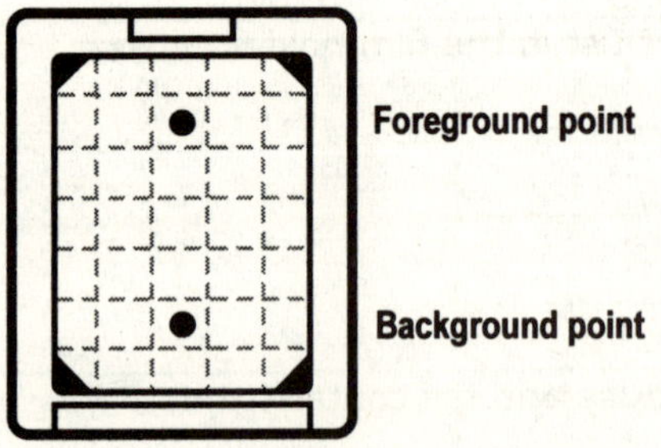

If you also want the plane of focus to tip from side to side around a horizontal axis, you need to perform the same procedure with a swing moment applied to the lens plane. Select two points that intersect the desired plane of focus and repeatedly focus on one and then the other while gradually applying swing to the front standard (as with tilt above). Once you are satisfied that they coincide, you need to check any tilt you applied again, since it has most likely moved a little (unless your lens rotates perfectly around its rear nodal point). Continue adjusting swing and tilt until focus is distributed exactly the way you intended. Some of these procedures may seem confusing to start with, so keep in mind that what you see on the ground glass is the image you will get. In other words, always trust your eyes above any step-by-step procedure.

14.5 JOURNAL

14.5.1 EXPOSURE INCREASE WITH BELLOWS EXTENSION

When the distance between the lens and the film plane is increased due to bellows extension, the amount of light reaching the film is reduced. To compensate for this loss, you must increase the exposure. Use these tables to record and determine your exposure increase. The formula below is used to calculate the entries, and you can also use this formula to make your own calculations:

$$\frac{\text{Bellows extension}^2}{\text{Focal length}^2} = \text{Exposure factor}$$

1 Measure the distance between the rear nodal point in the lens and the film plane.

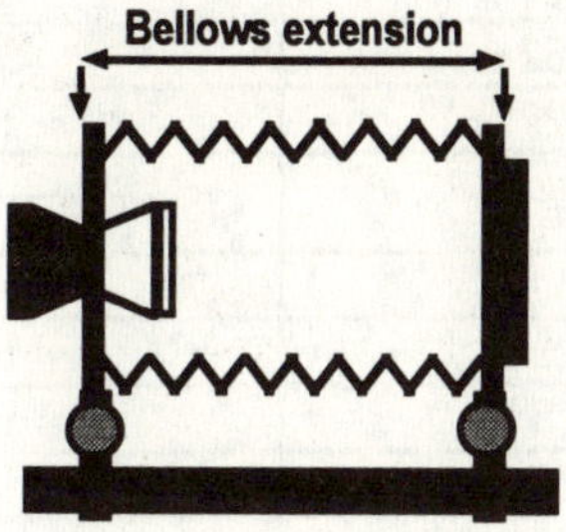

2 Note the measurement in mm.

140										

3 Note the focal length of your lens in mm.

90										

4 Find the exposure factor from the large table on the next pages.

2.42										

EXPOSURE FACTOR ▼									
1	1.2	1.5	2	2.5	3	4	5	6	8
0	1/3	2/3	1	1 1/3	1 2/3	2	2 1/3	2 2/3	3
EXPOSURE INCREASE IN STOPS ▲									

EXPOSURE INCREASE FOR A 4X5-INCH VIEW CAMERA

Bellows extension (mm)	Exposure factor	Bellows extension (mm)	Exposure factor
65mm lens focal length		**75mm lens focal length**	
65	1	**75**	1
85	1.71	**95**	1.60
105	2.61	**115**	2.35
125	3.70	**135**	3.24
145	4.98	**155**	4.27
165	6.44	**175**	5.44
185	8.10	**195**	6.76
205	9.95	**215**	8.21
225	11.98	**235**	9.81
245	14.21	**255**	11.56
265	16.62	**275**	13.44
285	19.22	**295**	15.47
90mm lens focal length		**135mm lens focal length**	
90	1	**135**	1
100	1.23	**145**	1.15
120	1.78	**165**	1.49
140	2.42	**185**	1.88
160	3.16	**205**	2.31
180	4	**225**	2.78
200	4.93	**245**	3.29
220	5.98	**265**	3.83
240	7.11	**285**	4.46
260	8.35	**305**	5.10
280	9.68	**325**	5.80
300	11.11	**345**	6.53
320	12.64	**365**	7.31
340	14.27	**385**	8.13
360	16	**405**	9
380	17.83	**425**	9.91
400	19.75	**445**	10.87
150mm lens focal length		**180mm lens focal length**	
150	1	**180**	1
160	1.14	**200**	1.23
180	1.44	**220**	1.49
200	1.78	**240**	1.78
220	2.15	**260**	2.09
240	2.56	**280**	2.42
260	3.00	**300**	2.78
280	3.48	**320**	3.16
300	4	**340**	3.57
320	4.55	**360**	4
340	5.13	**380**	4.46
360	5.76	**400**	4.94
380	6.42	**420**	5.44
400	7.11	**440**	5.98

420	7.84	460	6.53
440	8.60	480	7.11
460	9.40	500	7.72
480	10.24	520	8.35
500	11.11	540	9
520	12.02	560	9.68
540	12.96	580	10.38
560	13.94	600	11.11
210mm lens focal length ▼		**240mm lens focal length ▼**	
210	1	240	1
220	1.10	250	1.09
240	1.31	270	1.27
260	1.53	290	1.46
280	1.78	310	1.67
300	2.04	330	1.89
320	2.32	350	2.13
340	2.62	370	2.38
360	2.94	390	2.64
380	3.27	410	2.92
400	3.63	430	3.21
420	4	450	3.52
440	4.39	470	3.84
460	4.80	490	4.17
480	5.22	510	4.52
500	5.67	530	4.88
520	6.13	550	5.25
540	6.61	570	5.64
560	7.11	590	6.04
580	7.63	610	6.46
600	8.16	630	6.89
620	8.72	650	7.34
640	9.29	670	7.79
660	9.88	690	8.27
680	10.49	710	8.75
700	11.11	730	9.25

Notes

15 ZONE SYSTEM

15.1 GLOSSARY

Contraction In a Zone System context, a reduced development.

Expansion In a Zone System context, an increased development.

Full-scale Describes a print having a wide range of tonal values, from deep blacks through many shades of gray to brilliant white.

Gray card A card with 18 percent reflectance. The print value of the gray card corresponds to Zone V in the Zone System and the middle gray of your meter.

N Normal development.

N+1 (Normal-plus-one) Term used to describe overdevelopment by one stop. Usually requires a 25 percent increase in the normal development time.

N-1 (Normal-minus-one) Term used to describe underdevelopment by one stop. Usually requires development for 80 percent of the normal development time.

Tone The lightness or darkness of a particular area.

Visualize A mental process translating the values of a scene into a final print. In the Zone System, exposure and development decisions are based on this visualization and subsequent meter readings.

Zone A tonal value on the continuous grayscale that corresponds to a negative density and a print value.

Zone System A way to plan negative exposure and development to achieve precise control over the tonal values of various areas in a print.

Zone 0 The darkest possible print value. All the silver in the paper emulsion has been exposed.

Zone I Slight tonality without texture.

Zone II Some evidence of texture but no real detail.

Zone III The darkest tone that holds defined texture and full detail in the print.

Zone IV One stop less exposure than Zone V. A darker gray with full texture and detail.

Zone V Middle gray. Corresponds to a subject with 18 percent reflectance.

Zone VI One stop more exposure than Zone V. A lighter gray with full texture and detail.

Zone VII The lightest tone that holds well defined texture and full detail in the print.

Zone VIII Some evidence of texture but no real detail.

Zone IX Slight tonality without texture.

Zone X The lightest possible print value. Basically the white of the paper base.

15.2 SUMMARY

329 — **Zone System**

Have you ever looked at a scene and known just how you wanted the final print to appear: This is called visualization. **The Zone System is a method for controlling the black-and-white photographic process:** Based upon your visualization of a scene, you determine where you want values to fall and expose/develop your negative accordingly. **The Zone System lets you visualize how the tones in any scene will look in a print and to choose either a literal recording or a departure from reality:** Even if Ansel Adams initiated the Zone System, not every photograph produced by this method has to look like his prints.

330 - 331 — **The Zone System scales**

The Zone System has four scales that describe how light or dark an area is: The four scales are the meter-reading scale, the density scale of the negative, the print values, and finally the zones of the Zone System. **Subject values describe the amount of light reflected or emitted by various objects in a scene:** The scale is divided into 11 tones separated by a one-stop difference in value. **Negative-density values describe the amount of silver in various parts of the negative after it has been developed:** The scale of negative densities is divided into 11 densities separated by one-stop in exposure. **Print values describe the amount of silver in various parts of the print:** Again, the scale of values is divided into 11 tones. **The Zone scale is crucial because it links the values on the other three scales:** It provides a means of visualizing the relationship between a light-meter reading, exposure (and development), and the print. Decide how you want the subjects in a scene to appear as print values, and then determine the exposure and development to get a negative that will produce the desired print. The zone scale has normally been divided into 11 tones. These are divisions of what should be considered a continuous grayscale. Zone VI, for instance, represents the range of gray values found between the darker Zone V and the lighter Zone VII. There are many variations on the zone scale, some feature 14 and more tones. **Zone 0 (zero) is the deepest black print value that photographic paper can produce:** It represents no exposure, a clear film base, and the maximum black of the printing paper. **Zone X is the lightest possible print value – the pure white of the paper base:** It represents an overexposure with blocked highlights, an overly dense negative, and the white of the paper base. **Zone V corresponds to a middle gray, the tone of a standard-gray test card of 18 percent reflectance:** A reflected-light meter averages all the tones in a scene and gives a recommended meter reading based on this value. Page 331 illustrates where the zones of the Zone System will fall in a full-tonal-range print.

332 - 333 — **Using the zone scale while metering: Placing a tone**

Know the limits of your materials: In high-contrast scenes, the luminances of the subject may extend beyond the exposure range tolerated by the film. Metering with a reflected-light meter will allow you to place the most important values on the zone scale and determine where other values will fall. **When you meter different areas, you can determine where each lies on the zone scale for any given exposure:** Try to meter areas with a uniform value. They are easier to predict and place on the zone scale. Remember that the recommended meter reading for a value will produce a negative with a density that prints as a middle-gray tone – Zone V. **If you choose one of the f-stop and shutter speed combinations that are recommended by the meter, you will have placed the metered area in Zone V:**

Changing the exposure will expose the negative to reproduce the metered area as another, lighter or darker, value. One stop of overexposure will place the metered area on Zone VI. One stop of underexposure will place the metered area on Zone IV. **Once one tone is placed in any zone, all other luminances in the scene fall in zones relative to the first one:** Their relative brightness compared to the tone you placed (and exposed for) will determine where they will fall on the zone scale. Metering other areas and measuring the difference in stops from your exposure setting will give you the zone they will be reproduced as in the print.

334 - 335 **How development controls contrast**

Exposure plus development affect the tones in a scene: You can use development to increase or reduce the contrast (the range of zones) in an image. **Development can change the highlights and, as a result, control the overall contrast of the negative:** Done by altering the development time. **Increasing development increases contrast, decreasing development decreases contrast:** The density of high values builds more rapidly than lower values with increased development times. Adversely, reducing the time allows the lower values to develop further than their bright counterparts before the development time is cut short. **There are advantages to adjusting the negative's contrast:** It will print as predicted with a minimum of dodging and burning. **In Zone System terms, N stands for normal development:** Values fall where they were placed. **An expansion (Normal-Plus development) is produced by increasing development time:** N+1 development increases the values of bright zones and thereby the contrast - Zone VII will fall on Zone VIII. N+2 development will expand the contrast even further - Zone VII will fall on Zone IX. Values below Zone II will remain largely unaffected by N+1 development. **A contraction (Normal-Minus development) is produced by decreasing development time:** N-1 development contracts the zone scale by one zone in higher values. The change is less noticeable for zones below Zone II. N-2 is also possible, but rarely desirable. **Testing is the best way to determine your own development times:** The testing methods are described in literature dealing more extensively with the Zone System. See the Bibliography in the textbook. **However, here are some rough guidelines:** Use the manufacturer's film speed rating, place normal development on the time recommended by the manufacturer, and then increase the time by 25 percent for N+1, increase the time by 50 percent for N+2, develop for 80 percent of the time for N-1, and develop for 60 percent of the time for N-1. T-Max films require less of a change.

336 **Putting it all together**

The Zone System has four basic steps:

1. Visualize the final print.
2. Meter the most important area and place it on a zone.
3. Meter other areas to determine where they will fall.
4. Make development choices to adjust the contrast.

337 **Using the Zone System with roll film and color film**

Using the Zone System with roll film: You will alter the contrast of the entire roll, but since it may have been shot under similar conditions this is not necessarily a problem. Be aware that increased development will lead to an increase of grain in the negative. **With roll film, you can also plan on changing printing paper contrast:** Follow the old dictum; expose for the shadows and develop for the highlights. Make sure that your negatives have detail in the shadow areas, and you will most likely be able to adjust the contrast for each negative on an entire roll through development choices and paper contrast. **Using the Zone System with color film:**

You can place a value and predict where the other values will fall with color film. Extreme changes in development time, however, are not feasible due to color shifts. **With color negatives, place the most important shadow value:** Expose for the most important shadow area as with black-and-white film. You can ask your lab to push the film (overdevelop it) to increase the contrast. Some printing papers (Kodak's Supra and Ultra) come in different contrast "grades". **With color transparencies, correct exposure is vital because the film in the camera is the final viewing product:** Overexposed slides quickly lose detail in the highlights, so place the most important highlight no higher than Zone VII to retain texture and tone.

15.3 TEST

FILL IN THE BLANKS

1 The Zone System allows you to ____________________ a final print from a scene and then translate your vision through exposure and development decisions.

2 The zone scale consists of 11 or more divisions of a continuous ____________________.

3 Zone ____________________ is the deepest black print value.

4 Zone ____________________ is the lightest print value.

5 Zone ____________________ corresponds to the middle gray read by the light meter.

6 Zone ____________________ is the darkest zone that holds texture and detail in the shadow areas.

7 Zone ____________________ is lightest zone that holds texture as well as tonality.

8 If you use the exposure combination recommended by the meter to expose a subject with a uniform value, it will be reproduced with a Zone ____________________ print value.

9 If you expose a subject with a uniform value two stops more than a recommended meter reading, it will be reproduced with a Zone ____________________ print value.

10 Increasing the development time will ____________________ the negative contrast.

MULTIPLE CHOICE – CIRCLE ONE OR MORE

1 The zone scale:

a. is used for substitution readings instead of the gray card in scenes with more than one value.

b. establishes a relationship between negative density and print value that allows you to visualize your exposure and development decisions based on a final print.

c. is used instead of aperture settings on newer cameras.

2	When one tone has been placed on a zone, the other tones in a full-tonal-range scene will:	a.	fall outside the zone scale.
		b.	based on their luminance fall on zones relative to the placed zone.
		c.	fall on the same zone.
3	N+1 development means:	a.	overdevelopment of the negative.
		b.	an expansion of the negative.
		c.	a contraction of the negative.
4	With changes in development time, the dark values below Zone III are:	a.	affected more than the light values.
		b.	affected slightly less than the light values.
		c.	hardly affected at all.
5	After visualizing the print and metering the most important areas, you should:	a.	meter other areas to determine where these other values will fall.
		b.	always expose the film according to the meter reading to make sure that Zone V is reproduced in the print.
		c.	make sure that the most important shadow areas you metered were indeed of a Zone X value.
6	With color reversal film, the most important areas for metering and placement on the zone scale are:	a.	the darkest shadow areas with detail.
		b.	middle-gray values.
		c.	the brightest highlights.
7	A recommended increase in time for N+1 development is:	a.	25 percent.
		b.	50 percent.
		c.	100 percent.
8	The white of the paper base in a print corresponds to:	a.	Zone 0.
		b.	Zone V.
		c.	Zone X.
9	When the Zone System and development changes are used with roll film, it is best if:	a.	the entire roll is underexposed by 3 stops.
		b.	the entire roll is shot in similar contrast conditions.
		c.	extreme overdevelopment is avoided to prevent an increase in grain size.
10	If the metered difference in exposure between two areas is 3 stops, their print values will be:	a.	3 zones apart in the final print.
		b.	6 zones apart in the final print.
		c.	9 zones apart in the final print.

15.4 PRACTICAL TIPS

Sheet film development

Develop your sheet film in multiple trays.

The great advantage of developing your sheet film in tanks is the number of sheets that can be safely handled in one developing cycle. You can also place several sheets of film in a single tray and shuffle the pile during development for agitation purposes, but this can get scary when the film has a tendency to stick together. Besides, with all that handling, it is easy to scratch the wet emulsion. The potential problem that can arise with both the above methods is uneven development. Unless a large negative is exposed to a near constant flow of developer, it is likely to show signs of uneven density (caused by exhausted solutions) in uniform areas. One safe answer to these problems is to process only one or two sheets per tray with constant agitation, but this is often too slow for anyone eager to see the results.

Another method that truly works it to place 4 or more small 5x7 trays in a larger tray. Line up 3 large trays, each with a set of smaller trays containing developer, stop bath, and fixer. Place one sheet in each of the smaller trays and agitate them randomly by rocking the large tray.

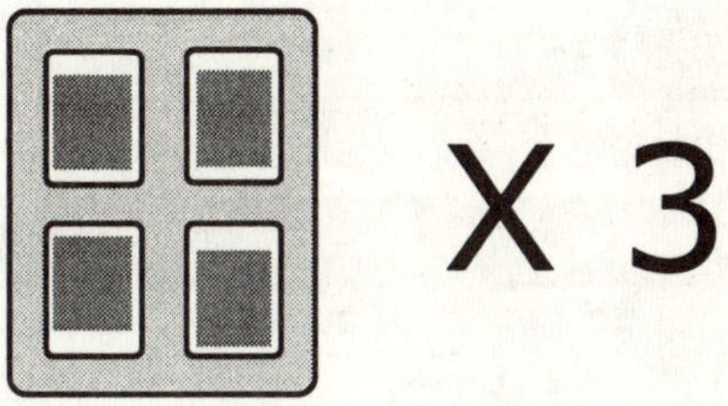

If you remember the order by which you inserted the sheets in the solutions, you can keep times constant for each negative by moving them to the next tray in the same order. Of course, for the advanced, there is also the possibility of reducing or extending the development time for one or more negatives in the same batch. If you use the Zone System for your work, you will most likely make some contrast adjustment in development. Once this film-processing procedure has been set up, it is actually very fast, even if you only do 4 negatives per cycle. The great advantage, however, is that you hardly handle the negatives, and they are of course unlikely to get scratched while moving around in their own solutions.

15.5 JOURNAL

15.5.1 ZONE-SYSTEM WORKSHEETS

These worksheets are intended to get you started with the Zone System. It is actually very easy to use once you have gained a little experience, and following the step-by-step procedure outlined in the tables below will assure that you get it right from the outset. To make the most of the precise control offered by the Zone System, you really need to use a spot meter to take reflected-light readings of local values in your scene. Spot meters are expensive when purchased on their own, so if you are considering a light meter to supplement your equipment, get one that covers all your bases, including reflected, incident, spot, and flash capabilities. With an averaging meter built into the camera, you need to move closer and isolate certain areas of the scene for your local readings. After completing these worksheets with a few exposures, you may want to draw up a similar outline of zones in a small notebook. Writing down your first placement and then jotting down the values where subsequent readings will fall can help in complex situations. The Zone System might seem very technical to start with, but you'll soon realize that it is simply a working method that makes large-format photography in particular far more predictable. It is after all based on your visualization.

ZONE-SYSTEM WORKSHEET EXAMPLE

1 Visualize a final print from the scene in front of you.

Examine the scene in front of you and search for creative solutions to how you want the final print to look. Remember that the Zone System gives you the tools to interpret the scene beyond a literal translation.

2 Meter the most important area, normally the deepest shadows with detail. Note the exposure.

f-number ▸		Shutter speed ▸	
	8		1/60

3 Place this area on the appropriate zone – the value you want in the final print.

0	I	II	III	IV	V	VI	VII	VIII	IX	X
			x							

4 Note the exposure you need to use to expose this area for the chosen zone.

f-number ▸		Shutter speed ▸	
	8		1/250

5 Meter other areas, especially the brightest highlights. Note the readings for these areas.

A – Deep shadow		B – Important area		C – Bright highlight		D – Brightest highlight	
f-number	**Shutter**	**f-number**	**Shutter**	**f-number**	**Shutter**	**f-number**	**Shutter**
8	1/125	11	1/500	11	1/1000	16	1/1000

6 Figure out where these areas will fall in relation to your initial placement. Adjust if necessary.

0	I	II	III	IV	V	VI	VII	VIII	IX	X
		A			B	C	D			

7 Consider equivalent exposures. Note the final exposure.

If all the placements above are satisfactory, consider equivalent exposures of your initial exposure reading.

f/number ▸		Shutter speed ▸	
	16		1/60

8 Based on step 6, make development choices to increase or reduce the contrast.

N - 2	N - 1	Normal	N + 1	N + 2
			x	

9 Evaluate your negative after development and include some comments below.

Negative reference ▸ # 35

The print from this negative turned out exactly as envisaged. The shadow area that I first metered and placed on Zone III turned out to be a deep black with both texture and detail. N + 1 development raised the values of the areas metered in C (Zone VI) and D (Zone VII) about one Zone to print with much better contrast. Overall a very successful use of the Zone System.

ZONE-SYSTEM WORKSHEET 1

1 Visualize a final print from the scene in front of you.

Examine the scene in front of you and search for creative solutions to how you want the final print to look. Remember that the Zone System gives you the tools to interpret the scene beyond a literal translation.

2 Meter the most important area, normally the deepest shadows with detail. Note the exposure.

f-number ▸		Shutter speed ▸	

3 Place this area on the appropriate zone – the value you want in the final print.

0	I	II	III	IV	V	VI	VII	VIII	IX	X

4 Note the exposure you need to use to expose this area for the chosen zone.

f-number ▸		Shutter speed ▸	

5 Meter other areas, especially the brightest highlights. Note the readings for these areas.

A – Deep shadow		B – Important area		C – Bright highlight		D – Brightest highlight	
f-number	**Shutter**	**f-number**	**Shutter**	**f-number**	**Shutter**	**f-number**	**Shutter**

6 Figure out where these areas will fall in relation to your initial placement. Adjust if necessary.

0	I	II	III	IV	V	VI	VII	VIII	IX	X

7 Consider equivalent exposures. Note the final exposure.

If all the placements above are satisfactory, consider equivalent exposures of your initial exposure reading.

f/number ▸		Shutter speed ▸	

8 Based on step 6, make development choices to increase or reduce the contrast.

N - 2	N - 1	Normal	N + 1	N + 2

9 Evaluate your negative after development and include some comments below.

Negative reference ▸	

ZONE-SYSTEM WORKSHEET 2

1	Visualize a final print from the scene in front of you.
	Examine the scene in front of you and search for creative solutions to how you want the final print to look. Remember that the Zone System gives you the tools to interpret the scene beyond a literal translation.
2	Meter the most important area, normally the deepest shadows with detail. Note the exposure.
	f-number ▸ Shutter speed ▸
3	Place this area on the appropriate zone – the value you want in the final print.

0	I	II	III	IV	V	VI	VII	VIII	IX	X

4	Note the exposure you need to use to expose this area for the chosen zone.
	f-number ▸ Shutter speed ▸
5	Meter other areas, especially the brightest highlights. Note the readings for these areas.

A – Deep shadow		B – Important area		C – Bright highlight		D – Brightest highlight	
f-number	**Shutter**	**f-number**	**Shutter**	**f-number**	**Shutter**	**f-number**	**Shutter**

6	Figure out where these areas will fall in relation to your initial placement. Adjust if necessary.

0	I	II	III	IV	V	VI	VII	VIII	IX	X

7	Consider equivalent exposures. Note the final exposure.
	If all the placements above are satisfactory, consider equivalent exposures of your initial exposure reading.
	f/number ▸ Shutter speed ▸
8	Based on step 6, make development choices to increase or reduce the contrast.

N - 2	N - 1	Normal	N + 1	N + 2

9	Evaluate your negative after development and include some comments below.
Negative reference ▸	

ZONE-SYSTEM WORKSHEET 3

1	Visualize a final print from the scene in front of you.
	Examine the scene in front of you and search for creative solutions to how you want the final print to look. Remember that the Zone System gives you the tools to interpret the scene beyond a literal translation.
2	Meter the most important area, normally the deepest shadows with detail. Note the exposure.
	f-number ▸ Shutter speed ▸
3	Place this area on the appropriate zone – the value you want in the final print.

0	I	II	III	IV	V	VI	VII	VIII	IX	X

4	Note the exposure you need to use to expose this area for the chosen zone.
	f-number ▸ Shutter speed ▸
5	Meter other areas, especially the brightest highlights. Note the readings for these areas.

A – Deep shadow		B – Important area		C – Bright highlight		D – Brightest highlight	
f-number	**Shutter**	**f-number**	**Shutter**	**f-number**	**Shutter**	**f-number**	**Shutter**

6	Figure out where these areas will fall in relation to your initial placement. Adjust if necessary.

0	I	II	III	IV	V	VI	VII	VIII	IX	X

7	Consider equivalent exposures. Note the final exposure.
	If all the placements above are satisfactory, consider equivalent exposures of your initial exposure reading.
	f/number ▸ Shutter speed ▸
8	Based on step 6, make development choices to increase or reduce the contrast.

N - 2	N - 1	Normal	N + 1	N + 2

9	Evaluate your negative after development and include some comments below.

Negative reference ▸

ZONE-SYSTEM WORKSHEET 4

1 Visualize a final print from the scene in front of you.

Examine the scene in front of you and search for creative solutions to how you want the final print to look. Remember that the Zone System gives you the tools to interpret the scene beyond a literal translation.

2 Meter the most important area, normally the deepest shadows with detail. Note the exposure.

f-number ▸		Shutter speed ▸	

3 Place this area on the appropriate zone – the value you want in the final print.

0	I	II	III	IV	V	VI	VII	VIII	IX	X

4 Note the exposure you need to use to expose this area for the chosen zone.

f-number ▸		Shutter speed ▸	

5 Meter other areas, especially the brightest highlights. Note the readings for these areas.

A – Deep shadow		B – Important area		C – Bright highlight		D – Brightest highlight	
f-number	**Shutter**	**f-number**	**Shutter**	**f-number**	**Shutter**	**f-number**	**Shutter**

6 Figure out where these areas will fall in relation to your initial placement. Adjust if necessary.

0	I	II	III	IV	V	VI	VII	VIII	IX	X

7 Consider equivalent exposures. Note the final exposure.

If all the placements above are satisfactory, consider equivalent exposures of your initial exposure reading.

f/number ▸		Shutter speed ▸	

8 Based on step 6, make development choices to increase or reduce the contrast.

N - 2	N - 1	Normal	N + 1	N + 2

9 Evaluate your negative after development and include some comments below.

Negative reference ▸	

ZONE-SYSTEM WORKSHEET 5

1 Visualize a final print from the scene in front of you.

Examine the scene in front of you and search for creative solutions to how you want the final print to look. Remember that the Zone System gives you the tools to interpret the scene beyond a literal translation.

2 Meter the most important area, normally the deepest shadows with detail. Note the exposure.

f-number ▸		Shutter speed ▸	

3 Place this area on the appropriate zone – the value you want in the final print.

0	I	II	III	IV	V	VI	VII	VIII	IX	X

4 Note the exposure you need to use to expose this area for the chosen zone.

f-number ▸		Shutter speed ▸	

5 Meter other areas, especially the brightest highlights. Note the readings for these areas.

A – Deep shadow		B – Important area		C – Bright highlight		D – Brightest highlight	
f-number	**Shutter**	**f-number**	**Shutter**	**f-number**	**Shutter**	**f-number**	**Shutter**

6 Figure out where these areas will fall in relation to your initial placement. Adjust if necessary.

0	I	II	III	IV	V	VI	VII	VIII	IX	X

7 Consider equivalent exposures. Note the final exposure.

If all the placements above are satisfactory, consider equivalent exposures of your initial exposure reading.

f/number ▸		Shutter speed ▸	

8 Based on step 6, make development choices to increase or reduce the contrast.

N - 2	N - 1	Normal	N + 1	N + 2

9 Evaluate your negative after development and include some comments below.

Negative reference ▸

16 SEEING PHOTOGRAPHS

16.1 GLOSSARY

Background	The areas of an image that surround the main subject.
Balance	Term used to describe a response to the arrangement of elements in an image. If the arrangement of tones or subjects is symmetrical, it is often referred to as "in balance".
Contrast	The difference between the darkest and lightest areas of a scene. Contrast is also used to describe the juxtaposition of seemingly opposing elements.
Convergence	The phenomenon in which lines that are parallel in a subject appear nonparallel in an image.
Crop	Trimming the edges of an image to include or exclude elements and thereby improve on the composition. Done in the camera through the viewfinder, during printing, by trimming the finished print, or overmatting the final image.
Depth of field	The area from near to far that appears sharp in a photograph.
Focus	The point where rays of light from the lens converge to form a sharp image. The term focus is also used to describe a center of attention or an action concentrating on such a center.
Frame	Used to describe the rectangular shape defined by the edges of the viewfinder window or a single negative on the film/contact sheet.
Framing	The process of selecting elements of the scene to be included in or excluded by the frame.
Light	Used to describe a photograph, light can have both a direction and a quality.
Line	A compositional element.
Meaning	The meaning of a photograph can be described as the articulation of a response to it in words.
Motion	A slow shutter speed can blur part of an image and create an impression of motion and time.
Pattern	An arrangement of shapes and/or tonal values.
Shape	A defined area. Larger than a spot.
Spot	An isolated point of interest in a photograph.
Perspective	The apparent size and depth of objects within an image.
Texture	Term used to describe the three-dimensional qualities of a surface.
Tone	The relative lightness or darkness of an area.
Viewpoint	The point of view from the camera position in relation to the subject.

16.2 SUMMARY

341 **Seeing photographs**

How do you learn to make better pictures: You start to explore the possibilities of how to photograph. **Your first step is to see your options, to see potential photographs in front of your camera:** Visualize the final print through the viewfinder. **Try to see how a picture communicates its visual content:** Concentrate on the resulting photograph, rather than just reproducing the scene in front of you as it "really" was.

342 - 343 **Basic choices: Content**

One of your first choices is how much of a scene to show: Single out the most important, or expressive, part of a scene or subject. **Get closer to your subject:** Closeness often simplifies the picture frame and focuses the attention on a subject. **What is your photograph about:** Decide on what you are intending to show or communicate and make your choices based on these decisions. **Try to visualize what you want the photograph to look like:** Explore the subject with the frame and make exposures for several options.

344 - 345 **Framing the subject**

The frame (the edges of a picture) isolates part of a larger scene: The photographer uses the frame to compose the picture and select the most important parts of a scene. **Every time you make an exposure, you make choices about framing – consciously or not:** The frame offers many options as to how a subject is either included or excluded within it. Be intuitive and daring in your selection. **Judicious cropping can strengthen a picture but awkward cropping can be distracting:** Obviously, your cropping of the scene can work to your advantage or disadvantage. There are no good rules, and "mistakes" can be more compelling than rigorous adherence to dubious principles. **Should your picture be horizontal or vertical:** Generally, hold the camera horizontally for horizontal subjects and vertically for vertical subjects.

346 - 347 **Backgrounds**

The background is part of the picture – obvious, but easy to forget: We tend to focus on the subject and forget about the background. The photograph, however, seems to lend the background an equal weight. **What do you do when your subject is in front of a less interesting or even distracting background:** Move yourself or the subject to simplify the background. **A busy background will call less attention to itself if it is blurred and indistinct rather than sharply focused:** Opening up the aperture and thereby reducing the depth of field will blur the background. Preview the effect. **Use the background when it contributes something:** Juxtaposing your main subject with the background can add to the picture.

348 - 349 **Spot/Line**

What good is design: Following certain design principles will provide you with a working vocabulary when photographing. **A single element of design seldom occurs in isolation:** A spot attracts attention, but rarely occurs in complete isolation within a photograph. Humans always seek out the human presence first. **Any small shape, not necessarily a round one, can act as a spot or point:** If the spot is your main subject, it directs the attention exactly the way you want, but a spot can also be a serious distraction. **The eye tends to connect two or more spots like a connect-the-numbers drawing:** When a picture is "read", the eye tends to move from spot to spot, from one focus of attention to another. **A line is a shape that is longer than it is wide:** Lines provide a shape for the eye to follow.

Lines are seen in relation to the edges of the frame. **According to some theories, lines have psychological overtones:** Both lines and colors may be perceived differently by different subjects. There are no objective effects inherent in the lines or colors themselves.

350 - 351 **Shape/Pattern**

A shape is any defined area: Shapes are always two-dimensional in a photograph, but variations in tone give them depth. Two or more shapes invite comparisons. Cropping a shape with the frame can actually accentuate its whole shape since the mind insists on completing it. **Objects that are close together can be seen as a single shape:** The photographer can position objects to join them. **Groupings can be visual as well as actual:** Grouping of objects can take place in the viewfinder. **Multiple shots, lines, or shapes can create a pattern that adds interest and unites the elements in a scene:** When combined, these arrangements give an impression of order, structure, and ultimately purposeful intent. Because of this, the photograph will appear more meaningful.

352 - 353 **Emphasis/Balance**

How do you emphasize some part of a photograph or play down another: You arrange your picture so that some parts are given more attention than others are. **Contrast attracts attention:** Placing a sharp subject against a blurred background or a dark figure against a white backdrop, or any other contrasting arrangement, directs attention. **Camera angles can emphasize a subject:** Remove distracting elements from the frame to focus on your subject. **Use surrounding parts of the scene to reinforce emphasis:** Use lines or other elements to point in the direction of your main subject. **People know when a picture is in balance even if they can't explain why:** Dark is heavier than light, large is heavier than small, an object at the edge has more weight than the same object placed at the center of the frame. Balance the frame by distributing these and other elements evenly. **Some tension in a picture can be an asset:** If the same formula is applied every time, it quickly loses impact. Try to explore new design solutions as you frame your subject.

354 - 355 **Using contrast and sharpness**

The sharpness of a photograph or of its various parts, is immediately noticeable: With normal vision, focus and sharpness is part of the mechanics of looking, but in a photograph sharpness is more conspicuous. **People tend to look first at the sharpest part of a photograph:** People tend to focus on sharp objects and ignore blurred, out-of-focus objects. **Depth of field affects sharpness from near to far:** Use focus and depth of field to distribute attention. **Motion can be photographed either sharp or blurred:** Freeze a moving subject with a fast shutter speed or give an impression of motion by blurring the subject with a slow shutter speed. **A gain in motion sharpness can mean a loss in depth of field:** A faster shutter speed means a smaller aperture and consequently less depth of field.

356 - 357 **Using contrasts of light and dark**

Contrast between light and dark draws a viewer's eye: Contrast also outlines and defines a subject sharply. **Contrast between two objects may be more apparent in color than in black and white:** The difference between two colors is more noticeable than the subtle change between two gray tones. Colored filters can be used to enhance the contrast between objects in black-and-white photography. **Light along the edge of an object can make its shape stand out:** Light falling from the back or front has this effect. **Shadows or highlights can be shown as separate shapes:** High-contrast images can take on graphic properties where shadows and highlights stand out as shapes.

You can adjust contrast somewhat during film processing and printing: To work with this effect, select development times and paper contrast grades to produce the desired result.

358 - 359 **Placing the subject within the frame**

Careful placement of a subject within the frame can strengthen an image: Consider your options creatively. **The most effective composition arises naturally from the subject itself:** There is on the contrary nothing natural about this. Compositional rules are a matter of convention. Make or break them as you see fit. **The horizon line – the dividing line between land and sky – is a strong visual element:** Place this line to distribute attention between land and sky. A tilted horizon, especially when it is clearly defined, is immediately noticeable and gives a sense of misalignment. **Stop for a moment to consider what you want to emphasize:** Place the horizon according to this emphasis. **Motion should usually lead into, rather than immediately out of, the image area:** This allows room for the motion to unfold. However, you may want to cut motion off by placing the moving subject close to the edge of the frame. **A subtler tension may be added by movement of a subject from right to left:** You are probably accustomed to "reading" from left to right and any motion extending the other way will go against your sense of a forward direction.

360 - 361 **Perspective and point of view**

The relative distance of objects from the lens and from each other affects perspective, the illusion of three dimensions in a two-dimensional photograph: Perspective is mainly produced by the relative difference in size between objects in the scene. The lens-to-subject distance affects the experience of perspective in a photograph. **Other factors affect perspective to a lesser degree:** Focus, lighting, overlapping of objects, colors, and tone affect the sense of depth in a photograph. A landscape that gradually recedes towards the horizon has a strong sense of depth. **Photographs of landscapes often gain from an impression of depth:** Position objects in the foreground, the horizon line in the upper half of the picture, or converging lines from foreground to background to add depth to a landscape photograph. **Your point of view or vantage point can have a strong influence:** Get away from the habit of photographing everything at eye level. A tilt, up or down, adds a distortion to your subject that can shape it to your advantage. Explore interesting angles through the viewfinder.

362 - 363 **Looking at – and talking about – photographs**

Photographs are made in order to convey a certain vision or idea, perhaps the beauty of a transcendent landscape or the gritty look of a downtown street: As a photographer, you quickly become aware that there is a decision-making process involved in every photograph. When you look at other pictures, you can consider how a photograph may have been composed, exposed, and printed to convey a certain meaning. You may ask yourself these questions:

1. What type of photograph is it?
2. What can you tell (or guess) about the photographer's intention?
3. What emphasis has the photographer created and how has that been done?
4. Do technical matters help or hinder the image?
5. Are graphic elements important, such as tone, line, or perspective?
6. What else does the photograph reveal besides what is immediately evident?
7. What emotional or physical impact does the photograph have?
8. How does this photograph relate to others made by the same photographer, in the same period, or of the same subject matter?

One caution when talking or writing about photographs: Keep it simple and honest. Please see page 362 in the textbook for a table of terms you can use when discussing photographs.

364 - 365 **Showing your work to editors and others**
Please see pages 364 – 365 for some informative comments from editors, gallery owners, and curators.

16.3 TEST

FILL IN THE BLANKS

1 It is equally important to consider the ____________________ when a subject is photographed.

2 The ____________________ is a crucial compositional device for the photographer.

3 A photographer's choice of focus and ____________________ are instrumental in directing attention to certain parts of a scene.

4 A ____________________ shutter speed is almost always desirable to prevent a blurred portrait.

5 The impression of depth (three dimensions) in a photograph is created by ____________________.

6 The quality of ____________________ in a photograph plays an important role in describing the subject and creating a mood.

7 By changing your ____________________, you can alter the way a scene or subject is seen.

8 Converging lines in a scene direct the eye towards a ____________________.

9 ____________________ between elements in a scene distributes and directs attention.

10 The ____________________ of a photograph can be considered the articulation of a response to it in words.

Notes

MULTIPLE CHOICE – CIRCLE ONE OR MORE

1	Perspective in a photograph is mostly influenced by:	a.	the focal length of the lens.
		b.	the angle of the horizon.
		c.	the distance between lens and subject.
2	Depth of field can also be used to:	a.	activate the edges of the frame.
		b.	change the focusing distance.
		c.	blur a distracting background into softer and less intrusive shapes.
3	It is best to frame a scene to your satisfaction rather than cropping the negative in printing because:	a.	it is ethically questionable to show anything but a full-frame photograph.
		b.	a photograph is only made when it is taken.
		c.	a negative enlarged enough to make a print of the cropped area will lead to an increase in grain and reduced sharpness.
4	When approaching a subject, a photographer should consider:	a.	framing.
		b.	exposure changes from the metered setting.
		c.	point of view.
5	Motion, and implicitly time, can be expressed through the use of:	a.	a slow shutter speed that blurs a moving subject.
		b.	an inherently blurred subject.
		c.	another perspective.
6	Responses to a photograph are:	a.	exclusively the viewer's own reactions.
		b.	clearly visible in the image.
		c.	formed by a viewer's interpretation of the photograph's content and its formal devices such as composition, contrast etc.
7	Compositional choices and exposure selections require that you:	a.	pre-visualize a print from the scene in front of you and make these decisions based on this visualization.
		b.	have a knowledge of how cameras and film work to make informed choices and selections.
		c.	immediately give up, switch to an automatic setting, and try to replicate a photograph you have already seen.

8	Breaking tentative rules of composition can have the effect of:	a.	adding a more unpredictable impact to your photographs.
		b.	escaping the boredom of repetitive solutions.
		c.	stirring the interest of a viewer.
9	When looking at and talking about a photograph, you can ask yourself the following questions:	a.	what were the photographer's intentions?
		b.	how did the photographer create this emphasis?
		c.	would it have been better with a dog in it?
10	There are perhaps:	a.	no objectively right or wrong responses to a photograph, only points of view.
		b.	no objectively good or bad photographs outside of the criteria used to make these distinctions.
		c.	creative possibilities in photography to formulate your own point of view on what makes a photograph wonderful and photography worthwhile.

16.4 PRACTICAL TIPS

Exposures

Explore and expose your options.

At the very beginning of this book, you were offered the advice of exploring the world through the viewfinder. By chapter 16, you have without doubt made significant progress on this suggestion, and you might find yourself trying several framing options for each shot before deciding on the best one. You might also have noticed how different what you saw when the photograph was made seems in comparison to the scene framed on the negative or contact sheet. Photography does strange things to people and places sometimes, and this level of unpredictability is often a welcome surprise that keeps your interest throughout the developing and printing process. However, after seeing the results from a roll of film, you may find that one of the discarded framing options that you debated at the scene might have been a much better choice. Weighing the pros and cons of your viewfinder image is undoubtedly necessary, but if you spend too long on this process, chances are that you will eventually discover some compelling argument to leave the shutter release untouched. It often feels safer to do nothing than to try something and possibly fail. While this practical tip does not encourage you to thoughtlessly squander film, it does advocate that you trust your intuition and make some exposures while you move around with a camera pressed to your eye. In a few cases, maybe even on your first roll, you might find that the final composition, which you believed to be the best when it was made, is in fact inferior to another framing after the images are developed. Covering your options all the way to the printing stage can in the end be a valuable insurance policy, especially since it only costs a few frames.

Practice

Look at photographs, examine how they are used, and read about them.

This chapter focuses mainly on visual elements that compose a photograph for aesthetic pleasure. These arrangements may be meaningful in the sense that they prepare us for a particular way of looking at photographs, and based on our preconditioned expectations, we can readily make exclamations of pleasure or disgust. Since the way we view photography is undoubtedly reflected in the kind of photographs we make, it seems fair to point out that the geometry and symmetry of visual elements explored in this chapter have met with several contesting positions in recent years. Many people believe that the formalism (which is a descriptive term for the practice of arranging formal elements in what is perceived to be an inherently meaningful way) it adheres to is no longer relevant for a postmodern outlook on images. Photography is so many things - an average Wal-Mart snapshot, an email attachment, or a framed masterpiece in the Museum of Modern Art. Some argue that photography must be seen as a system of signs, much like language, while others claim that it is our use and distribution of photographs that make them meaningful, not the photographs themselves. You hopefully appreciate how these disparate views influence the kind of photographs being made, and the extensive reading list in the next chapter of this Student Lab Manual contains titles that will introduce you to these positions and many more in depth. The bottom line here is that whether you are making art or working for commercial clients, you need to stay informed about the arguments and trends surrounding your chosen career to participate in the dialogue that constitutes it. Ever been in a group of friends when they discuss a book you never read or a television program you never saw? Well, trying to build a photographic practice of any sort without an up-to-date knowledge of the field will probably seem equally lonely and awkward. The best tip for seeing photographs must consequently extend beyond the immediate source material observed through the viewfinder in the world at large. It must involve looking at other photographs, thoroughly examining how they are used, and reading about different views on photography. With this kind of background in place, you are better equipped to build an involved and successful practice, whatever it might be.

16.5 JOURNAL

16.5.1 PROJECT DIARY

Every project or assignment, whether it is for a school critique, a gallery exhibition, or a commercial job, involves many decisions made by the photographer, but there is no single moment from initial conception to finished product where all the choices are made at once. All projects involve a continuous process of planning, photographing, and editing, but these steps do not necessarily unfold in this order. Sometimes the initial plan might need revision after the first results have been evaluated. A good photographer or artist will critically consider the range of choices at each step before deciding on a way to proceed, and then employ her or his technical skills to control the materials and direct them towards the expression sought. Use this first section as a diary for your projects or assignments. Plan, evaluate, and edit what you do, and include a running commentary of your decisions to become more aware of the process taking place. The working method outlined by these tables will seem very mechanical and ultimately predictable, but even when you make the best plan and execute it to perfection, you will most likely experience that your photographs rarely come out exactly as expected. When that happens (and it will), do not always return to your initial visualization. Look for potential and possibilities in the photographs you are making and let them inspire you to follow new and previously unthinkable expressions.

PROJECT TITLE ▸	Jumping the shadow	
Project description ▾		
For this project, you are asked to produce 5 self-portraits that reflect upon the act of representation. Photography is unique in that it allows you to see yourself as others may see you, but there might be more to you than appearances. How others choose to represent you may form the focus of your investigation. Keep in mind that this project is not a beauty pageant.		
?	?	?
What to photograph Where to find my subject What quality of light What time of day What is the intent	How to photograph Which film to use What framing is desirable What depth of field Any sense of motion	Which photographs worked Which exposures to print How to print What responses are evoked What meaning
All commercial studio portraiture is in essence a self-portrait, even if the subject does not trip the shutter. I go to the photographer to get the image I want, so I do select how to represent myself.	Research commercial studio styles and recreate them. Large- or medium-format color photography with soft light and frequent use of diffusing filters. (Try Vaseline on cheap UV filter). Narrow depth of field, elaborate backdrops, and use of props.	The first photographs shot of the actual finished set are surprisingly the most interesting. Everything is in place for the subject, so even if I am not in them, there is a vacuum at the center that I effectively fill. Print the two empty frames on roll 3.
In my wallet, I carry several IDs that serve to represent me, whether I go to a bar with a driver's license or check out books with a library card. Some of these, like a passport photo, demand a special pose that shows my ear in addition to my face. Play with these poses.	Look at all the IDs I can muster. Occasionally wanted criminals smile in mug shots. 35mm film is fine for this project. Use a lens of similar focal length to the Polaroid cameras used for passport photographs. Consider photo-booth strips also.	Print all images the same thumbnail size as requested by ID forms. Use a long lens, 80mm, in the enlarger and raise the easel from the baseboard. Present the images on small ID cards in a wallet to make the links more explicit. The more subtle alterations of the standard pose are better - roll 5.
Strange as it may sound, every self-portrait is in fact an act of blindness. The subject can never see it when it is made. There always seems to be two positions that are difficult to reconcile. There is the photographer/camera looking at the subject looking back. Can I collapse these positions?	I have to explore my options here with 35mm equipment. Obvious solutions may include mirrors and highly reflective windows, but I need to take this double presence into account for my framing, like I am trying to make sense of it and truly see myself. Consult - Lee Friedlander: Self Portrait - again.	This approach seems a little too predictable. The enigma I feel as a subject looking at myself is very real to me, but it does not quite resonate in the photographs. Maybe we have grown so accustomed to photographs that their strange madness no longer registers? Formally, some of the photographs are wonderful.

PROJECT TITLE ▶		
Project description ▼		
?	?	?
What to photograph Where to find my subject What quality of light What time of day What setting	How to photograph Which film to use What framing is desirable What depth of field Any sense of motion	Which photographs worked Which exposures to print How to print What responses are evoked What meaning

PROJECT TITLE ▸		
Project description ▾		
?	?	?
What to photograph Where to find my subject What quality of light What time of day What setting	How to photograph Which film to use What framing is desirable What depth of field Any sense of motion	Which photographs worked Which exposures to print How to print What responses are evoked What meaning

PROJECT TITLE ▸		
Project description ▾		
?	?	?
What to photograph Where to find my subject What quality of light What time of day What setting	How to photograph Which film to use What framing is desirable What depth of field Any sense of motion	Which photographs worked Which exposures to print How to print What responses are evoked What meaning

PROJECT TITLE ▸		
Project description ▾		
?	?	?
What to photograph Where to find my subject What quality of light What time of day What setting	How to photograph Which film to use What framing is desirable What depth of field Any sense of motion	Which photographs worked Which exposures to print How to print What responses are evoked What meaning

PROJECT TITLE ▸		
Project description ▾		
?	?	?
What to photograph Where to find my subject What quality of light What time of day What setting	How to photograph Which film to use What framing is desirable What depth of field Any sense of motion	Which photographs worked Which exposures to print How to print What responses are evoked What meaning

16.5.2 SCRAPBOOK

How do we know what a picture means or what it attempts to tell us? Through constant exposure to photographs and other images, we develop a visual vocabulary that somehow influences and shapes our understanding through common usage. This mode of communication may seem less definite than the spoken word or written language, but you probably agree that it can be equally meaningful and perhaps more persuasive. Have you noticed, for instance, how advertising almost always uses photographic imagery in some form to deliver its message? Together with your instructor, you may want to start investigating the impact photographs have on our experience and understanding of the world that surrounds us. Collect photographs, reproductions, or photocopies you find challenging in the scrapbook and consider your responses in terms of technical and aesthetic decisions that may influence your own photographic practice.

SCRAPBOOK SOURCE ▸ *Newspaper clipping*

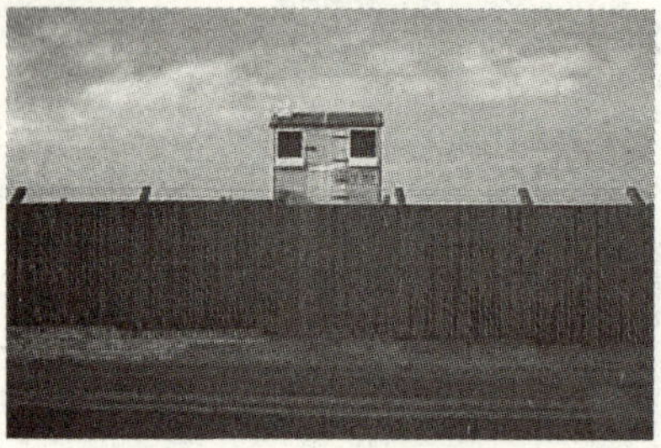

Comments

The tall barbed-wire fence with the tiny shed behind it reminds me of gated communities. The photograph uses juxtaposition of two elements quite effectively to make a point. The position of the photographer and the framing of the subject makes the photograph.

SCRAPBOOK SOURCE ▸ *Photocopy from library book*

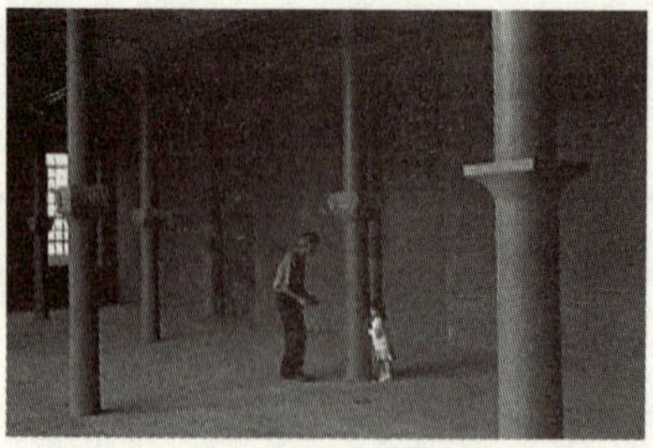

Comments

This photograph seems to be of the decisive moment school. A moment before or after, and this ambiguous yet poignant moment captured would not have been the same. Unlike the photograph above, this one truly relies upon the photographer being in the right place at the right time.

SCRAPBOOK SOURCE ▸

Comments

SCRAPBOOK SOURCE ▸

Comments

SCRAPBOOK SOURCE ▸

Comments

SCRAPBOOK SOURCE ▸

Comments

SCRAPBOOK SOURCE ▸

Comments

SCRAPBOOK SOURCE ▸

Comments

SCRAPBOOK SOURCE ▸

Comments

SCRAPBOOK SOURCE ▸

Comments

SCRAPBOOK SOURCE ▸

Comments

SCRAPBOOK SOURCE ▸

Comments

17 HISTORY OF PHOTOGRAPHY

17.1 GLOSSARY

Adams	Ansel Adams (American). Adams developed the Zone System as a general philosophy for his photography. Based for many years in Yosemite Valley, Adams photographs of nature in its Zone System splendor created a benchmark for what photographs should look like.
Albumen	Albumen is eggwhite. It was used to adhere a light sensitive solution to either a glass plate (for negatives) or paper (for prints).
Ambrotype	A collodion negative developed in a certain way and backed with a dark material to produce a positive image.
Atget	Eugène Atget (French). Prolific chronicler of Paris at the turn of the last century.
Autochrome	A positive color transparency made with an additive color process. Invented by the Lumière brothers in France and manufactured between 1907 and 1940.
Blueprint	A term often used to describe the Cyanotype process.
Callahan	Harry Callahan (American). Influential photographer and educator based in Chicago.
Calotype	The first positve/negative process invented by William Henry Fox Talbot and patented in 1841. Positive images, called salt prints, were made by contact printing the Calotype negative.
Camera obscura	Literally a darkened room. A box fitted with a lens and viewing mirror to let a draftsman trace the image projected by the lens on a piece of paper.
Cameron	Julia Margaret Cameron (British). Early portraitist with a romantic, if not mythical, vision.
Carte-de-visite	Usually a series of images taken by a single photographic plate and then mounted on a small piece of card. Popular in the 1860s.
Collodion	A wet-plate process where the negative is coated with a sensitized collodion emulsion. The plate is exposed and developed while wet.
Cyanotype	One of the first photographic processes. Iron salts and potassium ferricyanide are used instead of silver compounds to make a light-sensitive emulsion. Cyanotypes are distinctly blue in color.
Daguerre	Louis Jaques Mandé Daguerre (French). Early partner of Niépce and later inventor of the first photographic process (daguerreotype) suitable for widespread public use. Announced on January 7, 1839.
Daguerreotype	The first practical photographic process. A copper plate is covered with silver and sensitized in fumes of iodine to form silver iodide. Developed in mercury vapors. Daguerreotypes are unique objects.
Eastman	George Eastman (American). Launched the small roll-film camera in 1888 and thereby secured the immense success of his Eastman Kodak company.
Emerson	Peter Henry Emerson (British). An exponent for naturalistic photography in the 1880s. Emerson scorned artifice in photography and advocated the use of narrow focus to mimic the way the eye views a scene.

Evans	Walker Evans (American). Photographer with the Farm Security Administration. Evans eventually developed a range of works, and he has become one of the icons of American photography.
Ferrotype	See Tintype below.
Frank	Robert Frank (American). Photographer whose book "The Americans" (published in 1958) defined a new personal direction for documentary photography.
Lange	Dorothea Lange (American). Photographer with the Farm Security Administration, who produced one of the most celebrated images of that era – her "Migrant Mother".
Lumière	Antoine and Lois Lumière (French). Invented and marketed the Autochrome color process between 1907 and 1940.
Man Ray	Man Ray (American based in Paris). Man Ray's experiments with photographic materials are exemplary of the new vision that was developing with modernity.
Maxwell	James Clerk Maxwell (British). Devised the first additive color process in 1861.
Moholy-Nagy	Lázló Moholy-Nagy (Hungarian). A principal participant in the Bauhaus school's experiments with photographic materials. The aim was to develop a language for photography that was more compatible with modern life.
Muybridge	Eadweard Muybrdige (American). A pioneer in motion studies. A subject was caught by a sequential array of cameras at different moments to analyze movement patterns.
Niépce	Joseph Nicéphore Niépce (French). Generally credited with one of the first successful experiments aimed at fixing the camera obscura image. His "View from a Window at Gras", 1826, is commonly considered the first photographic image.
Photogenic drawing	An early method of producing paper negatives without a camera. Photograms are made with the same method today but with different materials.
Rayogram	Man Ray's own name for his photograms.
Robinson	Henry Peach Robinson (British). Early pioneer for artistic photography through the use of composite printing from different negatives.
Salomon	Erich Salomon (German). Major contributor to the birth of photojournalism and the picture essay.
Sander	August Sander (German). Produced a vast archive of portraits arranged according to occupation and social class. Sander was active in the late 1920s and early 1930s.
Siskind	Aaron Siskind (American). Influential photographer and educator based in Chicago. An abstracted vision with expressionistic intent.
Stereograph	Two views of the same scene photographed a small distance apart, mounted on a card, and then viewed through a special viewer to create a three-dimensional effect.
Stieglitz	Alfred Stieglitz (American). Influential photographer, gallery owner, and publisher active from about 1900 onwards.
Talbot	William Henry Fox Talbot (British). Inventor of the first negative/positive process, patented in 1841 as the calotype.
Talbotype	See the Calotype above.
Tintype	A positive image formed by using a thin sheet of iron coated with black lacquer and sensitized collodion. A cost-effective way of producing portraits.
Weston	Edward Weston (American). Weston's approach to photography favored sharp and detailed prints with a full tonal range. His straight photography was a strong influence from the 1930s to the 1950s.
White	Minor White (American). One of the most influential photographers in America from the 1950s onwards. White's philosophical and metaphorical take on photography opened up new avenues as to how the medium might be perceived.

17.2 SUMMARY

367

History of photography

Photography was one of the many inventions of the 19th century: They have all shaped the world we live in, but none of them have had the same impact as photography. **Photography took over what previously had been one of the main functions of art – the recording of factual visual information:** No technology reproduced and preserved a likeness better than photography.

368

The invention of photography

They said it couldn't be done: The ability to capture a reflection was thought impossible and it was furthermore considered blasphemy. **The camera obscura was the forerunner of the modern camera:** The effect of rays of light passing through a tiny opening had been known since Aristotle. In the Renaissance, a lens was added to the opening and the camera obscura was used as a drawing tool to trace an image reflected onto a piece of paper. **What remained to be discovered was a way to fix the camera obscura image permanently:** The darkening of silver compounds when exposed to light had been known since the 17th century, but the problem of halting (fixing) the action was not yet discovered. **The first permanent picture was made by Joseph Nicéphore Niépce:** Instead of a silver compound, Niépce used bitumen of Judea to create an image. He called the process heliography – sun drawing. **News of Niépce's work reached another Frenchman, Loius Jaques Mandé Daguerre:** From 1829 onwards, Niépce entered into a partnership with Daguerre to develop a permanent photographic process. **The mid-19th century was ripe for an invention like photography:** Portraiture was in demand and exotic travelogues had found a captive market. After Niépce's death in 1833, it would be another 6 years before the first photographic process to reach a wider audience was perfected by Daguerre and announced to the public.

369

Daguerreotype: "Designs on silver bright"

The response to the daguerreotype was sensational: The French Academy of Sciences announced the first commercially viable photographic process, the daguerreotype, to the public on January 7, 1839. Accounts of the process from the time marvel at the exquisite detail and wonderful finish of the objects. Daguerreotypes had an explosive development, and by 1853 an estimated 3 million were produced in the United States alone. **The daguerreotype was made on a highly polished surface of silver that was plated on a copper sheet:** The silvered plate was then placed in vapors from iodine crystals to form the compound silver iodide, which made the plate sensitive to light. After exposure, the plate was developed in mercury vapors and fixed before it was ready for viewing. **The daguerreotype was very popular in its time, but it was a technological dead end:** Its reflective surface made viewing difficult, the mercury vapors used for development were highly poisonous, and perhaps most importantly, each plate was unique and could not be reproduced as in a negative/positive process.

370

Calotype: Pictures on paper

Another photographic process was announced almost at once: Less than three weeks after the Daguerreotype became public property, William Henry Fox Talbot announced another method of permanently fixing the camera-obscura image. **Talbot made his images on paper:** First as "photograms" on paper sensitized with silver chloride and later with a camera obscura. **In June 1840 Talbot announced a technique that became the basis of modern photography:** He exposed a latent image and developed it.

Talbot realized the value of photographs on paper rather than on metal: They could be reproduced (and turned positive) through contact printing. Compared to the daguerreotype, however, the calotype was severely lacking in detail and sharpness.

371 **Collodion wet plate: Sharp and reproducible**

The collodion wet-plate process had the best feature of the daguerreotype – sharpness- and the best of the calotype – reproducibility: It was also more light sensitive, which allowed for shorter exposures. After its introduction in 1851, it became the most common process. Collodion was used to attach the light-sensitive emulsion to a smooth glass plate. **The disadvantage of collodion was that the plate had to be exposed and processed while it was still wet:** The plate was coated and sensitized, exposed while wet, and then developed and fixed immediately. This meant that a complete darkroom was part of the equipment at all times - in the studio as well as the field. **Collodion could be used to form either a negative or positive image:** A clear glass plate could be printed on albumen-covered paper. A glass plate covered with dark material on one side turned into a positive image called an ambrotype. Coated on dark enameled metal, it became a tintype. **One of the most popular uses was to make stereographic photographs:** By taking two photographs a small distance apart, they can be placed in a viewer for a three-dimensional effect. **By the 1860's the world had millions of photographic images; 25 years earlier there had been none:** Photography was everywhere, from portrait studios to battlefields.

372 **Gelatin emulsion/Roll-film base: Photography for everyone**

Until the 1880s, few photographs were made by the general public: Up until that point, people had mostly sought out professionals for portraits and other commissions. **By the 1880's, the perfection of two techniques not only made possible a fast, dry plate but also eliminated the need for the clumsy, fragile glass plate itself:** Gelatin emulsions were soon applied to another invention of the time – roll film. **Much of the credit for popularizing photography goes to George Eastman:** His Eastman Kodak Company first developed a portable roll film. **Roll film made possible a new kind of camera:** The small and inexpensive Kodak camera was developed in 1888. Camera and film (100 pictures) were sent back to Kodak for processing. **The Kodak camera became an international sensation almost overnight:** With the invention of plastic (in place of paper) backed roll film, the Kodak products geared toward the amateur photographer soon became immensely popular.

373 **Color photography**

Daguerre himself knew that only one thing was needed to make his wonderful invention complete – color: To reproduce the world as it was seen, color was desired. **After several false starts, one of the first successes was demonstrated in 1861 by the British physicist James Clerk Maxwell:** Through three separate negatives in red, green, and blue, Maxwell demonstrated a color process based on projection and additive color mixing in 1861. In 1869, the Frenchmen Lois Ducos du Haroun and Charles Cros, working independently, presented their research into subtractive color mixing, using the primaries cyan, magenta, and yellow. Three images in these colors were superimposed in the three-color carbon process and the carbro process. The method remains in use for the modern dye-transfer process. **The first commercially successful color was an additive process:** The Lumière brothers' autochrome process reached the market in 1907. **Kodachrome, a subtractive process, made color photography practical:**

The efforts of Leopold Mannes and Leopold Godowsky combined with researchers at the Kodak labs resulted in the Kodachrome in 1935. The film contained 3 layers sensitive to red, green, and blue, which formed a positive color image through a single exposure. This forms the basis for all modern color emulsions. **Today it is difficult to imagine photography without color:** Color has become the standard for most applications of photography, both amateur and professional.

374 - 375 **Early portraits**

People wanted portraits: Despite painfully long sitting times (often requiring a head clamp to keep the subject still), people flocked to the portrait studios. In the 1860s, a series of small portraits on a single card became a popular item. These were called cartes-de-visites. **Photographs had an almost mythical presence:** A presence haunted by an absence, which was impossible to fully comprehend yet incredibly desirable.

376 **Early travel photography**

Early travel photographs met a demand for pictures of faraway places: The world was being explored, but the means of travel were still fraught with hardship and danger. Photographs made it possible to almost directly experience the new wonders of the world from the comfort of your own home. **The Near East was of special interest:** Ancient cultures and biblical references made the subject matter especially rich. Early daguerreotypes were reproduced as engravings, and actual photographs were not readily available in large numbers until the collodion process was invented. **The most spectacular scenery of the western United States was not much photographed until the late 1860s:** As part of government expeditions intent on mapping and documenting the geological features of the western States, photographers like Timothy O'Sullivan and Alexander Gardner provided a record of the sights they encountered. William Henry Jackson and Carleton Watkins photographed the areas that were to become Yellowstone and Yosemite National Parks. Their images were used as arguments in Congress to preserve this wilderness.

377 **Early images of war**

Photographs made war scenes more immediate for those at home: However, as in the case of Roger Fenton's record of the Crimean War, views tended to be idealistic rather than realistic. **Photographs from the American Civil War were the first to show the reality of war:** Mathew B. Brady hired a team of photographers to document battle scenes from the Civil War. His business investment turned out to be failure. Few people wanted to remember what they sought to forget, but the images have become an invaluable record of the conflict.

378 **Time and motion in early photographs**

The earliest photographs required very long exposures: People would blur or disappear entirely in most cases. **Stereographic photographs were the first to show action as it was taking place:** Because of the faster lenses in stereo cameras, they were able to stop motion. **These "instantaneous" photographs revealed aspects of motion that the unaided eye was not able to see:** Some movement patterns were "seen" for the first time in the motion studies done with multiple cameras exposed at short intervals. **Eadweard Muybridge was a pioneer in motion studies:** His elaborate set ups with multiple cameras and a grid for a backdrop turned photographic motion studies into a science.

379 **The photograph as document**

Photographs can be documents on many levels: They are both objective records and subjective arguments. **Eugène Atget's work went beyond simple records:** His photographs of Paris from around the turn of the century convey the experience he had of the city at that time. **August Sander chose to document a people:** His staged and formal portraits categorized the German people according to occupation and social class.

380 - 381 **Photography and social change**

Photography soon went from documenting the world to documenting it for a cause: Jacob Riis picked up photography as a means of showing and hopefully correcting living conditions in New York slums. Lewis Hine photographed child labor to initiate labor reforms. **The photographers of the Farm Security Administration recorded the depression of the 1930s:** Lead by Roy Stryker, Dorothea Lange, Walker Evans, Russell Lee, Marion Post Wolcott, Arthur Rothstein, and Ben Shahn, among others, worked for a government agency to capture the depression and the effects of the New Deal policy initiated by President Roosevelt.

382 - 385 **Photojournalism**

Whatever the news event – from a prize-fight to a war – we expect to see pictures of it: News used to be dominated by text. Photographs were translated into woodcuts and reproduced as black-and-white line art. **The halftone process, perfected in the 1880s, permitted photographs and type to be printed together:** Halftones reproduce the grayscale in a spatial arrangement of black and white areas. Seen close up, the halftone pattern is easily discernible. This reproduction process made photographs an integral part of the news. **The photo essay, a sequence of photographs plus brief textual material, came of age in the 1930s:** Picture magazines like *Life* and *Look* made this format popular. Small 35mm cameras allowed photographers to work in a more unobtrusive way, which gave their pictures a more candid and authentic feel. Picture magazines have been overcome by television, but the news is still carried by images.

386 **Photography as Art in the 19th Century**

Was it just a photograph or was it art: Photography immediately looked to the conventions of representation outlined by other art practices such as painting and drawing. The debate about whether photography is simply an objective record or a subjective representation surrounds its categorization as art. **Many photographers adapted styles of painting to the photographic print:** By manipulating photographic materials in prints made from multiple negatives, artists such as Oscar G. Rejlander and Henry Peach Robinson sought to remove the objective criteria that prevented photography from becoming a personal expression. **By the 1880s a new movement championed naturalism as artistic photography:** The image shaping properties of the camera, and especially the ability it has to focus on one point at a time while rendering the rest of a scene slightly soft (much like the eye), convinced Peter Henry Emerson that the artistic qualities of photography were inherent in the descriptive powers of the medium itself.

387 **Pictorial photography and the Photo-Secession**

Was photography an art: Photographers were still concerned with this question at the turn of the century. The international movement of pictorialism sought to separate its photographic expressions from those of other uses of the medium.

Art for art's sake was their goal, and an aesthetic was defined through numerous exhibitions selected by juries. **Many pictorialists believed that artistic merit increased if the photograph looked like some other kind of art:** Works of art where the unmistakable touch of a hand lent them an interpretive character were favored. To achieve these effects, pictorialists often used printing techniques to which handwork was added. This perceptively reduced the photographic content to the extent that the artificial reproduction of nature was replaced by art. **In America, Alfred Stieglitz was the leader and catalyst for photography as an art form:** Through his galleries, publications (Camera Work), and own photographs, Stieglitz set an agenda for photography that gradually lent it recognition as a serious art form.

388 **The direct image in art**

Some photographers interested in art in the early 20th century made images directly related to the photographic process: The straight image was eventually considered by Stieglitz, Paul Strand, and later Minor White to have a strong sense of equivalence. Considered a metaphor, the photograph would stand in for a state of mind. **Straight photography dominated photography as an art form from the 1930s to the 1950s:** Photographers such as Edward Weston, Ansel Adams, Paul Caponigro, and Imogen Cunningham promoted a photography where the final image existed in the mind before it was visualized through the camera. To bring this vision out with the utmost clarity, they preferred glossy papers and small apertures to emphasize sharpness and a full tonal range in their images.

389 **The quest for a new vision**

The beginning of the 20th century saw great changes in many areas: The world was changing and art was supposed to change with it. **At the center of radical art, design, and thinking was the Bauhaus:** Located in Berlin, the Bauhaus philosophy had an impact on both European and American philosophies. László Moholy-Nagy sought a new expression in the use of photograms and collage. Man ray, drawn to Dada and surrealist thinking, used solarization as a means of expanding the language of photography.

390 - **Photography as art in the 1950s and beyond**

A tremendous growth has taken place in the acceptance of photography as an art form: Photography is now part of the curriculum in schools. Museums and galleries show photographs regularly. They are bought and sold as art and included in large collections. Magazines are devoted to writing about and publishing photography. **American work of the 1950s was often described in terms of regional styles:** Chicago was known for the abstract yet expressive work of Aaron Siskind and Harry Callahan. The west coast had the purism of Ansel Adams and Minor White (only a tenuous connection in agendas here). New York was the center for social documentary through the work of the Photo League. Amidst all this, there was the salesman for a personalized documentary, Robert Frank, touring America to produce that eponymous book "The Americans". **An increasing number of colleges and art schools in the 1960s offered photography courses:** Partly due to the co-existence with other disciplines within art departments, photography has experienced a cross-fertilization with other techniques. Photography today is less straight and more involved in multi-media productions. The influx of digital photography has exaggerated this development.

17.3 TEST

FILL IN THE BLANKS

1 Nicéphore Niépce named the process for his fist successful attempts at securing the camera obscura image ____________________.

2 The daguerreotype is a copper plate coated with ____________________.

3 On January 7, ____________________, the daguerreotype was announced to the public before the French Academy of Sciences.

4 William Henry Fox Talbot's calotype process allowed paper negatives to be ____________________.

5 From 1851 onwards, most photographers used the ____________________ process.

6 ____________________ was the first person to take full advantage of the gelatin emulsion and roll film inventions.

7 The first Kodak camera reached the marketplace in ____________________ and from that moment onwards photography secured a mass appeal.

8 The first color photographs produced by James Clerk Maxwell employed an ____________________ color process.

9 ____________________ was a subtractive color process that made color photography available to a wider audience in 1935.

10 A ____________________ consists of several small images on one card, and they were popular in the 1860s.

MULTIPLE CHOICE – CIRCLE ONE OR MORE

1 The following photographers were responsible for the first photographic surveys of the American West:
- a. Daguerre, Lumière, Niépce.
- b. Siskind, Callahan, Frank.
- c. O'Sullivan, Gardner, Jackson.

2 Mathew B. Brady established a team of photographers to provide commercial images of the:
- a. Rocky Mountains.
- b. Civil war.
- c. Colorado River.

3 Some of the first motion studies were produced by:
- a. August Sander.
- b. Eugéne Atget.
- c. Eadweard Muybridge.

4 The photographs of the Farm Security Administration were intended to:
- a. show the effects of the depression.
- b. document the effectiveness of Roosevelt's New Deal policy.
- c. display the beauty of the cultivated landscape.

5	The photo-essay pioneered by magazines such as Look and Life contained:	a.	photographs only.
		b.	photographs and very little text.
		c.	photographs and long explanatory captions.
6	Photographs by Julia Margaret Cameron and Henry Peach Robinson:	a.	relied on the clarity of the image to show artistic intent.
		b.	show signs of manipulation to highlight the illustrative and allegorical properties of the medium.
		c.	closely resemble those of Peter Henry Emerson.
7	Pictorialists aimed to make their photographs look like:	a.	charcoal drawings.
		b.	sharp and detailed daguerreotypes.
		c.	true documents of a scene.
8	In the 1930s, a group of photographers (including Ansel Adams) emerged that favored:	a.	what they termed straight photography.
		b.	sharp prints on glossy paper with a full tonal range and an attention to detail and texture.
		c.	visualization of the final print as a way of recording a subject.
9	With the influx of modernity came the desire to represent a changing world in new ways, as exemplified by photographers such as:	a.	Man Ray.
		b.	Lázló Moholy-Nagy.
		c.	Paul Strand.
10	Photography since the 1950s has been marked by:	a.	a return to the traditional values of the naturalist photographers.
		b.	the entry of photography into the school curriculum.
		c.	a wider range of aesthetic approaches to photography.

Notes

17.4 PRACTICAL TIPS

Essay guidelines

Analyze the photographs and support your arguments.

Every history of photography class will require you to write several essays, and you might also write shorter pieces as part of a studio assignment. The first rule when it comes to writing assignments in an academic setting is to carefully read the essay questions. What exactly are they asking, and what are you required to do? Discuss the questions with your instructor if you are in doubt. Once these guidelines have been clearly answered, you are ready to start compiling research and develop your ideas for the essay of choice. If you know what you are doing from the outset, there will be fewer blind alleys to follow and less time wasted on excursions that will not directly benefit your work. With regards to the structure of the essay itself, it usually follows a breakdown of introduction, main essay, and conclusion. The French film director Jean-Luc Godard once said that his films always come with a beginning, a middle, and an end, but not necessarily in that order. You also write your essays in parts that are not necessarily sequential. Start with the main body of the piece to develop your arguments, proceed to clarify them in the conclusion, and then write the introduction after you have a better idea of what will follow. Without fail, starting with the introduction will require a rewrite after you have had time to think through the material over a few pages. The key to a good essay is to anchor your arguments in the photographs you are writing about. Look carefully at the images and contextualize them with research and your own thoughts. Not only will this mode of analysis impress your instructor; it will give you something concrete to consider. Examine the images, read what others have had to say about them, and suddenly you have a wealth of information to write about. This approach is both better and easier than any attempts at constructing your arguments from thin air. When you write in response to something without trying to figure out what comes next all the time, your thoughts and words will also flow much faster. Finally, always support your position. It is bad psychology to impress an opinion on someone without explaining why you see something in a certain way. Instead of simply telling your reader how a photograph should be read, which will most likely solicit the wrong response, persuade them with eloquent arguments supported by authoritative opinions and evidence you see in the images themselves.

Research guidelines

Stay organized with your research and document sources as you proceed.

Academic writing assignments will require you to use footnotes and to compile a bibliography. If you neglect this important part of your assignments early on, you pay a higher prize later. Imagine having to look up every source again for bibliographical references, or to search for the page numbers of a quote throughout an entire book after your essay is done. You really don't want to waste time on this. The trick is to make a habit of writing down what you need during your research. When you consult a book, record the complete information, and always make a note of the page numbers when you come across a quote that might be used in the essay. With this approach, you are effectively compiling your bibliography as you read, and if you insert the completed footnotes as you write, the essay will practically be done the very moment you type your last period. Imagine that compared to desperately chasing down library books you consulted that are now loaned to someone else.

Writing guidelines

Create an outline first and then fill in the pieces.

When you first start writing, even a page or two might seem like a long train of thought to string together. As you proceed to more advanced classes, or even a doctorate degree, this feeling of being overcome by a mammoth task never really goes away. There will always be a next level that both increases the number of pages that you have to write and the research requirements. Instead of procrastinating and getting nothing done when there is too much to do, approach the overwhelming task at hand in the only way possible: break it down into smaller pieces and then compile and complete them in a methodical manner. Once you have gathered a significant amount of research and jotted down some ideas on where you are heading, create an outline of how your argument will flow. As you do this, write down the points you would like to make in shorthand and critically consider how various elements are linked. To make your essay easy to read, you need to make transitions between sentences, paragraphs, and perhaps most importantly, the various elements of your argument. Once the outline has taken on a shape that starts to make sense, consider if there is more research that needs to be done before the actual writing can start. Fill in any gaps in the argument at this stage. When you eventually sit down to write the essay, your head will be filled with thoughts on the subject, and the outline will guide you from sentence to sentence. It helps if you do not worry too much about the actual style at this point. Not every sentence needs to be a masterpiece, and there is always the opportunity to polish them later. Writers write in different ways, and a final anecdote about two masters of American literature will illustrate the distinctions. Jack Kerouac wrote his epic book "On the Road" in a three-week spell on sheets of paper taped together for a continuous flow into his constantly tapping typewriter. Upon hearing the story, Norman Mailer humorously exclaimed that this was not writing but typing to defend his slower rate of output. In a way he was right, because Kerouac spent several years revising his lengthy scroll before it was published.

17.5 JOURNAL

17.5.1 A PHOTOGRAPHY READING LIST

Please find two separate reading lists dealing with the history and criticism of photography below. The lists have been prepared to help you locate the books, and they do not follow proper guidelines for bibliographical references, nor are they always complete. In other words, do not compile your bibliography this way for essays or other assignments. To list a source in these contexts, please use this complete format as an example:

Batchen, Geoffrey; Burning with Desire – The Conception of Photography
(Cambridge, MA: MIT Press, 1997)

The topical suggestions below are designed to be a study guide. You can enter the call number for a particular book in the space allocated while you research your library's catalog. Once recorded, there is no need to look it up again. Beneath each title, there is a frame where you can make some shorthand references to material covered in that particular book. This might be very useful in the initial stages of an essay, or if you are planning to research a favorite photographer in depth. Finally, every book in this selection deserves a star rating, but only a few have received that distinguishing mark of quality. Needless to say, this author has not read every title included, so the stars are reserved for a selection of books with an established reputation in the field (and the author has indeed read most of them and will vouch for their excellence).

✓	CALL NUMBER	HISTORY
❑	TR 184.23B	**Burning with Desire – The Conception of Photography ★** Geoffrey Batchen *(MIT Press, 1997)*

The list of people who claimed to have invented photography – page 35.
Discussion of H. Bayard photograph – pages 158–173.

✓	CALL NUMBER	HISTORY
❑		**A Guide to Early Photographic Processes** Brian Coe, Mark Haworth-Booth *(V&A Museum and Hurtwood Press, 1983)*
❑		**A History of Photography: Social and Cultural Perspectives** Jean-Claude Lemagny, André Rouillé *(Cambridge University Press, 1987)*
❑		**A History of Women Photographers ★** Naomi Rosenblum *(Abbevile Press, 1994)*
❑		**A New History of Photography ★** Michel Frizot *(Könemann, 1998)*
❑		**A World History of Photography – 3rd edition** Naomi Rosenblum *(Abbeville Press, 1997)*
❑		**Africa Then: Photographs, 1840 – 1918** Nicolas Monti *(Alfred A. Knopf, 1987)*
❑		**America and the Daguerreotype** John Wood *(University of Iowa Press, 1991)*

❑ **American Photography, 1890 – 1965**
Peter Galassi
(Museum of Modern Art, 1995)

❑ **American Photography: A Critical History**
Jonathan Green
(Harry N. Abrams, 1984)

❑ **Art and Photography: Forerunners and Influences**
Heinrich Schwarz
(Visual Studies Workshop and Peregrine Smith, 1985)

❑ **Beauty of Another Order: Photography in Science ★**
Ann Thomas
(Yale University Press, National Gallery of Canada, 1997)

❑ **Before Photography: Painting and the Invention of Photography**
Peter Galassi
(Museum of Modern Art, 1981)

❑ **Burning with Desire – The Conception of Photography ★**
Geoffrey Batchen
(MIT Press, 1997)

❑ **Bystander: A History of Street Photography**
Colin Westerbeck
(Bulfinch Press, 1994)

❑ **Cameras: From Daguerreotypes to Instant Pictures**
Brian Coe
(Crown, 1978)

❑ **Care and Identification of 19th Century Photographic Prints**
James M. Reilly
(Eastman Kodak Co., 1986)

Color Photography: The First Hundred Years
Brian Coe
(Ash & Grant, 1978)

Each Wild Idea: Writing, Photography, History ★
Geoffrey Batchen
(MIT Press, 2001)

Focus East: Early Photography in the Near East
Nissan Perez
(Harry N. Abrams, 1988)

Forgotten Marriage: The Painted Tintype and the Decorative Frame, 1860 – 1910
Stanley B. Burns
(The Burns Press, 1995)

History of Photography
Josef Maria Eder
(Dover, 1978) Originally published in 1945

Image and Memory: Photography from Latin America, 1866 - 1994
Wendy Watriss, Lois Parkinson Zamora
(University of Texas Press, Austin, 1998)

Industrial Madness: Commercial Photography in Paris 1848 – 1871
Elizabeth Anne McCauley
(Yale University Press, 1994)

Latent Image: The Discovery of Photography
Beaumont Newhall
(University of New Mexico Press, 1983)

Mirror Image: The Influence of the Daguerreotype on American Society
Richard Rudisill
(University of New Mexico Press, 1971)

❑ **Modern Photojournalism**
Tim N. Gidal
(Collier, 1973)

❑ **Out of the Shadows: Herschel, Talbot, and the Invention of Photography ★**
Larry J. Schaaf
(Yale University Press, 1992)

❑ **Paper and Light: The Calotype in France and Great Britain, 1839 – 1870**
Richard R. Brettell
(D. R. Godine, 1984)

❑ **Photography and Surrealism**
Rosalind Krauss, Jane Livingston, Dawn Ades
(Abbeville Press, 1986)

❑ **Photography and the American Scene**
Robert Taft
(Dover Publications, 1964)

❑ **Photography in America: The Formative Years, 1839 – 1900**
William B. Welling
(Crowell, 1978)

❑ **Photography in Brazil, 1840 – 1900**
Gilberto Ferrez
(University of New Mexico Press, 1990)

❑ **Photography in Nineteenth-Century America**
Martha A. Sandweiss
(Harry N. Abrams, 1991)

❑ **Photography in the Modern Era: European Documents and Critical Writings, 1913 – 1940**
Christopher Phillips
(Metropolitan Museum of Art and Aperture, 1989)

❑ **Photography Until Now**
John Szarkowski
(Museum of Modern Art, 1989)

❑ **Photography: Discovery and Invention**
(J. Paul Getty Museum, 1990)

❑ **Photospeak: A Guide to the Ideas, Movements, and Techniques of Photography**
Giles Mora
(Abbeville Press, 1998)

❑ **Picturing Modernism: Moholoy - Nagy and Photography in Weimar Germany**
Eleanor M. Hight
(MIT Press, 1995)

❑ **Second View: The Rephotographic Survey Project ★**
Mark Klett, Ellen Manchester, Joann Verburg
(University of New Mexico Press, 1984)

❑ **Secrets of the Dark Chamber: The Art of the American Daguerreotype ★**
Merry Foresta and John Wood
(Smithsonian Institution Press, 1995)

❑ **Seeing Straight: The f.64 Revolution in Photography**
Therese Thau Heyman
(The Oakland Museum, 1992)

❑ **Sleeping Beauty: Memorial Photography in America ★**
Stanley B. Burns
(Twelvetrees Press, 1990)

❑ **Techniques of the Observer: On Vision and Modernity in the Nineteenth Century ★**
Jonathan Crary
(MIT Press, 1990)

❑ **The Age of Collodion, Part II of two volumes**
Helmut Gernsheim
(Thames and Hudson, 1988)

❑ **The American Daguerreotype**
Floyd Rinhart and Marion Rinhart
(University of Georgia Press, 1981)

❑ **The American Space: Meaning in Nineteenth-Century Landscape Photography**
Daniel Wolf
(Wesleyan University Press, 1983)

❑ **The Art of French Calotype**
André Jammes and Eugenia P. Janis
(Princeton University Press, 1983)

❑ **The Art of Photography 1839 – 1989**
Mike Weaver
(Yale University Press, 1989)

❑ **The Art of the Autochrome: The Birth of Color Photography**
John Wood
(University of Iowa Press, 1993)

❑ **The Daguerreotype in America**
Beaumont Newhall
(Dover, 1976)

❑ **The Daguerreotype: Nineteenth-Century Technology and Modern Science**
Susan M. Barger and William B. White
(Smithsonian Institution Press, 1991)

❑ **The Era of the French Calotype**
Janet Buerger
(International Museum of Photography, 1982)

❑ **The Golden Age of British Photography, 1839 – 1900**
Mark Haworth-Booth
(Aperture, Philadelphia Museum of Art, 1984)

❑ **The History of Photography from 1839 to the Present ★**
Beaumont Newhall
(Museum of Modern Art, 1982)

❑ **The Illustrated History of Color Photography**
Jack Coote
(Fountain Press, 1994)

❑ **The Magic Image: The Genius of Photography from 1839 to the Present Day**
Cecil Beaton and Gail Buckland
(Little, Brown & Co., 1975)

❑ **The Mechanical Eye in Australia: Photography, 1841 - 1900**
Peter Stanbury, Alan Davies
(Oxford University Press, 1985)

❑ **The Origins of Photography ★**
Helmut Gernsheim
(Thames and Hudson, 1982)

❑ **The Origins of Photojournalism in America**
Michael L. Carlebach
(Smithsonian Institution Press, 1997)

❑ **The Photograph Collectors' Guide**
Lee D. Witkin, Barbara London
(New York Graphic Society, 1979)

☐ **The Picture History of Photography from the Earliest Beginnings to The Present Day**
Peter Pollack
(Harry N. Abrams, 1969)

☐ **The Rise of Photography: 1850 to 1900, Part I of two volumes**
Helmut Gernsheim
(Thames and Hudson, 1988)

☐ **The Scenic Daguerreotype: Romanticism and Early Photography**
John Wood
(University of Iowa Press, 1995)

☐ **Through Indian Eyes: 19th and Early 20th Century Photography from India**
Judith Mara Gutman
(Oxford University Press, 1982)

☐ **View Finders: Early Black Women Photographers**
Jeanne Moutoussamy-Ashe
(Dodd, Meade, 1986)

✓	CALL NUMBER	CRITICISM

☐ **A New History of Photography ★**
Michel Frizot
(Könemann, 1998)

☐ **A Visual Culture Reader ★**
Nicholas Mirzoeff
(Routledge, 1998)

☐ **An Introduction to Visual Culture ★**
Nicholas Mirzoeff
(Routledge, 1999)

- [ ] **Another Way of Telling**
John Berger
(Pantheon, 1995)

- [ ] **Anthropology and Photography 1860-1920**
Elizabeth Edwards
(Yale University Press, 1992)

- [ ] **Artspeak: A Guide to Contemporary Ideas, Movements and Buzzwords**
Robert Atkins
(Abbeville Press, 1999)

- [ ] **Beauty in Photography: Essays in Defense of Traditional Values**
Robert Adams
(Aperture, 1996)

- [ ] **Burning with Desire – The Conception of Photography ★**
Geoffrey Batchen
(MIT Press, 1997)

- [ ] **Camera Lucida ★★★**
Roland Barthes
(Hill and Wang, 1981)

- [ ] **Camera Work: A Critical Anthology**
Edited by Jonathan Green
(Aperture, 1973)

- [ ] **Clicking in: Hot Links to a Digital Culture**
Lynn Hershman-Leeson
(Bay Press, 1996)

- [ ] **Crisis of the Real**
Andy Grundberg
(Aperture, 1999)

❑ **Critical Focus**
A. D. Coleman
(Nazraeli Press, 1994)

❑ **Criticizing photographs: An Introduction to Understanding Images ★**
Terry Barrett
(Mayfield, 2000)

❑ **Each Wild Idea: Writing, Photography, History ★**
Geoffrey Batchen
(MIT Press, 2001)

❑ **Electronic Culture: Technology and Visual Representation ★**
Timothy Druckery
(Aperture, 1997)

❑ **Illuminations: Women's Writings on Photography from 1850 to the Present ★**
Liz Heron, Val Williams
(Duke University Press, 1996)

❑ **Image – Music – Text ★**
Roland Barthes
(Hill and Wang, 1977)

❑ **In Our Own Image**
Fred Ritchin
(Aperture, 1999)

❑ **Iterations: The New Image**
Timothy Druckery
(MIT Press, 1993)

❑ **Literature and Photography: Interaction 1840 to 1990**
Jane M. Rabb
(University of New Mexico Press, 1995)

☐ **Lone Visions, Crowded Frames: Essays on Photography**
Max Kozloff
(University of New Mexico Press, 1994)

☐ **Looking at Photographs: 100 Pictures from the Collection of the MOMA**
John Szarkowski
(Museum of Modern Art, 1976)

☐ **Occam's Razor**
Bill Jay
(Nazraeli Press, 1992)

☐ **On Photography ★**
Susan Sontag
(Anchor, 1990)

☐ **Overexposed: Essays on Contemporary Photography**
Carol Squiers
(New Press, 1999)

☐ **Photographers on Photography: A Critical Anthology**
Nathan Lyons
(Prentice Hall, 1966)

☐ **Photography – 1900 to the Present**
Diana Emery Hulick, Joseph Marshall
(Prentice Hall, 1998)

☐ **Photography After Photography: Memory and Representation in the Digital Age ★**
Hubertus von Amelunxen
(G & B International, 1997)

☐ **Photography Against the Grain: Essays and Photoworks ★**
Allan Sekula
(Press of the Novia Scotia College of Art and Design, 1984)

❑ **Photography at the Dock ★**
Abigail Solomon-Godeau
(University of Minnesota Press, 1994)

❑ **Photography in Print: Writings from 1816 to the Present**
Vicki Goldberg
(Simon and Schuster, 1981)

❑ **Photography: A Critical Introduction ★**
Liz Wells
(Routledge, 2000)

❑ **Photography: Essays and Images**
Beaumont Newhall
(Museum of Modern Art, 1980)

❑ **Photovideo: Photography in the Age of Computers**
Paul Wombell
(Paul and Co., 1991)

❑ **Picturing Us: African American Identity in Photography ★**
Deborah Willis
(New Press, 1996)

❑ **Simulations**
Jean Baudrillard
(Semiotext(e), 1983)

❑ **Snap to Grid – A User's Guide to Digital Arts, Media, and Cultures**
Peter Lunenfeld
(MIT Press, 2000)

❑ **Surface - Contemporary Photographic Practice**
Simon Browning
(Booth-Clibborn Editions, 1996)

❑ **Techniques of the Observer: On Vision and Modernity in the Nineteenth Century ★**
Jonathan Crary
(MIT Press, 1990)

❑ **The Burden of Representation: Essays on Photographies and Histories ★**
John Tagg
(University of Minnesota Press, 1993)

❑ **The Contest of Meaning: Critical Histories of Photography ★**
Richard Bolton
(MIT Press, 1992)

❑ **The Digital Dialectic – New Essays on New Media ★**
Peter Lunenfeld
(MIT Press, 2000)

❑ **The Engine of Visualization**
Patrick Maynard
(Cornell University Press, 1997)

❑ **The Medium is the Massage: An Inventory of Effects**
Marshall McLuhan and Quentin Fiore
(HardWired, 1996) Originally published in 1967

❑ **The Photograph: A Strange Confined Space**
Mary Price
(Stanford University Press, 1997)

❑ **The Photographic Image in Digital Culture**
Martin Lister
(Routledge, 1995)

❑ **The Reconfigured Eye**
William J. Mitchell
(MIT Press, 1994)

❑ **Thinking Photography ★**
Victor Burgin
(Macmillan, 1982)

❑ **Trace and Transformation**
Joel Eisinger
(University of New Mexico Press, 1999)

❑ **Truths and Fictions**
Pedro Meyer
(Aperture, 1995)

❑ **Veronica's Revenge: Contemporary Perspectives on Photography**
Elizabeth Janus
(Scalo, 1998)

Notes

18 TEST ANSWERS

SCORE-SHEET	Fill in the blanks / 10	Multiple choice / 10	Test score / 20
1.3			
2.3			
3.3			
4.3			
5.3			
6.3			
7.3			
8.3			
9.3			
10.3			
11.3			
12.3			
13.3			
14.3			
15.3			
16.3			
17.3			
FINAL SCORES			

18.1 TEST ANSWERS

FILL IN THE BLANKS		MULTIPLE CHOICE	
1	Aperture	1	b.
2	Focusing	2	b. – c.
3	Sensitivity	3	a. – b. – c.
4	DX-code	4	a. – b.
5	Positive	5	b. – c.
6	Shutter speed	6	b.
7	Background	7	a.
8	Shutter	8	b.
9	Aperture	9	a. – b.
10	Counter	10	a. – b. – c.

18.2 TEST ANSWERS

FILL IN THE BLANKS		MULTIPLE CHOICE	
1	Reflex	1	b.
2	Motion	2	a.
3	Aperture Shutter speed	3	b. – c.
4	Sharpness	4	a.
5	Increases	5	a. – c.
6	Increases	6	b. – c.
7	f/16	7	a. – b.
8	1/60	8	b. – c.
9	Focal-plane	9	c.
10	1/30	10	a.

18.3 TEST ANSWERS

FILL IN THE BLANKS		MULTIPLE CHOICE	
1	Angle	1	c.
2	Human	2	c.
3	Short	3	b.
4	Aperture Focal length Subject	4	a.
5	Hyperfocal	5	b.
6	Macro	6	b.
7	Focal lengths	7	b. – c.
8	Subject	8	a.
9	One	9	a.
10	Circles	10	b.

18.4 TEST ANSWERS

FILL IN THE BLANKS		MULTIPLE CHOICE	
1	Emulsion	1	a. – c.
2	Panchromatic	2	c.
3	Slow	3	a. – b. – c.
4	ISO	4	c.
5	Infrared	5	a. – c.
6	Transparency	6	a. – b.
7	Slow	7	b.
8	Fast	8	a. – c.
9	Factor	9	a. – b. – c.
10	Complementary	10	c.

18.5 TEST ANSWERS

FILL IN THE BLANKS		MULTIPLE CHOICE	
1	Aperture Shutter speed	1	b.
2	Exposure	2	b.
3	Latitude	3	a.
4	Reflected	4	a. – b.
5	Middle gray	5	b.
6	1	6	b. – c.
7	Manual	7	a. – b. – c.
8	Bracketing	8	b.
9	Film speed	9	a.
10	Average	10	c.

18.6 TEST ANSWERS

FILL IN THE BLANKS		MULTIPLE CHOICE	
1	Latent	1	b.
2	Developer Stop bath Fixer	2	a. – b.
3	Water	3	a. – c.
4	Temperature	4	b.
5	Overdeveloped	5	a. – c.
6	Underexposure	6	c.
7	Even	7	a. – b. – c.
8	Fixer	8	b.
9	Working	9	a.
10	Wetting agent	10	b.

18.7 TEST ANSWERS

FILL IN THE BLANKS		MULTIPLE CHOICE	
1	Contact	1	b.
2	Developer Stop bath Fixer	2	b. – c.
3	Density	3	a.
4	Magnifier	4	a. – c.
5	Dodging Burning in	5	a. – b. – c.
6	Test strip	6	c.
7	Cropping	7	a.
8	Aligned	8	b.
9	Glossy	9	b. – c.
10	Archival	10	a. – c.

18.8 TEST ANSWERS

FILL IN THE BLANKS		MULTIPLE CHOICE	
1	Dry-mount tissue	1	a. – c.
2	Archival	2	a. – b. –c.
3	Spotting	3	b.
4	Overmat	4	a.
5	Brush	5	c.
6	Bleaching	6	a. – c.
7	Ply	7	c.
8	Tacking iron	8	b.
9	210	9	b.
10	Dark	10	b.

18.9 TEST ANSWERS

FILL IN THE BLANKS		MULTIPLE CHOICE	
1	3	1	c.
2	Reversal	2	b.
3	Cyan Magenta Yellow	3	b.
4	Short	4	c.
5	Kelvin	5	a.
6	Instant	6	b.
7	3200	7	b.
8	Daylight	8	b.
9	Density	9	a.
10	Magenta	10	a.

18.10.3 TEST ANSWERS

FILL IN THE BLANKS		MULTIPLE CHOICE	
1	Scanner	1	a. – b.
2	CCD	2	a.
3	Memory	3	b. – c.
4	Pixels	4	a. – c.
5	Monitor	5	c.
6	Megabytes	6	b.
7	Compression	7	a. – b.
8	8	8	b.
9	Increases	9	a. – b. – c.
10	Lossy	10	a. – b.

18.11 TEST ANSWERS

FILL IN THE BLANKS		MULTIPLE CHOICE	
1	Resolution	1	b.
2	72	2	b.
3	Pixels	3	b.
4	Discarding	4	b.
5	Increase	5	a.
6	PSD	6	a. – b. – c.
7	Compression	7	b.
8	Tools	8	c.
9	Undo	9	b.
10	Selection	10	b.

18.12 TEST ANSWERS

FILL IN THE BLANKS		MULTIPLE CHOICE	
1	Direct	1	b.
2	Diffused	2	b.
3	Diffused	3	a.
4	Direct	4	a. – b. – c.
5	Inverse square	5	b. – c.
6	Main	6	a. – b.
7	Synchronized	7	a.
8	Incandescent	8	c.
9	Bounce	9	c.
10	Guide number	10	a. – b. – c.

18.13 TEST ANSWERS

FILL IN THE BLANKS		MULTIPLE CHOICE	
1	Cross	1	b.
2	Sabattier	2	a.
3	Cyanotype	3	a.
4	45	4	b.
5	Polarizing	5	b.
6	Depth of field	6	c.
7	Photogram	7	a. – b.
8	Contact	8	a. – c.
9	Installation	9	b. – c.
10	Paralell	10	a. – b. – c.

18.14 TEST ANSWERS

FILL IN THE BLANKS		MULTIPLE CHOICE	
1	Movements	1	b.
2	Bellows	2	c.
3	Fall	3	c.
4	150	4	b.
5	Further	5	c.
6	Shape	6	b.
7	Circle	7	b. – c.
8	Intersect	8	b.
9	Level	9	b.
10	Emulsion	10	b.

18.15 TEST ANSWERS

FILL IN THE BLANKS		MULTIPLE CHOICE	
1	Visualize	1	b.
2	Grayscale	2	b.
3	0	3	a. – b.
4	X	4	c.
5	V	5	a.
6	III	6	c.
7	VIII	7	a.
8	V	8	c.
9	VII	9	b. – c.
10	Increase	10	a.

18.16 TEST ANSWERS

FILL IN THE BLANKS		MULTIPLE CHOICE	
1	Background	1	c.
2	Frame	2	c.
3	Depth of field	3	c.
4	Fast	4	a. – b. – c.
5	Perspective	5	a.
6	Light	6	c.
7	Viewpoint	7	a. – b.
8	Point	8	a. – b. – c.
9	Contrast	9	a. – b.
10	Meaning	10	a. – b. – c.

18.17 TEST ANSWERS

FILL IN THE BLANKS ▾		MULTIPLE CHOICE ▾	
1	Heliography	**1**	c.
2	Silver	**2**	b.
3	1839	**3**	c.
4	Printed	**4**	a. – b.
5	Wet-collodion	**5**	b.
6	George Eastman	**6**	b.
7	1888	**7**	a.
8	Additive	**8**	a. – b. – c.
9	Kodachrome	**9**	a. – b.
10	Carte-de-visite	**10**	b. – c.

Notes